Chaldean Numerology
For Beginners

About the Author

Heather Alicia Lagan (Chilliwack, British Columbia) is a lifelong metaphysician and spiritual practitioner. She is a Master Chaldean numerologist with over twenty years experience, and she has used this system to conduct hundreds of readings for clients. Visit Lagan online at TheReadingRoom101.com.

To Write to the Author

If you wish to contact the author or would like more information about this book, please write to the author in care of Llewellyn Worldwide, and we will forward your request. Both the author and the publisher appreciate hearing from you and learning of your enjoyment of this book and how it has helped you. Llewellyn Worldwide cannot guarantee that every letter written to the author can be answered, but all will be forwarded. Please write to:

Heather Alicia Lagan
℅ Llewellyn Worldwide
2143 Wooddale Drive
Woodbury, MN 55125-2989

Please enclose a self-addressed stamped envelope for reply, or $1.00 to cover costs. If outside the USA, enclose an international postal reply coupon.

Chaldean Numerology

For Beginners

How Your Name & Birthday
Reveal Your True Nature & Life Path

HEATHER ALICIA LAGAN

Llewellyn Publications
Woodbury, Minnesota

FIRST EDITION
Ninth Printing, 2022

Book format by Bob Gaul
Cover art © iStockphoto.com/Alan Merrigan
Cover design by Ellen Lawson
Editing by Patti Frazee
Interior cards from *Universal Tarot* by De Angelis,
  reprinted by permission from Lo Scarabeo

Llewellyn Publications is a registered trademark of Llewellyn Worldwide Ltd.

Library of Congress Cataloging-in-Publication Data
Lagan, Heather Alicia
   Chaldean numerology for beginners : how your name & birthday reveal your true nature & life path/Heather Alicia Lagan.—1st ed.
      p. cm.
   Includes bibliographical references.
   ISBN 978-0-7387-2624-3
1. Numerology. 2. Names, Personal—Miscellanea. 3. Birthdays—Miscellanea.
I. Title.
   BF1623.P9L34 2011
   133.3'35—dc23
                            2011034467

Llewellyn Publications
A Division of Llewellyn Worldwide Ltd.
2143 Wooddale Drive
Woodbury, MN 55125-2989
www.llewellyn.com

Printed in the United States of America

Scientists acknowledge that everything in our universe vibrates to its own level of energy. Numbers and letters are central to this knowledge and when combined and "read," present the vibrational story behind any given word or name and reveal the hidden pathway each energy is to follow.

… words, like nature, half reveal and half conceal the soul within …

—Lord Alfred Tennyson (1809–1892)

Words have meanings and names have power.

—author unknown

… the invisible thing called a Good Name is made up of the breath of numbers that speak well of you …

—George Savile (1633–1695)

Words are the keys to the heart.

—Chinese proverb

contents

Dedication

Dedicated to every one of you
and
the connections between
every one of us

Acknowledgments

This has been a journey twenty years in the making. I have learned so much from so many people and clients and had no idea at the time that all of this education would take the form of a book. I simply did not keep track of it all, other than on my posterboard "book" and in my brain. So many people have been a part of this journey into print, some in little ways and others in larger ways, but all of you supported my goal and my writing in your own inimitable ways and I value your contributions beyond measure. You know who you are and so does Universe. I want to thank all of you and I apologize to any particular persons or sources of inspiration that should ideally be named herein.

That said, I do want to acknowledge a few people who have made a world of difference in my journey. Gratitude and lots of love go to my sister, Claudia Lagan, for being my rock and the most treasured gift of my life next to my son, James; Catherine Lang-Murphy for her years of encouragement; Sylvaine Lelong for her unfailing support; Jose Alberto Canhas for his kind and generous heart and for showing me the reality of the dream; Leeya Brooke Thompson for sharing her thoughts, precious support, and friendship; Amy Glaser for her invaluable advice; David Hill for always being there; and the entire crew at Llewellyn for their faith in this project and in me. Last, but certainly not least, I thank you, dear reader, for reading these words. I hope the ones that follow will bring a smile to your lips and a lightness to your heart.

introduction

The Chaldean System

While there are several numerology systems in use today, only Chaldean (pronounced *cal-day-yan*) numerology has proven itself to me over the years to be almost eerie in its accuracy. Essentially, the Chaldeans were the first to recognize that *all things are energy* and connect sounds to vibrations, vibrations to numbers, and numbers to letters. Highly spiritual in nature, this system is an original in the numbers game and was the first to connect the original meanings of the letters to name analysis. It looks *beyond* your name to the individual letter energies and what they mean to you, and *beyond* your date of birth to the specific vibrations of your Lifepath, or what you are here to do, be, or learn.

Despite having a reputation as being difficult to learn (which is why it was almost lost to history in the first place), this system is actually quite easy to master. Once you know its long-held secrets, it will become a unique and invaluable tool in your personal and daily life. Not only does it provide you with a personal "blueprint," it also offers insights into others.

The Ancient Chaldeans

Over two thousand years ago, the ancient Chaldeans lived around the southernmost tip of Babylonia, near the lush mouths of the Tigris and Euphrates rivers. While the origins of these rather mysterious peoples were and still are unknown, they did overtake the Babylonian throne (the most famous of their kings being Nebuchadnezzar, who ruled from approximately 606 to 561 BCE), where they remained for more than seventy-five years. While many fundamental structures such as housing, agriculture, and manufacturing were already in place when the throne was assumed, the Chaldeans contributed advanced astrology, mathematics, and spiritual elements to the society, which included an interesting blend of Lunar worship, esoteric observations, and methods of magick and divination. It is hardly surprising then that Babylonia as a whole is often considered the "cradle of civilization"—the fact that relatively few recordings of the Chaldeans and their origins, belief systems, and practices were written by the people themselves only serves to underscore the overall mystery

surrounding them and the part they played in the subsequent spread of knowledge and science throughout
the Western world. However, despite this lack of original
recordings, the system of numerology attributed to the
Chaldeans has not only survived, it has proven itself to be
an incredibly accurate method of measuring energies. Try
it out for yourself and you will be amazed at its accuracy
and uniqueness.

What's Your Vibe?

Have you ever wondered how you "come across" to others?
Or, what kind of vibe you give off? This multi-faceted oracle will tell you that, along with many other things.

Chaldean numerology tracks the energy fluctuations
created when you think or speak—or when someone else
does. Simply put, the sound that emanates from your
mouth sends out frequencies that affect both you and those
around you.

The most common words associated with you are
found in your name—and their vibrations speak volumes
about you, your attitudes, characteristics, power levels, and
much more, but only to the educated ear.

To illustrate the concept of sound vibrations, consider
what occurs when a piano is played: it produces different
tones, some sharp and some soft, but all resonate throughout the room, even when a note is only hit once. Beyond
being heard or felt, Chaldean numerology allows letter
energies and number vibrations to be "read." In a name,
for instance, each letter holds a meaning and a history,
and letter placements and number frequencies reveal

characteristics, patterns, strengths, weaknesses, pathways, spiritual connections, and challenges. Basically, your name is like a song—many might be able to hum the tune, but its true meaning can only be ascertained by knowing how to read the lyrics.

What's in a Name?

Letters and numbers are like the individual strokes that make up a painting of word energies. Words are *alive*. They live. You most certainly know that words can wound in that "the pen is mightier than the sword." In fact, wordplay is everywhere; look closely at "words," move the "s" and you have "sword." There is definitely more to the alphabet and its components than meets the eye, and this is true of your name as well.

Let's look at the letter D. This letter primarily represents a "Door" and carries a traditional meaning of foundational stability. Its supporting number is 4, the number of firm foundations. The two combined produce a fixed, routine, predictable, and sometimes stagnant energy that, like a door, carries two sides and can be open or closed in attitude. There are often significant challenges or struggles in the life of a Cornerstone D that go beyond the norm; that said, the D is also tenacious and does not give up easily. Beyond being reliable and fairly domestic, the D can be stubborn and uncompromising, to the extent that no amount of entreaty or persuasion will convince it to open its door, much less to go outside of its comfort zone to explore new terrain. On the other hand, the positive D will be open to possibilities and opportunities and eager to explore the "other side," but it will always want to go home and retire behind the privacy of its own closed doors.

Now, think of someone you know whose name begins with a "D." Do any of the above descriptions ring any bells?

Therefore, just knowing someone's first name, or even their initials, will tell you a lot about them. Imagine what a complete chart will reveal.

What's in a Number?

Now let's have a quick peek at how number energies work. Imagine holding a big bucket with one lonely penny sitting on the bottom, then imagine that same bucket holding 10,000 pennies—the addition of several ciphers (or zeros) has created an occasion worthy of a trip to the bank. Placement of number elements will always affect other numbers, much as 10 percent of a stock is preferable to .01 percent of it. This rule holds true for all number (and letter) arrangements; each affects the other in some way.

Think about the computer in your house. Then think about all of the other computers out there and the massive reach of the World Wide Web. At the core of this system, you will find the number 1 and the cipher 0, which is a pretty amazing thought if you dwell upon it. The fact is that everything on this Earth can be traced back to numbers, and you are affected by them just like everyone else.

The Dark Side of Numbers and Letters

Also like everyone else, you undoubtedly have days when you feel lighter than air and others when you feel heavier than cement. Everything and everyone carries the potential for both positive and negative reactions and moods—and since everything is energy, numbers and letters are no exception. They do not, however, suffer from mood swings; rather, they carry both potentialities (for positive and negative) within their frame work: each number has a negative vibration, as does each letter. While I do list some of these at the end of each description, the easiest way to ascertain the negatives is by reversing the listed positives.

The one thing that has become evident to me is that what I call "undeveloped" people will have little or no interest in self-improvement/spirituality themes or applications and thus will rarely, if ever, be found reading a book such as this.

The most dangerous of the negative manifestations comes in the most powerful numbers; for example, numbers that carry very forceful or elevated levels of potential are the ones to look out for—because of their force, drive, and hunger for achievement, power, and control, numbers 1 and 8 are two of the more potentially negative numbers (and the 9 has its moments as well), while elevated Masters like the 11 (in particular) and sometimes the 22 can also create "monster" energies, which I will expand upon later. If you do have someone in your life that fits the negative and often dangerous descriptions of *any* number, you will likely find that you *already knew*—the intuition is an amazing gift. Listen to its warning and leave or get help. Dark energies take a while to get that way and are not likely to change their spots overnight. If they are well established, chances are good that these energies can truly become harmful to others.

That said, do not be surprised if some of the negative descriptions apply to you—as long as they are not ongoing or accentuated traits you have nothing to worry about. We are all a blend of dualities and opposites and a relatively *balanced* blend is considered normal. Even the Sun has its off days.

What's the Difference Between Systems?

One of the more popular numerology systems, known as Western Numerology and attributed to Pythagoras (circa 500 BCE), differs in major ways from Chaldean. The Pythagorean system is based on sequential patterns rather than on sound vibrations. The alphabet is arranged in order and under a number chart that runs from 1 through 9. One major difference is in the 9: the ancient Chaldeans viewed this number with tremendous respect; therefore it was not included in the number chart, although it could still be found as a name total. In the eyes of these ancients, this number was sacred, perhaps partly due to its connection to infinity (it is the only number that can be multiplied by any other number and consistently reduce back to its core); however, Pythagoras paid it no special mind, even assigning the letters I and R to its domain. Further, the latter system relies on information gleaned only from the birth or given name while Chaldean numerology focuses only on the name you are currently using—after all, it is *those* energies that are affecting you at any given time, not the ones you carried long ago. Another aspect to consider here are name changes. Whether by virtue or choice—adoption, marriage, divorce, and even through the development of nicknames—names can and do change, thereby altering energy vibrations. Most importantly, no other systems specifically address the meanings of the *letters* within a name energy, nor do they carry or convey the spiritual messages that are intrinsic to the Chaldean system. Suffice it to say that the Chaldean system is one of a kind ... and it works.

The History of Our Alphabet

The ancient Chaldeans used a different set of symbols than we do today. Called cuneiform (which looks rather like straight nails with wedged tips), this method was used by necessity more than anything else. Most record keeping was accomplished using wet clay tablets, and making straight marks was much more effective than trying to draw curves. However, sounds and symbols remained a predominant theme throughout the many years of subsequent integration and adaptations involving pictographs, Egyptian hieroglyphics, Greek additions, Roman stylizations, and contributions from the Phoenicians and Hebrews, among others, but the central essence of Chaldean numerology has remained intact. Its core essence has been preserved for thousands of years and is as accurate now as it was in ancient times.

What began as a relatively simple connection between sound and symbol morphed into the alphabet as we know it today, a process that took many hundreds of years—but it is more than that. Our alphabet speaks its own language, and Chaldean numerology allows us to translate what is truly being said without the necessity of calculating vowels and so on. This system is complete unto itself and it will tell you all you need to know about your "self." Calculating your own numbers using this method presents the beginning of a journey that is all about you.

What Makes Me an Expert?

While visiting my local library more than twenty years ago, a proverbial book fell off the shelf and into my arms. Naturally, I took it home and opened it with a normal amount of curiosity. However, upon reading an early entry, my curiosity became wide-eyed fascination. While books are designed to speak to us, this one took that theme into the twilight zone. The book informed me in no uncertain terms that the *book had found me* and that if I became absorbed in its contents, I would then become bound and obliged to share this information with others to assist them in their journey through life. I remember feeling as though I had received a direct communication from an unknown realm. Like someone or something was talking specifically *to me.* While I certainly felt inadequate to the task at the time, that message stayed with me.

I never found that book again, despite concerted efforts. I do not recall its cover, its title, or the author's name. Its visit with me and its deposition of knowledge was as mysterious as its subject matter and swift and utter disappearance.

In the many years that have passed since reading those words, I have prepared and read hundreds of Chaldean reports for clients and friends, and without exaggeration, no one has been less than impressed with its accuracy and spiritual insights. Chaldean numerology has taught me so much about myself and has blessed me with a deep understanding of the subtleties and shades, the depths and the heights, the repeating patterns and links that form the language of our alphabet and its connected number values in a way I could never have imagined possible. As a result, I have *bonded* with this subject: it has become a natural extension of who I am.

I thought the time would never come, but after years of living with Chaldean numerology and its attendant gifts, I finally find myself equipped to fulfill my end of the unspoken agreement that I believe originated from Universe itself: to share this knowledge with you.

I sincerely hope you enjoy the end result as much as I enjoyed being a part of its creation.

What's in a name?
—Shakespeare (circa 1591), *Romeo and Juliet*

one

Chaldean Numerology Chart

B elow is the original Chaldean chart that we will use for all calculations (you might find it helpful to hand-draw a version of your own). Here is where you will begin to discover and uncover the challenges, strengths, and lessons that are held within the mysterious and spiritual vibrations of your name and Lifepath.

1	2	3	4	5	6	7	8
A	B	G	D	E	U	O	F
Q	R	C	M	H	V	Z	P
Y	K	L	T	N	W		
I		S		X			
J							

Again, it is important that you use the name you are most commonly known by or use the most frequently. If you were born Terrence, but go by Terry, then Terry is the name you will use. Similarly, if you still carry a married name legally but use your maiden name for daily purposes, then your maiden name is the one you will use. The most important thing to remember here is that whatever you are called or call yourself on a regular basis is the energy you are projecting and is the only name of current importance.

Numbers as Years

A less obvious but nevertheless relevant aspect of names and numbers involves the number of years each letter covers. The numerical value of each letter also refers to the number of years it takes to transit that letter energy. For instance, my name totals to a sub 27, which means I completed the first energy transit of "Heather" at age 27. The second time I will complete the transit, I will be 54, and so on. When you look at the Chaldean chart, think of those numbers as *years*, not just energies. As you calculate and record your own name number and Lifepath results, keep in mind that each letter is commenting on the stages you will be going through from birth until, well, until you graduate from this Earth plane.

A Word on the Process

Once you have ascertained your particular numbers and letters and I have explained the various departments that your names, letters, and numbers fall into, we will then move into the ancient meanings of the symbols: first, the numbers, as they are, by comparison, quicker to learn and subsequently understand when referred to in the alphabetical section and second, the letters of the alphabet, which will add deeper dimensions to the meanings of the numbers.

The process of analysis is highly individual and personal, so be sure to allow the connections or messages that come through when studying your numbers, subs or otherwise, a moment or two of contemplation, for every number in your chart is there for a reason and holds its own special message for you. All you need do is be open to the seemingly random thoughts that pass through your mind.

Learning how to decipher and delve into the mysteries in your names is easier than it might sound. Just follow the categories I have listed and make a note of your results: they will explain how the different forms of your names can be separated and what they will reveal. Be sure to track your results because the final visual summary of your numbers will often show you connections that could otherwise be missed.

Chaldean
Name Analysis

How to Calculate Your Numbers

First, find yourself a large sheet of paper and a pen and write your first, middle, and last names in block letters across the top of the page. Further down, write the month (1–12) and day of your birth. Leave enough room above, below, between, and beside your names for notes and additions. Above each letter in your name, note the number that it falls under on the Chaldean chart as illustrated in the following example:

J O H N	A D A M	S M I T H
1 7 5 5	1 4 1 4	3 4 1 4 5

Now, total each of your names individually.

J O H N	A D A M	S M I T H
1 7 5 5	1 4 1 4	3 4 1 4 5
=18	=10	=17

These sub numbers (18, 10, and 17) are now reduced to their single digit.

J O H N	A D A M	S M I T H
1 7 5 5	1 4 1 4	3 4 1 4 5
=18	=10	=17
=9	**=1**	**=8**

So we now know that John Adam Smith's numbers are 9, 1, and 8. Follow the same procedure to reach your own set of numbers. If your sub number is still a double digit (e.g., 19/10), keep adding until you reach a single-digit number (10/1) unless it is a Master Number (11, 22, 33).

As we move through the various categories in name analysis, note each category result beneath your main name heading.

Master Numbers 11, 22, 33, etc.

If by chance, one or more of your names total to a final sub number composed of Master Numbers like 11, 22, or 33 (which I will get into later), do not reduce these to single numbers. These are higher manifestations of the regular 1 through 9 number scale and stand on their own.

These are the most commonly seen Master Numbers, although they do run all the way up the number scale. (If you do happen to discover several Master Numbers in your names, you are among a rare group and will have access to elevated power sources, which will be explained later. Generally speaking, however, higher Masters are the exception rather than the rule.)

So, a first name of 11 combined with a second name of 22 will total to 33. This is the only time when the numerological law of addition does not apply. Master energies are impossible to "vibrate to" for long periods of time, so during off or down times, they will function at a lower connective level, or as what I call "quiet" numbers, like 2 (11), 4 (22), and 6 (33), respectively. But for purposes of calculating, leave these numbers as they fall and count them as final numbers.

Your Daily Name

Your Daily Name is the name you are most often called and known by and holds the most immediate impact when calculating your name energies; it is the overall energy that we project or allow others to see on a daily basis. Like the hardcover of a book, the Daily Name represents that which is seen from the outside. It is a semi-casual outer view which offers a bit of information while concealing the entire story and offering a layer of protection from damage or mistreatment.

Much will certainly be revealed through a person's first and last names, but the inner soul, or middle name, remains securely tucked away to be shown only to a special few. (Don't worry if you do not have a middle name or if you have more than one—that will be covered, too.)

To reach the final total for your Daily Name, simply add the digits of your first name to the digits of your last name. This will produce a combination composed of sub numbers, much as the 18 of John and the 17 of Smith form a sub number of 35. The Daily Name total for John Smith is reached by adding this sub number digit together (3+5), so his Daily Name is 8. This means that his general persona while functioning in the social realm would reflect the style of the average 8.

Your own Daily Name will reflect your general outer presentation, characteristics, personality, challenges, and interaction styles. It is not only how you choose (even subconsciously) to be seen, it is also how others see you and the manner in which they will respond to you and to your projected energies.

Sub Numbers

All sub numbers comment on the inner workings of your personality, including your natural energies and how they might best be used in this lifetime. Subs often reveal your thoughts, intuitions, natural talents, secret longings, and habits and are good indicators of the platform that will serve you best and from which you may learn the most while on your journey through this life. For example, a sub number of 35, because of its high level of physical and mental agility and change, may indicate that a career involving activity and stimulation may be favorable to one that involves sitting in one spot for eight hours. The latter scenario does not honor the need to feed the mind and body (3), nor does it honor the hunger for independence and freedom (5). Sub numbers can shed light on different areas and in different ways.

The general rule of thumb is that all subs count, however, the last sub (the one just prior to your final number) will hold the strongest message for you. If any of your names break down into more than one sub number (for example 48/12 = 3), consider the first sub number and what connections are there for you, but focus mainly on the last sub number (in this case, 12), before reaching the final name number as it often holds the most pertinent messages. Sometimes these messages will refer to actual events, sometimes they will comment on what type of job would make you happy, sometimes it will be a very personal message that will only make sense to you. All subs add different nuances and shades to the Total Name Number—they show the specific undertones of predispositions, preferences, personal needs, tendencies, unexpressed desires, and add that personal touch to your individual name energies.

What If You Don't Have a Sub Number in Your Name?

If by chance, one or more of your name energies totals to a single number without reaching a sub number first, this is similar in meaning as having no middle name; it means this name energy *is what it is.* It is upfront about who it is and what it cares about. Consider the name Mia—this name is composed of 4+1+1 and totals directly to 6. There is no sub number. In this event, the meaning of the number in question is very true to its traditional descriptions: the number 6 is all about love and home and community, and that is where it will perform the best—doing something that is much loved, spending time with those who are much loved, and assisting within the home and community in the most effective manner. This is true for any direct single digit; the number energy reached will encompass its traditional meanings without the sometimes distracting presence of sub energies. There are rarely hidden agendas or subversive qualities, and game playing is not usually a priority. A single-digit name energy is often a clean expression of its number value.

Your Total Name Number

Your Total Name Number is exactly what it sounds like: it is the grand total of all of your names combined and includes your first, middle, and last names. The final number of these combined names will offer insights into the potentialities your energy carried upon entering this Earth plane. This is how John Adam Smith's Total Name Number calculations look:

J O H N	A D A M	S M I T H
1 7 5 5	1 4 1 4	3 4 1 4 5
=18	=10	=17
=9	=1	=8

Sub#	Total Name#
45	9
18	9

John's first sub number is 45; his second (and main) sub number is 18 and his Total Name Number is 9.

Your own grand total is the one used for assessing what your ultimate and "proper" potential is, which would be why it is also the energy that represents how we are viewed by official organizations or persons, like the government, the medical and court systems, or anything similar. Overall, though, it is indicative of what you *could* achieve in your life if you so choose. This is the gift Universe sent here with you—whether it is made use of or not is an individual decision, but the message of the main sub number (18 for John) is usually a nudge in the right direction. This sub number can point to what needs to be achieved, overcome, accepted, or honored before we can tune in to the Universal wavelength of our Total Name Number. (In case you are curious, John would need to investigate his own fundamental beliefs or patterns [4], and make some serious changes [5] thereto in order to overcome his need or urge [1] to feel in control [8] before he would be able or equipped to step into the rewarding, intuitive, creative, and spiritual aspects of his Total Name Number 9.)

Whole Name Numbers

Whole Name Numbers are the individual totals reached for each name much as the separate total for the name John is 9. (If you have completed your Daily Name and Total Name Numbers, you will already know your Whole Name Numbers.) Whether these number energies are connected to the first, middle, or last name, the Whole Name Number always refers to the complete addition (or the final digit, except in the case of Master Numbers) of an individual name. In the case of the first, or social, name, this energy will reflect the general essence of the image you project while out and about. The middle or "inner" Whole Name Number shows how you feel about your "self" or what your inner attitude is, while your last or domestic Whole Name Number will comment on your experiences while growing up or while married … or, in the case of a name change, which energies you linked with by doing so.

Whole Name Number calculations can serve you well in social settings when a last name is not known—the benefits of being able to determine someone's overall social energy will become more evident as we proceed, but the point here is that any Whole Name Number, be it first, middle, or last, will outline the overall vibrational energy that is intrinsic to that name: the *letters* that shape the name will tell you much more about the person's styles and tendencies.

Having said that, let's start with a few basics, like which aspect of *you* each Whole Name represents.

Your First Name—Social Persona

Your first name is always a mirror of how others see you, or how you present yourself in public—the energy you carry and project and the one people respond to on a primarily social and sometimes subconscious level. This will cover work, friends, neighbors, casual dates, parties, and other social gatherings. This is the face we wear when out shopping, going to the movies, sitting on the bus, or chatting with the waitress. This is not to say that we are not being ourselves; it simply says that we all feel somewhat vulnerable and would prefer not to display the sensitive parts of our individual souls for all to see. Our social name energy is a protective shield some wear lightly and discard easily, while others wear it rigidly and rarely remove it. Our first names serve as our social introduction energy so that we may interact with others with ease. Of course, on a deeper level, it also indicates our interests, our personalities, our likes and dislikes, our habits, and our "state" in life.

Two First Names

Should someone carry two first names, that person will have a choice (usually subconscious) of two different ways of presenting themselves, or will be able to adjust their behavior more readily to different situations. On the other hand, two first names can also be an unfortunate indicator of dual characters, or two distinct and different personalities that can emerge depending on the situation, person, or emotion involved. For example, a two-namer might be the nicest guy in the world, but while you both are enjoying a lovely meal at a restaurant, his steak arrives well done, but he ordered it rare. This two-namer may then suddenly display his alter energy and embarrass you right under the table, and maybe even right out the back door of the restaurant. Such unexpected and perhaps out-of-character behaviors can easily connect back to the name that carries the more powerful vibration (like an 8) and be demonstrative of its energies.

However, the majority of us have only one first name, and even if you have two, it just makes you a more complex and enigmatic personality. If you feel uncomfortable with one of your names, trust that feeling and drop the use of it.

In a nutshell, a double first name is still reflective of your social energy, what you do with it, and how it appears and feels to others.

Your Middle Name—Inner or Soul Energy

Your middle name, as I have mentioned, is perhaps the most important energy in the entire analysis, for it reveals the truth about your inner soul. It shows hidden talents, true motivations, desires, and the level your soul is at or is trying to reach—it is like the place we all can be alone with our "self." Often it will reveal strange shadow messages from divine realms, explain certain feelings or yearnings, or simply solve puzzles a person has been aware of but unable to put together on their own for whatever reasons. Sometimes, though, the middle name can provide invaluable validation by confirming that the direction being pursued or the path being traveled is the right one, despite the poor condition of the road. Strong spiritual encouragement gets to the heart of the matter and offers insight into the true character and into where and how each person's unique gifts might be best utilized, both for the good of others and also for the good of the self. The inner essence often reveals insecurities, severe self-doubt, and periodic setbacks; in fact, this is where the key to freeing ourselves from "jail" is often found—it can show you what is missing from your life and which key will get you out the quickest. Here is also where personal attributes will make themselves known and usually in no uncertain terms, which can also inspire the warmth of recognition. Unacknowledged or buried strengths often come to light and are finally and happily owned.

An important link to look for involves the middle name and the energies found in your Lifepath, or day and month of birth. When connected or even identical vibrations are evident (for example, my middle name and day of birth are both 10 values), this will point to specific talents or abilities or goals that have every possibility of being realized once the ego has been accepted for what it is—the *human* side of the equation. You are undoubtedly familiar with one of my favorite sayings—we are *spirits having a human experience* and not the other way around. But the fact is that the human ego is strong, sometimes stronger than faith. Should you find this link in your numbers (and even if you don't), know that no matter how difficult present circumstances may appear (especially if you are following your dream), honorable quests and intentions are always supported by Universe, although it can prove difficult for spirit to out-talk ego. And truth be told, this is what the entire process of analysis is about: ego versus spirit. Even the most spiritually aware suffer periodic struggles between faith and doubt; the latter promotes doubt that anything good will happen and then doubt it when it does. After all, how long can a good thing last? We doubt that we truly deserve anything good; in fact, we doubt that we are even good people. We doubt that others really understand us—and wouldn't they run for the hills if they did? Doubt is the underminer of faith.

This is where the struggle lies—between human emotions and spiritual beliefs. Name analysis can reassure us that we do, indeed, have goodness at our core, even if it is deeply buried. Since we are spirits engaged in human experiences, we are not perfect; we do need to accept our human elements and frailties—they are an important part of us and of our lessons. This is a large part of Chaldean numerology: to accept the lessons provided us and to accommodate, absorb, and grow *with* them rather than waste time trying to explain away, ignore, or justify our negatives. The middle name is often home to hidden gems and revelations that can serve as catalysts to awakenings of all kinds.

Two Middle Names

Like the first name, the middle can also be composed of two or more names and this will indicate the presence of two (or more) separate energies; and since these energies are on the *inside* and not at a social level, this indicates the presence of two diverse energies or directions in the deep psyche. Put even more succinctly, the more middle names a person has, the more confused and confusing they may be to themselves and others because of assorted and sometimes contrary energies conflicting within. In such cases, a close look at the individual energies will usually identify a central conflict (for example, the forceful 1 may not quite jive with the tender and loving 6), which can be addressed and even resolved once recognized. Occasionally, of course, a hyphenated (first or) middle name can hold two different yet positive energies that can work quite well together. On the other hand, two inner energies can conflict with one another, in which case, dropping one or the other name can help soothe the inner fluctuations.

What If You Don't Have a Middle Name?

The absence of a middle name can actually prove beneficial; it means you are very upfront about who you are—what you see is what you get. If you are a nasty badass, you are a nasty badass and make no attempt to hide it. Or, you can be very regal, collected, and reserved and that too will show your true nature shining through. Folks with only first and last names tend to say it like it is and appear fairly straightforward and genuine; whether that be a positive or negative will depend on the numbers, letters, and Lifepath energies connected to the name.

Your Last Name—Domestic Influence

Your last name is related to the domestic history of the family, or the male hierarchy. As such, it is of lesser import, as it comments only on the energy present when you joined the circle, so to speak, in much the same manner as the year of birth is of least import, as it merely comments on what phase the Earth was in when you made your initial appearance here. Obviously, both energies will affect a person, but are not as important as *who they are,* which is reflected in the first and middle names and day and month of birth. The domestic name often holds the source of major life lessons, especially if the last name is inherited from male relatives or, put another way, if it is the name you grew up with. Here is where the foundational building blocks are laid that will influence adult interactions and belief systems. These energies, however, are not *you*—they were already here when you arrived.

If your last name is your married name, this is reflective of the male hierarchy that originates with your husband and his ancestors and again, this is not *your* energy. It will, however, affect you and your family, so making yourself aware of its frequencies can assist you in communicating with your family members, especially when touchy subjects arise, such as between yourself and your spouse and even your children.

Lifepath Number

Lifepath Numbers tell you what you are here to learn, to become, to do. It will highlight the direction you are to take in order to achieve your goals or lessons while here, and it is not unusual for Lifepath lessons to introduce a few harsh learning curves, learning curves that will be repeated if the point is not taken or simply not understood. This will manifest as negative cycles that repeat themselves: some will point out your need to take responsibility; some will point out your need to honor your creativity; some will advise you against living lifestyles that are oil to your water. The possibilities are as significant and as unique as you are. Whatever the message of your Lifepath, you will find a direction therein—a confirmation of something you already suspected or a push down that road you have always wanted to investigate. If you have ever wondered why you are here, your Lifepath will help you find the answer.

The Lifepath Number is found in the combination of your day and month of birth. For example, let's say your birthday is September 5. You would calculate it as follows:

September + 5
9 (month) + 5 = 14/5

Your Lifepath would be 5 and your sub number would be 14.

Ideally, you should be able to link one of your main names or totals to your Lifepath Number or a component thereof. This simply intensifies and focuses your energy and ability to complete your lessons while here and also comments on the more mysterious aspect of this art: it is almost inevitable that you will see repeating numbers in your own chart. Don't worry, however, if this is not the case. While it is usually a fairly simple matter to adjust a name to line up with a Lifepath energy, a Lifepath Number that stands apart from all name energies (for instance, it is the only major number of its kind in your entire chart) is not necessarily a bad thing—it just indicates the presence of something that will need to be honored at some point in your life. For example, imagine a woman whose chart is filled with the loving number 6 essence, but her Lifepath is the driving force of number 1. This woman seems utterly domestic and devotes herself with complete focus to her home and kids for twenty-odd years before (out of the blue, her friends say) starting her own company, into which she pours the same level of devotion that she afforded her kids. In short order, her business venture becomes highly successful.

This woman had to honor the loving domesticity of the 6 in her chart as much as she did the driving force of her number 1 Lifepath.

That said, keep in mind that Lifepath Numbers can indicate a lifestyle that is already being pursued, and as such, it serves as a strong confirmation that the road you are upon is the correct one. This is usually the case when such confirmation is indeed, *needed.*

The flip side of the coin involves a kick-in-the-pants kind of energy. This occurs when an awakening of sorts is required. This can come in the form of something that has been submerged or subjugated, which needs to be honored, and the Lifepath will call attention to it in no uncertain terms. Oftentimes, there will be a sense of relief and almost of having been given permission to pursue that which the heart truly desires or a wry recognition in the truth of its message.

Either way, you will know what yours is saying. It will *resonate* with you in a way that will be undeniable.

Your Day of Birth

The actual day you were born is also very important: it is almost like your main sub number for your Lifepath, but its message is more personal, more intimate. This is the supreme comment on the single-most influential energy that is personal to you—it celebrates your introduction. It's like your "coming out" or debut (into reality), and its ramifications cannot be understated. If your day of birth falls in the 1 to 9 scale, those energies are fairly straightforward, as they are composed of single and fairly direct energies. If, however, your day of birth holds two digits, here is how you will read them. First, look at the initial number, which can only be a 1, 2, or 3. Ascertain the meanings for the number specific to you. Then look at the second number for its connections. And finally, look at the number that both reduce to. For example, if your day of birth is the 25th, you would consider the meanings of the 2 (the impact of couples, pairs, and relationships) and the 5 (changes, freedom, experimentation of the senses). These two energies suggest that while relationships of all kinds are important (2), they may take a back seat to the desire to explore, to travel, to chase stimulation and freedom (5). The final total of the

25 takes us to a Lifepath Number 7, which is a completely different vibe in that it rules the functions of the brain and relates to intense and investigative thought—this is an introspective and generally reserved energy. This suggests that the Lifepath will ultimately lead down a new path: one of logic, practicality, introspection, meditation, and wisdom. There is much more to the 7 than this, but we will save that for later. Suffice it to say that this example shows two opposing forces: one is changeable and even thrill-seeking (25), while the other is controlled, dignified, analytical, and possibly (depending on the development stage of the individual) mystical, imaginative, and spiritual (7). So the struggle here might be whether to allow the senses to dictate the direction of the mind or to allow the mind to dictate the direction of the senses.

When you have calculated your own Lifepath, simply apply the number meaning to your own life. Follow your intuition and the connections and messages will come.

Remember to allow yourself the time for contemplation as your brain knows all and is highly attuned to the receipt of thought-form messages. Something you read today might not connect until two days from now.

Your Current Energy Phase

Your current energy phase will indicate where you are in terms of transiting your name energy, as shown in your (first) sub number for each name; this is the number of years the energies in each name will take to pass through. Each letter holds its own nuances and characteristics, and the corresponding number value expands its meaning.

When calculated, your "code" will signal the prevailing forces currently at play in your life, and by truly understanding their characteristics and tone, you will be equipped to understand and relate and possibly align yourself and your actions to these energies and use them to attain the best possible results. Here is an example of how to calculate your current energy phase, and we will use our old friend, John, once again as an example.

J O H N	A D A M	S M I T H
1 7 5 5	1 4 1 4	3 4 1 4 5
=18 (years)	= 10 (years)	= 17 (years)

Let's say John is 40 years of age. Since the main sub number of his first name is 18, we automatically know that he has transited the energies of John at least twice (18+18=36), which would leave him back at the J at the age of 37, which covers 1 year, so at 40, he would be in the 3rd year of the O letter energy. Looking at his middle name and following the same process leaves us in the last year of the M cycle while his last name completes the code with another M. So his current code is OMM or 744, which are the number values assigned to each letter. Added together, this code reduces to 15/6. Since we have already talked about the number 6, you will know that family, domesticity, community, nurturing, and love, or the lack of these elements, will be the focus for John during this energy phase and that the forces of change (15) will also play a role. Again, the way phases are read and the meanings attached will become clearer as we proceed, but in the meanwhile, follow the above pattern to uncover your own energy phase and record it for future reference.

Your Identity Initials

Here is yet another code of sorts and can be called a short-hand version of all that you are and also of the (usually) three main influences of your life, which makes sense since initials are composed of your Cornerstone energies. Follow the same method of calculation to reach your Initial energy as you did with your current energy phases: simply add the number values of your initials together, reduce them, and look at the sub number and final digit as well as the letter energies to glean more information about your complete shorthand handle. (Mine is HAL, the total of which also matches my first name number of 9.)

Try this yourself and see if your Identity Initials connect anywhere to your name chart or Lifepath number. Connections will continue to appear as you compile your various numbers and codes.

Predominant Letters

The highest quantity of repeating letters in your entire name will tell you all about the prevailing *event* energies that have the strongest effects for you—their influences never really abate, especially if there are four or more of one-letter energy present and more so if one or two are Cornerstones. For example, if your name contains one C, you will know that you are a natural communicator of some kind and that the urge to investigate this angle will manifest at some point in your life (count through your name in years to ascertain when a certain phase will be highlighted for you). If, however, your name contains four of these letters and one is a Cornerstone, you will know that the meaning of the C will be emphasized and will create a *necessity* to use your communication skills in your daily life. So, if you've always wanted, for example, to write music and sing or become a photographer, the multi-C would be telling you to *start doing* it as opposed to *just thinking* about it. The more repetitions, the more important the messages held in the letter (or letters) will be.

Predominant Numbers

The highest number of specific numbers in your entire name offers yet another view into your name. This one involves an *energy* or *speed* snapshot. Let's say you have six number 1 values in your handle. It would be a safe bet to say that you are not likely to give up and throw in the towel when things get rough—you are the survivor, and survivors don't just lie down and die. Let's take this further and presuppose that your second-highest number quantity is the number 6: this suggests that while giving up is not an option, neither is the search for a loving and nurturing home and partner and all that this would entail. Looking at my own numbers, there are a total of seven number 1 values (four of which are in my Soul energy), which means that, thankfully, I am a survivor. There is a core energy within that will not allow me to give up or give in. I will keep going despite setbacks. What do yours say about you?

Words in Names

If by chance your name contains another name or word, the meaning of the attached sound energy often points out a subtle message. Consider my first name: it contains the words

"heat" and "her," which confirms my major issue with heat—
I hate it. This peculiarity roots back to my childhood when
being hot all the time earned me the nickname of "Heater."
On the other hand, as I grow older, the reverse is also becoming true; the cold bites through my bones in a way it never
has before, therefore, "heat her" has taken on a whole new,
and just as accurate meaning—but I still hate heat!

Look carefully at your names and be open to sub-level
energy messages. If you should find some, listen to what
they are saying to you. It may be nothing of major consequence, but it may also provide confirmation of peculiar
details, much as my "heat" and "her" does, or, it can refer to
something more important. Again, this is something that
only you will truly connect with.

How to Read Your Name

Like reading a sentence, the letters in your name are read
from left to right. Each letter symbol flows into the next
and creates a pattern of energies. For example, let's look at
the letter energies in the word HEAT. The basic meaning
for each letter is as follows: the H is a ladder that offers two
different directions—up or down. The E is sheer Energy
that accentuates and exaggerates, especially that which
comes before it. The A creates a new and original force.
The T is additional in nature; therefore, it "adds to" or
"makes stronger."

So, the word HEAT is read like this: we have a rise in
something (H) that is beyond the norm (E) that creates a
considerable force (A) and keeps building (T).

Taking this further, both the H and E are 5 values, which are connected to the senses and the stimulation of those senses. The A is a 1 value, which begins something new and points to survival, and the T is a 4 value, which refers to fundamental issues and includes the health of the body. We all know that HEAT involves *rising* temperatures that are inherently *excessive* and that it can easily create a heavy and almost-unbearable *force*, which will only get heavier as the heat *increases*. This HEAT can negatively impact the body and its senses, and when it soars to unbearable degrees, it can even threaten human survival.

Your name is also a blueprint. Look to the individual letter meanings and their supportive numbers for descriptives and then link those elements together. This can take some practice, but it can be done; *feel* the letters in your name, link them together, and trust your intuition when doing so.

The Love Thing

Have you ever wondered about the connections between yourself and your mate? Here is a way to find out about the vibrations and, indeed, the lessons and challenges that have brought the two of you together.

There are two ways to do this: the first is to add your first names together and the second is to add your Daily Names together. Your first name additions will address your personal interactions with one another while the second will comment on the likely outcome or result of your union. Each method takes both the final sub number and single digit into consideration when looking for messages.

Let's say that your first name additions total to a 6. This would mean that the two of you respond and react to each other with loving and caring energies, but that care must be taken to avoid each becoming so absorbed in the other that individual identities are blurred. Taken further, let's say that the combination of your Daily Names totals to a 5; this would indicate the need for freedom, independence, changes, and sensory stimulation *on both sides.* Needless to say, this combination can easily indicate an ultimate separation—the 5 energy is usually not overly attached to domestic bliss and routine. If, however, each partner can honor the other's need for personal space, this union can flow with the changes of the 5 while also providing each other the safe haven of the 6.

Extended Connecting Numbers

Extended connecting numbers are to be found in a variety of areas that can include everything from the total count of the actual letters in your name to addresses and phone numbers. Write down the last four numbers in each of your landlines or cell phone numbers (the area codes and first three numbers are excluded, as the area and exchange codes are shared by many others—only the last four numbers connect directly to you). Add those numbers until they reduce to a single digit. These calculations will tell you about the energy surrounding each number. This can also be applied to your home and work address (include the street name as well, but do pay close attention to the actual numbers in the address), your Social Security/Insurance number, your driver's license, license plate, charge card numbers (again, check online for the actual numbers that point to you; for example, one company's card shows that the first six numbers are multiple-use and that the last one is also a reference number—hence, the nine numbers between the two are your personal account vibrations), bank accounts (again, stick to your actual account number)—any number that has a personal connection to you. See how many of those numbers correspond with numbers from your chart. If there are any number energies that do not fit, look closely at the things they represent. For instance, if a prominent number in your personal chart is a 6 (the gentle and loving domesticity), but you are living in an 8 energy home, you might be more comfortable elsewhere, as the 8 energy generally carries overtones of power, control, and authority, which can override and overwhelm a gentle 6 energy.

To be aware of the number energies that constantly surround us is revelatory in itself and often provides answers to questions one may not even be aware need asking. Take a serious look at the numbers *before* moving into that new house, accepting a new name (through marriage, for example), naming your child, hiring an employee, or simply picking out a new PIN number at the bank. And always remember your own numbers so you will have a point of reference.

The numbers and letters in your life affect you in direct and indirect ways. Consider even the date on which you've decided to begin a new project or set up that all-important meeting. Do you choose the 1st (good) or the 9th (not so good)? You want to ask that special person out for the first time? Try it on the 6th, the energy of love, rather than the 5th, which, while being an energy of communication and sensory input, is also the energy of change and non-commitment.

Chaldean numerology is a tool of many uses. It can be used to do some deep digging into your own soul or to measure the energies of others. It can offer commentaries on people, places, and things, or just tell you about the essence behind your favorite numbers.

Its uses are countless and invaluable. Just keep this book nearby and use it as a reference.

… perfect numbers, like perfect [people] are very rare …
—René Descartes (1596–1650)

three

The Numbers

In order to illustrate the dynamics of the number scale, I have included brief snapshots of the journey of one man and how he started out alone, met his mate, fathered a child, built a home, adjusted to changes, contemplated his existence, reached a spiritual balance, and finally, left this plane of reality. This Lone Man travels through the vibrational pictures and experiences that are inherent to the number scale and serves to bring the subtleties involved to light. He is a simple tool designed to provide understanding of the number energies that are really just a narrative of the journey of mankind—from beginning to end and back again. (This is not the only system to do so—the Major Arcana of the Tarot also follows this same route, something that I will expand upon as we proceed.) In other words, each number introduces new elements to those that came before, so the 5 for example will be a compilation of the qualities and characteristics of the numbers 1 through 4 while also introducing the specific vibrations of the 5.

You will find the traditional characteristics, as well as the Lifepaths and challenges for each number, listed at the end of its section (Master Number Lifepaths are listed under Master Numbers).

Nothing and Everything: The Majesty of Zero (0)

The zero was not considered a number by the ancient Chaldeans because it held no quantity and therefore no purpose, but in keeping with progress and amalgamation, I have included it here, as its importance cannot be denied and its uses are instrumental and necessary in analysis.

The subject of the 0 (shared in the letter O) is often up for debate: is it a number or not? Whether it is a member of the set of "natural numbers" or "real numbers" has nothing to do with anything—the zero or cipher plays a pivotal and impressive role in numerology and in our very existence, and, as such, it is worthy of a paragraph or two. The intensity and potential of the 0 is not to be underestimated.

The 0 contains both mystical and multi-level dynamics that defy simple explanation. Its mathematical essence is "no thing"—nothing, zip, and zero (00.00)—however, with a tiny addition, it can become everything (1,000,000). The symbol itself has no beginning and no end and its connection to eternity is characterized by the figure 8 laid on its side, which forms the lemniscate—the symbol of infinity. One of the more prominent manifestations of its meaning can be found in the matching circles of a pair of wedding rings: one hopes the union lasts forever. It is also the big fat 0 on a test or its complete opposite, 100 percent. It is the bubbles you blow in the bathtub, the drain down which the water flows, and the eyeballs staring back at you in the mirror. It is the O in Open and the O in clOsed. It is the shape of an atom, a human cell, a donut, a crop circle, and a lollipop. It is the protective circle cast by the metaphysician and the circle of yin and yang worn about many necks.

While the 0 is practically limitless in its applications, it does seem to focus on either the increase or decrease of matter. It is power, intensity, and creation, but it can take away as easily as it gives.

I have always noticed connections between the energies of numbers and the meanings of the 22 Major Arcana cards in the Tarot deck.

The first Major Arcana tarot card, the Fool, is numbered 0 and represents the world of possibilities that are open and waiting to be discovered. The Fool (complete with two O vibrations) is the blank slate that exists as man steps into the picture. This energy is rife with anticipation and prospects: choices in direction are imminent and any actions taken will lead to results of some kind.

Since the figure on this card appears either oblivious to or not worried by the cliff at his feet, he is often seen as a brave risk-taker. He can also be seen as a flat-out fool, for who else would be watching the sky while they are negotiating a dangerous cliff? The truth lies somewhere in the middle: this Fool is not a fool at all—he is fully aware of where he is and what he is doing; after all, he has thought long enough on the matter to have brought along his necessary possessions (in the little bag) and his loyal companion (the little dog). The deeper truth of this image is found in the symbolic rose he holds: roses are usually connected to love or emotions, and his gaze heavenward is simply illustrative of his strong level of faith; he is looking to Universe for guidance and trusts this guidance implicitly. The Fool is not stupid. He is simply following his dreams and his intuition and is preparing for new beginnings ... and any new beginning involves an element of risk. This figure has no visible history; therefore any forward movement will introduce scenarios in which anything is possible.

Which sets the stage perfectly for Act 1 to begin.

Number One (1): Beginning of All—Original Force

Here we will open with our Lone Man; consider him the caveman of this story. He has no one to turn to for aid or advice. He is *alone,* a single entity who has "no thing" in his past; therefore, he is the initiator of all things. Our Lone Man is, at heart, a *survivor,* and in true keeping with his instincts and intuition (although he may not recognize them as such), he must provide himself with basic necessities such as food and shelter. He must do for himself, as there is no one else to do for him—here is the individual who is tightly bound to his natural ego and instincts. He is the one who begins the search for experiences and achievement.

The number 1 is masculine in its approach, which means it has all of the attributes society often assigns to successful men. The 1 is brave, ambitious, goal-oriented, pro-active, and confident. The 1 energy displays a strength of will that often lands that person at the top of the heap, even if getting there takes a while—the 1 often has to start over from square 1. But if the person with this number essence finds and sets its focus on a project, position, or person, they will move buildings, hills, or mountains in order to reach their goal. To say that the 1 is motivated would be a slight understatement: the pure, "1 and only" forerunner to the entire number system will stop at almost nothing to get what they want if they want it badly enough. Progress is what matters, and if compassion is not thrown into the mix, a strong 1 vibration can become dominated and directed by the ego, and even fail to notice the damage their trail-blazing attitudes and activities can leave in their wake. Most number 1s will display some level of these qualities at some point, however, the more number 1 values in a name, the more exaggerated these qualities will become. While the 1 is all about moving forward and experiencing as much as they can about everything, they can also come across as arrogant, self-centered, unemotional, and even selfish while doing so—but that is the nature of the vibration. This energy is gifted with an insatiable and endless curiosity—"initial glows" can and do wear off—so old jobs, stagnant relationships, and boring hobbies can all be up for review... constantly. After all, there are so many other things to investigate and experience. This tendency can leave many projects unfinished, lessons not learned, and friendships unattended.

Since the 1 can be seen as somewhat self-absorbed, intimate relationships can be difficult propositions as well, for as much as this energy loves to be in love, it is the *idea* of love, the perfect *ideal* of love that the number 1 chases. Unfortunately, reality rarely lives up to fantasy and the 1 often keeps looking ... and looking ... and looking. Attempting emotional involvement with the average (multi)1 can be a lonely and confusing challenge, as the 1 character will blow hot and cold and draw close before pulling away. If, by chance, the 1 should find something or someone of interest, there their attention will focus, and quite intently. Unfortunately, their focus usually shifts. They may return after a time, but the damage will have been done. This can make committed, straightforward love unions, marriages, and even friendships a struggle at times. Work and other interests tend to take precedence over intimacy, and since the 1 is driven to succeed, constant action and busy-ness can become repetitive to the point of predictability.

So, if you are looking for a soft, cuddly lovey-dove who will rub your feet each night, bring you dinner (cook it, too?), lend a sympathetic ear, and offer genuine, gentle advice before tucking you into bed, I would strongly suggest you look elsewhere, perhaps to the domestic 6 or the couple-based 2.

Perhaps paradoxically, this number is also open to the instinctual aspects of survival and, therefore, usually does not question similar messages from intuition. This actually helps to explain why the 1 advances and achieves: they follow the lead laid out for them and do not doubt its source—although they may well think that the source of such messages is self-generated.

From an aesthetic and spiritual point of view, the single, straight line a man might draw in the sand to indicate him "self" is appropriate to his condition. It is the basis for the first-person singular and incorporates the "I" as in the self and the ego: "I be," "I exist," and "I am." On a more evolved level, the I illustrates the link between God and man. It is the umbilical cord that connects us to "out there" and thereby allows us to have hope and faith, and to experience love. Intuition is the voice of Universe and connects us to the bigger picture, whether consciously realized or not.

An almost-perfect example of the concept of Original Force is to be found when contemplating and analyzing the scientific term used to describe the twin coils that hold our individual strands of DNA: this particular abbreviation even *totals* to a 10 (1). This is truly a unique, progressive, original, and creative force that dictates the human code and yet assigns incredible differences in each person so they become true individuals. As such, it is the ideal representation of the Original Force of the number 1.

The number 1 personality can be almost overwhelming in terms of their personal power, creative abilities, and ultimate achievements, but this usually only comes after considerable experimentation with a variety of careers. When they do find their focus, usually later in life, it will often involve a unique or different topic, method, activity, or trade. It is truly an original and is drawn to all things inspiring. The dull and boring do not attract the number 1—they prefer anything that fits into the categories of different, unusual, odd, bizarre, or downright weird.

When the Original Force of the number 1 is understood, harnessed, and directed, the results can be awe inspiring. Here you might find an award-winning architect who quietly runs homes for the needy, a top military advisor who is also a volunteer teacher to the disabled, or an honest-to-goodness billionaire who lives in a small community home and anonymously donates a large percentage of his income to humanitarian charities. These number 1 vibrations will have consciously realized the spiritual side of existence and combined it with the natural force of their ruling number. The point is that *if* a 1 energy can gather all of its power and steer it in the direction decided, the results can be dramatic. This energy, especially when compounded with more 1 values, can become one of the most penetrating and compelling forces in the numbers game. The pure will, intent, intuitive prowess, and creative abilities contained in the number 1 will give them the strength to survive, the drive to keep going, and the compelling urge to escape, all of which come in very handy if 1s should find themselves in dire circumstances or abusive situations. Rarely will a strong number 1 be held down for long. They will find a way out.

I find it more than interesting that the Major Arcana tarot card valued by the number 1 is the Magician, who is nothing if not dynamic, focused, and in charge of himself and his destiny. This figure has all of the tools he needs to accomplish his goals and takes action both in his mind and with his body to create that which he desires. The Magician is resourceful, intuitive, curious, and adventurous, and he moves ahead with purpose and focus. One might say that this figure has a remarkable level of power at his or her disposal (ancient societies may have labeled this energy as a witch; however, modern-day translations would be more in line with practicing the Law of Attraction) and anything is possible.

The Major Arcana tarot card of the Sun (number 19) reduces to an Original Force number 1 as well. It represents energetic creation and new beginnings. In fact, the Sun is the most sublime of all number 1 energies. It is like a gigantic light bulb in the sky without which the world, her people, her animals, and her crops would perish. The world would plunge into darkness and nothing would ever be right or normal again. The Sun is the life-giver (the term  "the Sun" totals to a 10/1, as well) and is the consummate example of the energy behind the Original Force number 1; it allows us to survive. As previously mentioned, its number is 19, and this combines the Original Force with repeated endings and beginnings, which makes absolute sense as we

all know that the Sun rises and sets... for all of us.

Yet another Major Arcana tarot card, called the Wheel of Fortune (number 10), also reduces to the power and originality of the 1. Its overall tone is one of unexpected change. It appears when one situation changes rather quickly, thus introducing something completely new into the life ("Fortune" totals to a 10/1, as well—and we all know that it can bring good or bad with it). The Wheel is ever-turning and represents the ongoing theme of endings and beginnings we all experience. The Wheel speaks to starting new phases, dealing with changes, and adjusting to the surprises life can throw at you when you least expect it—all of which result in necessary shifts in place or circumstance, be it for the positive or the negative (notice that the four corner figures are all reading from what I call the "book of life" in which all things are possible). On another level, the number 10 depicted does hold a positive message, which is that the Wheel often brings success and reward: picture spinning the Wheel your whole life and finally hitting the jackpot. This ties into the meaning of the 10, which we will get into later; for now, let's just say that it indicates rewards after a long struggle and achievements that can affect mankind in a small or rather large way.

All of these Major Arcana energies support the meaning of the one-and-only 1 in their own unique ways.

Multi 1 Values

I have found the unadulterated and "uncut" multiple 1 energy to be similar to the proverbial bull in a china shop. This refers to the purest form of this energy, unaffected by any nearby influential or softening letters. When the 1 appears more than four times in a chart (including within the name itself and also as Whole, Daily, or Total Name and Lifepath numbers), it compounds the pure thrust of this Original Force energy, which can be quite intimidating and even ruthless. Curiously, while the number 1 is generally non-demonstrative and non-emotional, at least on the surface (being *first* theoretically means having no frame of reference), the 1 can be quite the talker, very charming, and socially active. However, despite this apparent openness, the 1 often finds it difficult to share deep emotions; they maintain a certain distance even while apparently deeply involved and wear a protective mask on a daily basis. The presence of too many 1s translates into the inability to truly immerse into an intimate/love relationship due to the aforementioned lack of a frame of reference. There is hope for the lonely 1: if they are successful in learning their challenges well and learning to control their ego, the 1 can become compassionate, intuitive, and loving with a level of faith and openness that could transform the 1 into a truly warmhearted energy and something of a rare breed.

When a chart is filled with 1s, this indicates someone who will try and try again, as mentioned. The 1 is a new start, so it stands to reason that many 1s show the necessity for many new starts. This is the true "tell" of the survivor.

A Chart that Holds No 1 Values

This can indicate a personality who needs to tap into their own abilities and move forward with confidence and determination. A lack of 1 values can also indicate a personality who will back down more often than not and who possesses no particular goals in life. There is a marked lack of drive and motivation, but this is not necessarily a bad thing—it just indicates a softer personality.

Traditional Descriptives

Typical traits of the 1 energy include ambitious, determined, progressive, active, instinctual, curious, original, and creative. More negative descriptions include superior, arrogant, impatient, controlling, ego-driven, and sometimes cruel and abusive.

Words that Total to Number 1

The following words demonstrate the very essence of an Original Force in their meanings and totals. Consider the following as individual forces: death, soul, spirit, faith, passion, devil—and even the core words used to describe the 1 energy: origin and forces.

Lifepath for the Number 1

Anyone with a number 1 Lifepath will be or become a leader of some type, whether that is as a supervisor of an office or as the owner of a multi-million-dollar business. The number 1 Lifepath is all about striving and starting over as many times as required to achieve success. As a pioneering vibration, the 1 often has difficulty in intimate relationships and often prefers to live alone (and if in a relationship, it is advisable that the number 1 have a room or a space that they can call their own). The number 1 needs to understand that they are not necessarily here to build a family and home. They are here to accomplish something—something they can leave behind when they go, and preferably something that will prove beneficial in some way to mankind. Commitment to that aim or goal is a large part of this Lifepath lesson.

Challenge for the Number 1

The challenge for the number 1 is to overcome the ego through the use of the intuition and acknowledgement of a higher power or element. The 1 needs to "gentle" itself through connections with others and learn to allow emotional vulnerability—they need to learn how to drop their guard. The number 1 is challenged to never give up on doing and pursuing that which they love, for it is there that the 1 will find the success they seek.

Quirky Phrase to Remember the 1 By

1 Angry Queen Yells In Jail

This should help you remember that number 1 represents the letters A, Q, Y, I, and J.

Number Two (2): Pairs and Duality

Okay, so now our Lone Man has found some food and has built a shelter. As mentioned, he is alone. This is where the energy of the number 2 comes in, and it comes in the form of a woman who suddenly appears at the border of his campsite; he is no longer alone. Now there is another person involved and the lone man has now become part of a duo or couple. The jump from one person to two introduces a completely new situation.

As with any combination of original or unique energies (combination of 1+1=2 or male/female), there will be natural conflict, as each have different personalities, likes and dislikes, preferences, interests, methods of communication, traits, and idiosyncracies. In a "couple" type of situation, these differences can manifest in many ways. One sleeps late, the other rises early. One prefers silence, the other is constantly chattering. One is quite untidy, the other is a neat freak. The possibilities are endless. As you can imagine, conflict can easily become an issue and a *duel* based on *duality* can occur. The key word here is *compromise*, and it is one of the challenges for the number 2.

However, luckily for our Lone Man and for contemporary man/woman, the 2, or addition to the scene, is generally known for its ability to see both sides of an issue, is a peaceful and generous energy and seeks romance, domesticity, and is not forceful or domineering. As such, any conflicts that may arise will likely be short in duration, then overcome and settled by the gentle 2. It is a feminine energy, one that is soft and diplomatic and compliments the individualism of the number 1. A necessity of the 2 is the existence of another element, opinion, or person. Consider "2 halves of the whole," "the better half," or "2 peas in a pod": the dual aspects inherent in the 2 form the basis for the "Cosmic Parents and the Family of Man" (20). This would indicate that most positive 2 energies have a high potential of becoming truly supportive and loving parents, friends, employees, and partners.

Unfortunately, when unsure of its place, or emotionally threatened, the 2 personality is also known to be overly sensitive, indecisive, insecure, possessive, moody, sulky, reproachful, and vengeful. There is a strong risk of passive aggressiveness here, which can be one of the most difficult duels to fight and win. However, if all is fairly mellow in the world of the 2, they will give all of themselves to friendships, family members, job, and home. The 2 is the peacemaker; it will do all in its power to calm troubled waters and makes a wonderful arbitrator or mediator because of its innate ability to see both sides of an issue.

The 2 needs people and things around them. They need a comfort zone (which is composed of familiar objects and people) in order to function effectively. For this reason, you may well come across many 2s who are collectors... of anything, from plastic stir sticks to people. It would not be uncommon to find a 2 energy surrounded by several pets, running a day-care, or housing a few relatives.

It must be added that while an obvious result of combining energies may result in conflict, it also results in intimacy. Number 2 *needs* closeness, sharing, honesty, and reassurance in its relationships but, most importantly, the 2 needs to be *in* a relationship that ultimately leads to physical intimacy. This number is very tactile and thirsts for the reassurance of hugs, kisses, and other displays of affection. This need can be so intense that oftentimes the 2 will *settle* just to have someone near. Too many 2s in a chart would indicate a foundational lack in formative relationships, for example, between parent and child. The 2 in question would then spend a majority of their time searching for that elusive love connection they were deprived of at the beginning of their lives here. As you can imagine, such a search in terms of an adult relationship may lead to a fair amount of heartbreak, as the search would be for the nurturing and care of a parent rather than the sharing and equality of a spouse. The 2 must ideally find a middle ground between the yearning for an absolute union and maintaining a sense of self. Generally speaking, though, the 2 is all about the *love thing.* Enough of the right stuff will help any seeking 2 to recognize and break cycles that belong in the past. In fact, the high compassion level present in several 2 energies indicates a predisposition towards becoming effective counselors, therapists, or teachers. They are great listeners and very sensitive to the emotional states of others.

Flashback to our Lone Man and Woman. It is a dark and stormy night. Lightning sparks, thunder rolls, and the skies open in a deluge. The woman is frightened and scurries into the shelter and safety of the man's arms. Of course, a fire is crackling and throwing golden warmth and dancing shadows upon them as they stand together, gazing raptly into one another's eyes. After they have discovered the thrill of a first kiss, a nap is suddenly in order and they lie down upon the warm, soft bearskin rug next to the fire. And while they may not actually think about it, they have just initiated the beginnings of a creative process of the Highest Order. The fertile, active, creative, and even magickal energy of the number 3 has begun to work its wonders. They will see this extraordinary event develop over the course of the next nine months.

More on this miracle later.

The Major Arcana tarot card attached to the number 2 is the High Priestess. I think of her as full of secrets and sacred and sometimes dangerous knowledge, which is implied in the heavy book she carries in her lap (the TORA is often thought to refer to the TAROT backwards, with the T hidden; TORA is also found on the Wheel of Fortune ... others, like myself, believe this to be the Book of Law). The High Priestess is

the female equivalent of the Magician and holds much of the same mystery and magickal prowess and powers, but her strongest sense is that of her intuition.

In human form, she represents someone who is just as open to the reality that surrounds her as she is to the inner world of the intuition and spirit. She is the two joined as one: she is the cover of the book and its contents and represents the connection between units of two, specifically that of Spirit and man. Notice also that the number 2 is visually highlighted on this card as she sits between two columns, of which one is white and the other black; again referring to the two different worlds of the High Priestess. However, she is neither black, nor white; her truth lies in the shade between the two.

The Major Arcana tarot card of Justice (11) also reduces to the number 2 and refers to the two components of the law: innocence versus guilt. Other ways of saying this are "lies versus truth" or "good versus evil" or "right versus wrong." Justice's job is to discern the truth (notice again the two pillars Justice sits between) and to achieve some manner of balance, which is symbolically evident in the (2) plates that form the scale of balance shown on the card, and in the sword held in the opposite hand. The scales register only when something is added and that something is represented here by the sword, which is an air element and refers to the power of the spoken word. Therefore, words that are spoken play a significant role here and will determine the outcome when placed on the scales. It will come as no great surprise that Justice does indeed refer to the Justice system, which governs "legal versus illegal" acts. This is another way of saying "as above, so below." Justice keeps things even and fair, down to the legal contract and the fine print, for what is printed may secret away a lie.

The Major Arcana card of Judgement shows a value of 20, which also cores down to the number 2. As you can see, the Archangel Gabriel blows a horn over the figures who seem to be standing in their coffins and who do seem to be part of a grave-yard. My own feeling about this card is that it offers a second chance—another life, an alternate route. Another take on this card is that it offers the opportunity to rise above the limits of our human bodies and egos. Either way, Judgment has two sides: for and against. As such, it ties in to the duality of the 2 as well.

As you can see, the energy of the 2 is of paramount importance in terms of the content and meanings for all of these cards: two sides, two verdicts, and two realities.

Multi 2 Values

As mentioned, the name that is heavy in 2 values often experiences difficulty in personal relationships. The desire or need to "join with another" in a significant way is strong and usually cores back to an unsatisfactory union with either parent (not necessarily both). As such, the adult 2 will be prone to seeking out the perfect mate and can spend far too much time and energy trying to please those it cares for or loves. This can and does include friends, family, lovers, homes, jobs—anything that is composed of opposite or separate entities. The peacemaking number 2 seeks soft and kind emotions and personalities, which can, understandably, result in frequent disappointments. Predictably, these disappointments can also usher in periods of depression, caution, and a sense of insecurity. Should they become involved in obsessive or abusive situations or relationships, the number 2 can withdraw from life and become vulnerable to addictive habits, unethical or illegal behavior, and emotional instability.

A Chart with No 2 Values

A personality with no 2 values in their read will tend to treat intimate relationships in a rather lighthearted manner, or so it may appear. They may avoid emotional entanglements or will not feel the necessity to meld themselves with another. This type of energy will generally not require the presence of someone else to make them feel complete or valid. In fact, a chart showing low or no 2 vibrations may not feel the need to connect with others at all.

Traditional Descriptives

Some traditional descriptives of the number 2 personality are as follows: tactful, friendly, helpful, diplomatic, loyal, trustworthy, gentle, romantic, compassionate, nurturing, domestic, and shy. A negative 2 can be emotionally manipulative, moody, insecure, timid, mentally unbalanced, and passive-aggressive.

Words That Total to Number 2

The following words total to the number 2 and reflect both the nature of the 2 and the two-sided nature of this number essence: tactful, friendly, parental, spiritual, helpful, sharing, loyalty, balance, duality, door, window, bed, and telephone.

Lifepath for the Number 2

The number 2 is all about sharing, caring, and compromising. They will need a mate or someone to care for—relationships are the core essence of the 2. Work should involve one-on-one situations where social connections will be many. A natural negotiator, the 2 is calm in the face of conflict and will go out of its way to restore or maintain the peace. Kind and loyal, the 2 will thrive when surrounded by family and friends. They do need to learn compromise, though—not everyone is as complacent or as gentle as they are.

Challenge for the Number 2

The challenge for the 2s is to retain individuality even while within a loving group and to differentiate between themselves and others. In its search for love, they must come to understand that the source of love is at once cosmic and inner; it cannot be supplied by another person. The 2 needs to focus upon their own fulfillment and less on the fulfillment of others. This is not selfish; it is being true to the self. The challenge for the number 2 is to learn not to compromise themselves for love. The typical 2 also needs to learn to stand up for themselves and to speak their mind in an effective and clear manner.

Quirky Phrase to Remember the 2 By
2 Big Red Kisses
This should help you remember that the number 2 represents B, R, and K.

Number Three (3): Creativity and Magick

If you can picture our Lone Man and his woman a few months down the road and can see the lady as pregnant, you will have a good idea of the energy that surrounds the number 3. This number rules creativity, fertility, activity, thought, and a certain element of magick and luck. It speaks to the combined energies of two elements that produce a third and rather special one, in this case, a baby. I view this number essence as primarily feminine as well, although other sources see it as male. I suppose the most appropriate comment would be that it is a blend of the two.

There has been an incredible jump in physical and mental activity for these parents. The addition of a child has created a family (the triangle, trinity, or "3rd dimension" of the "mother, father, and child") and the parents are run off their feet. They are 100 percent focused on the birth of their baby and its needs, which are many. They often wonder about this magickal miracle, the perfection of this tiny entity and its creators, these 2 who are now 3. The point here is that the adults are solely focused on the needs, wants, and outright demands of the baby. When they are not busy *physically* caring for the needs of the child—which include feeding, changing, protecting, educating, encouraging, entertaining—they are *thinking* of the child and its future. Constant activity in thought and in body—that is the primary energy of the 3. That and its connection to magickal fortunes (creation of the child) and never-ending entertainment.

We shall now leave the frenetic abode of the Lone Man's family and translate the 3 energy into a person of modern times. As its main associations of creativity, fertility, activity, and luck might suggest, the 3 is always in motion. Both ancient and modern investigators consider the number 3 as the energy that creates all things as it overcomes the 2 of duality with the introduction of another aspect, such as the birth of a child. It is the trinity of body/mind/spirit, birth/life/death, thought/action/result, past/present/future, and beginning/middle/end. It holds the entire spectrum within its structure and energy; thus, the brain is always active, as is the body if not more so—it is poised for "ready, set, go."

This energy is always occupied with something—be it at work or at play. Common among 3s is physically doing one thing, while the brain or mind is on a completely different playing field, like being out shopping for shoes while wondering what color to paint the living room and whether or not to go to the office party next week. Typical 3s have short attention spans, which is why you won't find many of them engrossed in reading *War and Peace*. They prefer not to focus on one thing for too long; there are just too many other things to think about and do. Number 3 energies are very creative and are great communicators and, as such, make fantastic entertainers, comedians, artists, singers, or authors. Threes are touched by magick, as in the vision afforded by an open "3rd eye" (the mystical awakening thought held in the pineal gland, which is a tiny gland found in the center of the brain and behind the eyes). "Third time's the charm," "Father, Son, and Holy Ghost," "3 strikes, you're out!" (being given 3 chances), "3 wishes," and the 3-D world we live in. Or you can click your heels 3 times to go home.

So the 3 character would seem to refer to someone in possession of plenty of luck, dumb or otherwise. Threes tend to rise to the top of their profession because of their constant brain activity, level of creativity, energy, curiosity, and originality. To be honest, though, I never stop wondering what all these 3s are so industriously running from or to. Yes, part of the energy is natural and integral, but, unfortunately, there is usually a motivational factor in the level of energy expelled and such motivation generally sources back to childhood and holds a negative vibe, hence the drive to keep going, keep moving, never stop—for if the 3s stop, they will have to face not only themselves, but that from which they run so dogmatically. With the luck factor of the 3 rising through the roof, chances are good that no matter what the past might reveal, the 3 will make it through—maybe because of its challenge, which is to "rebirth," or to gather and assimilate all aspects of the self (body, mind, and spirit) into one balanced energy.

It is no great surprise that an older, unenlightened 3 is prone to running out of steam or, worse, hitting the wall. Translated, this speaks to the need to slow down as age encroaches, for the human body is not made to operate at high speeds for extended periods of time. The parts will naturally wear down or out and health problems will force the animated number 3 to take a time out…and it could be a long one.

Romantically, the partner of a 3 would need to be very independent and secure, as the constant activity of their partner would leave them to their own devises more often than not. The 3 might do well with a more grounded energy, like the 4, who will offer a stable home environment and the sense of steadiness an overactive 3 might just need and appreciate. Of course, that would mean that the 4 in question would need to relax some of their own natural impulses for order and routine, but, then again, doesn't love conquer all?

The energy of the 3 is evident once more when we look at the Major Arcana tarot card of the Empress: she is fertility at its finest. Sometimes referred to as Mother Earth, she is often portrayed as pregnant (and nearby sits the symbol for femininity), which can point to an actual birth of a child, relationship, or project. Anything that is fertile and growing is her domain. Most depictions of the Empress show her sur-

rounded by budding or blooming flowers, healthy trees, and flowing waters that are necessary to growth (and also represent emotions). She is the *mother*—and we all know how typically busy mothers are and the awe and respect with which they are usually perceived by their children. The Empress personifies feminine power, creativity, and magickal abilities (bringing forth a child). As such, she is to be regarded with the utmost respect and treated with care ... like our own Mother Earth should be.

The Major Arcana tarot card of the Hanged Man (number 12) also reduces to 3 and represents *taking action to cease action,* which is accomplished by voluntarily hanging upside down from a tree or post—all the better to see

situations from different angles and to take a time-out in order to contemplate and regroup. This card points to *stopping* the ever-active 3 energy; putting a hold on it or suspending it long enough to see things from a different perspective. Worthy of note is the number 12, which signifies a completion of some kind. This figure has reached the end of one stage and is pausing before continuing on. So this card's message is perhaps a bit odd in that it endeavors to *reverse and stop* activity and to impose rest—a deed that is done using rather unorthodox methods. The "halo" that surrounds our figure's head indicates new understanding and spiritual awakening.

The Major Arcana tarot card of the World (21) brings to mind the old saying that the world is your oyster, and this is indeed its meaning. There is a sense of balance in this card, which is reflected in the two wands the lady holds and the two lemniscates (symbols of

infinity), which can be seen at the upper and lower ends of the laurel wreath surrounding her. This is the reward at the end of a long road: it offers success, travel (an excellent example of activity), and a perfect oyster that opens (like magick) to reveal your own perfect pearl.

This is the last Major Arcana card, and it encompasses all previous activity and thought and identifies the conclusion to at least one chapter of the life, which is generally seen as rewarding. It is interesting to note that the human body has generally ceased its development by the age of 21 and that legal recognition is afforded in many countries when one reaches the age of 21. This points to levels of completions and feelings of wholeness and acceptance—a new base from which further action springs.

So here we have 3 very different cards that all support and demonstrate the power of the number 3 in very different ways, which are all tied together in the end.

Multi 3 Values

Too many 3 values in a name points to overactivity. Quite simply, the overly charged 3 energy can produce far too many interests, hobbies, directions, or connections. In other words, the multi 3 can be found moving from project to project, job to job, home to home, city to city, person to person—this is a search without definite destination or reward. The attention span of the 3 is limited and this can lead to infidelity, unreliability, and general chaos. On the flip side, the loaded 3 can also live an enviable lifestyle that can include considerable travel, excitement, and freedom—which is great, as long as it is what is truly desired. However, care must be taken to avoid misrepresentation of the self to others who may see things differently. For example, a 2 who is longing to settle down with a 3 may have a long wait, and the 3 should make their intentions clear in order to avoid misunderstandings and hurt feelings. This holds true for any connections in a heavily ruled 3 life … consideration of others is of major import.

A Chart with No 3 Values

Someone with no 3 values in their read will have a balanced lifestyle: physical activity is usually normal as is the level of thought patterns. They could, however, perhaps use a bit of good, old-fashioned luck (hang a horseshoe!), and may wish to incorporate a form of exercise in their routine.

Traditional Descriptives

Typical descriptions of the 3 include energetic, positive, creative/artistic, visionary, hypnotic, attractive, humorous, entertaining, flirtatious, charming, and sensual. When the 3 turns negative, it can be unreliable, vain, arrogant, wasteful, bored, evasive, illusive, and frustrating to deal with on any level.

Words that Total to Number 3

Some words that hold the energy of the 3 and/or stimulate the body, brain, or spirit are three, empress, love, magic, energy, comedian, entertainer, nurse, administrator, philosophy, activity, and hurricane.

Lifepath for the Number 3

The 3 is always up to something—they love adventures and new projects and would do well in positions that offer variety and spontaneity. Very social, charming, and entertaining, the number 3 Lifepath indicates creative self-expression (in whichever form it may come to the individual) as a natural gift that should be pursued. The road of the 3 can be an exciting one that includes routine travel, changes, and new experiences, and should ideally include a like-minded mate.

Challenge for the Number 3

The challenge for the 3 is to stop; to be still long enough to allow all aspects of the body, mind, and soul to unify. The 3 must learn to feel comfortable in their own skin. Doing nothing and allowing the mind to travel where it will (which is a form of meditation) is one of its challenges, while another is to honor their artistic and creative talents (or gifts). Attached to this last one is to learn to focus on one thing (the favorite pastime or hobby) and pursue it to the exclusion of all else. There is magick in doing so, and rebirth and spiritual satisfaction.

Quirky Phrase to Remember the 3 By
3 Grey Cats Lick Sauce
This should help you remember that the number 3 represents G, C, L, and S.

Number Four (4): Solid Foundations

Back at the Lone Man camp, there now exists a family. And the one thing most families like is a house: a safe, solid, and secure place to call home. Our Lone Man is no different. He has been chopping, molding, and clearing space so that he may plot the 4 corners of his structure and lay down firm and stable foundations upon which to build a house. Therein lay the base elements of the foundational 4: form, dependability, routine, safety, laws, proper procedure, stability, and durability.

The conventional number 4 of today is representative of the hard worker: someone who is practical, logical, productive, and protective. The pure 4 is grounded—it is firm and solid. Think of the 4 winds, the 4 seasons, the 4 directions, the 4 wheels on a car, the 4 legs of a chair, the 4 corners of a house, or even the traditional 4 members of a family. This energy, which I think of as male, is down-to-earth, responsible, logical, cyclical, repetitive, and practical, and usually represents a family-oriented, loyal, and patriotic person. An unfortunate side effect of this routine steadiness is boredom due to the simple repetitiveness of a persistent cycle, which is bound to become mundane at some point. The 4 needs to guard against becoming excessively bored and against procrastinating, for this can cause the more argumentative, opinionated, humorless, stubborn, and downright mean side of the 4 to emerge because of sheer frustration.

But overall, the 4 is one of the more favorable number energies, if one likes responsibility, honesty, reliability, and dependability. Other qualities that are particular to the 4 personality are meticulousness, perfectionism, and a seemingly natural dislike of some type concerning authority figures or anyone in a supervisory role. This is because of the 4's inherent ability and desire to take control and shoulder responsibility; they do not need another to do it for them or to show them how it is done. Accordingly, although 4s generally make excellent employees, they are more suited to self-employment. Some 4s can also have a case of having-to-have-the-last-word syndrome, a by-product of their built-in tendency to dominate (4 is connected to the 8, which is a controlling number). The

4 also has the strange ability to switch views or take opposing standpoints, similar to a debate with the same person arguing for both sides. And doing so convincingly, as well.

As mentioned, the 4 is one of the more consistent energies in the number scale simply because of the fact that it is dependable, loyal, genuine, and faithful. However, the 4 can also come in another, perhaps less desirable form—their lesson may involve *learning* how to be dependable and personally responsible. The difference between the two shouldn't be too hard to spot.

The Major Arcana tarot card of the Emperor (4) is the ultimate Father Figure and provides and personifies rules, authority, law, routine, reliability, and solid advice. In other words, he is a foundational, wise, and grounding energy and is not one to be challenged; this man has seen the world and knows its truths. The confident, assured, and relaxed attitude of the bearded man who sits upon his throne as though it were an extension

of himself speaks to his experiences just as his armor speaks to his past history of fighting the good fight. The image of the Ram that often accompanies him is yet another verification of the strength, determination, and leadership the Emperor embodies and serves to confirm the energies of the 4 he is ruled by. This man is law and experience combined; he knows that the answers to all questions rest upon truth.

Another Major Arcana tarot card which carries the 4 energies is Death (number 13): however, this grounded and foundational energy manifests in a slightly different way— it offers fundamental and often permanent changes to the elemental parameters of life itself. Its core meaning is of something that has been a key part of life coming to an end or changing in a significant way. The Death card rarely means actual physical death: it refers to basic issues and the shifts that take place within those basic structures. Thus, although its tone is disparate, Death grows from the same roots as the Emperor, and both figures are equally respected and perhaps even slightly feared because of the ultimate authority they both symbolize. However, upon taking a closer look at Death, the pure white horse he rides is actually a comment on clear and clean energy. Further, the Sun is on the rise in the distant sky. So this is not an ending as we think of it, rather, it is a beginning of something else; something that we may not be familiar with but which holds the promise of a new day, one that comes after experiencing a few dark nights.

I do want to add here that the tarot deck is composed of 22 Major Arcana cards (a Master Number that refers to building something of note, which also totals down to 4—the core issues and events that form life itself) and is composed of the suits of Pentacles, Wands, Cups, and Swords. These suits translate into the 4 prime elements of existence: our physical bodies, money, and career (Pentacles); our spirit, ability to create, passion, and intensity (Wands); our emotions, their consequences and rewards (Cups); and our thoughts and words, what we do with them and how they can affect those around us (Swords).

The sturdy and grounded number 4 is the very foundation upon which this entire spiritual divination system rests—a strong commentary on the fundamental essences of this vibration.

Multi 4 Values

Anyone with a preponderance of 4 values in their name analysis will likely have issues with family members. This can manifest as *wanting* to be responsible and dependable but finding this a somewhat difficult desire to realize (especially if the sub number is 13). The 4 is stable and functional, so a person who is heavy in this energy is going to swing one way or the other. They will take the responsibility and pragmatism of this grounded vibration too far in daily life, the results of which can be excessive meticulousness, unbending rules, and even such a potent level of "a place for everything and everything in its place" that frustrations can lead to abusive behaviors. The fanatical 4 can be infuriatingly stubborn and immovable—"set in their ways" comes to mind. This can make the multi 4 a good business partner, boss, and employee—as long as they do not become so caught up in details that they miss the bigger picture.

As a domestic partner, the 4 can wind up treating the mate in a business-like rather than romantic fashion, which can lead to all kinds of problems.

As just briefly mentioned, the multi 4 can also show an alarming lack of awareness as far as the basics of life are concerned. Everything I just said about the 4 can be reversed, and this type of 4 will find it hard to commit, to stick to one career or relationship or place, and can find themselves constantly moving on in order to avoid laying down foundations or getting stuck in one place, with one person, or at one job. Ultimately, this type of 4 will have to learn to depend on themselves rather than others (in such a case, some form of the 4 will usually show up as part of the Lifepath).

A Chart with No 4 Values

A personality with no 4 values featured in their read will not find personal accountability or duty to be an issue; they will have a naturally developed sense of duty and a balanced understanding of the responsibilities of life. Sometimes, no 4 values can be indicative of needing to take personal responsibility for the mundane responsibilities and details of daily life.

Traditional Meanings

A traditional 4 energy can be seen as reliable, hard-working, loyal, patriotic, family-oriented, honest, meticulous, and methodical. A negative 4 personality can be arrogant, opinionated, irresponsible, defensive, evasive, argumentative, uninspired, rebellious, and even controlling, cruel, and abusive.

Words that Total to Number 4

A few words that illustrate the energy of the 4 are tied to recognized fundamentals and include fundamentals, element, basics, regular, domestic, authority, reliable, control, sex, bible, and thunder. (An interesting one is graphology, which is the study of handwriting. This practice reveals the identity or the "state of mind" of a person much like the fingerprint does, although its uses are a bit more psychological.)

Lifepath for the Number 4

This path is one of work and taking responsibility for the contents of life. This number essence points to reliability, accountability, strength, determination, and the satisfaction of earning one's way. Charity is not something the developed 4 will feel comfortable accepting. Often seen as organized and methodical, the number 4 is the number that seeks security and routine and takes great personal pleasure in being able to provide for themselves and their family.

However, this number also can point to someone whose path involves *learning to take personal responsibility* for their life rather than seeking security from outside of themselves. This kind of 4 may have a difficult financial life until this lesson is learned and incorporated into the psyche, which usually does happen, albeit sometimes later in life.

Challenge for the Number 4

The challenge for the number 4 is to blend responsibility with fun. This energy needs to either loosen up and enjoy life a little bit more, or they need to learn how to take and accept responsibility for themselves in foundational ways. The number 4 is challenged to work (often with their hands) at a job they truly love, but that presents many challenges in and of itself. The key is to lay down the plan and to follow through despite any and all detours or potholes.

Quirky Phrase to Remember the 4 By
4 Drunk Men Talking
This should help you remember that the number 4 represents the letter D, M, and T.

Number Five (5): Changes and Freedom

The years have passed and our Lone Man family is doing quite well, all things considered. The key element that illustrates the influence of the number 5 revolves around their child, who is now a teenager. Since teens come in both sexes and the following can be experienced by both, I tend to assign both masculine and feminine energies to its vibrations.

What the average teen experiences involves a waking up of sorts; we become aware of our senses and of our physical body (think of the five points of the starred pentagram as an overlay for the figure of man). We also seek the thrill of experimentation, of new faces and places and our right to express (and indulge) ourselves in whichever manner we see fit. This energy phase introduces the realization that we are beings separate from our parents, and as such, we are independent and free to do as we please. Or so we think. And so the Lone Man's teenager thinks. So if you can imagine the possible antics of this particular teenager, you may have a good idea of the vibrations that surround this enigmatic and sometimes baffling number.

The number 5 is all about freedom and changes and individualism and the senses. Even within an established family unit, these urges and titillations can and do affect *everyone,* especially after a time of stability and routine. Five often kicks in to counteract boredom, which is one of the things the number 4 needs to look out for as well.

Time to translate the 5 into someone you might know. The 5 energies root to the yearning for something *more*— for change and adventure and freedom. There exists a deep restlessness and a corresponding desire for stimulation, particularly of the senses. As a person, this energy can translate into someone who is fascinating, but very illusive and transitory.

The 5 is the administrator; the one calling the shots and the one who will do as he or she pleases. This energy is also the communicator. They love to vocalize, write, draw, paint, or sculpt—anything which sends messages along artistic avenues.

Because of its many meanings, one might think that this number vibration holds potential chaos within its structure—and it does. Thankfully, a further characteristic of the 5 is that it carries a natural balance point (it sits in the middle of the regular number scale of 1 to 10). It is the middle of the road, the half empty or full, the naturally positioned set of scales that speak to the normal and natural state of neutral. What effect does this have on the strength of the need for experimentation? Communication? Freedom? Oddly enough, the high frequency charge of the unadulterated 5 is balanced out by its middle-of-the-scale placement, so despite changes galore, the 5 always seems to stay on an even keel, even when the boat is tipping. Change is, after all, a natural part of life and is to be anticipated, expected, and absorbed or adjusted to, and thankfully, the 5 is the best at doing so.

A true 5 personality will be very difficult to get a handle on. They represent all of the things I mentioned above. They are true independents, authoritarians, freedom and, sometimes, excitement junkies. At its highest vibration—as found in a chart with many 5s—the need for thrills, challenges, and stimulation of the senses, and yes, I do mean *all* of the senses, is keen. The number 5 needs constant diversity and change or they will stagnate and sink into negative attitudes, withdraw into themselves, and entertain destructive habits or behaviors.

Although the 5 is also quite the charmer and can put on a mask of reliability for a time, it would be unwise to entirely depend on a 5, as they tend to live in the moment and are easily moved and swayed should something take their attention and hold it. The 5 is under the influence of freedom: they do not respond well to being tied down, controlled, contained, or stuck in a routine of any kind. If they are in such a situation, the 5 will adjust, but the truth about what they are thinking or planning will be deeply hidden, and change will come once more, sometimes, of others. unexpectedly for others involved. As mentioned, they are, at all times, the authoritarian: the boss of themselves and, sometimes inadvertently, others. This makes the 5 a potentially challenging choice in a mate or even in an employee. Although they are thoroughly likable and engaging energies, they still will ultimately do things their own way, which in turn tends to leave people, places, and things behind, often without warning.

These brave adventurers are the ones you will find in unusual careers, traveling to unusual spots, jumping from airplanes, driving race cars, climbing mountains, and experiencing life to the fullest while sometimes even (consciously or unconsciously) cheating death. Depending on placement and other details, this can also involve courting the fates in less-than-positive ways such as experimentation with alcohol, sex, and drugs, as the 5 is also ruled by the senses. People with a plethora of 5 values are often mentally high strung and hard to "put a finger on." Because of a connection with Mercury, they can display quicksilver moves and moods. Since they prefer to be in charge of themselves, the 5 is constantly seeking new opportunities and challenges and can switch from one situation or person to another in a heartbeat. The 5 is the most potent of sexual attraction vibrations and can, if they so choose, attract the opposite (or the same) sex as easily and naturally as the proverbial flame attracts the moth.

The unfettered 5 who is free to do and be as he or she sees fit is the sparkle in the champagne, the flash in the pan (meaning the gold found therein), and the wings on the bird. Take away their champagne, stomp on their pan, or clip their wings and you will have a restless, edgy, and frustrated energy on your hands. The best advice I can give for handling the 5 is to give them free reign. Hanging on to a 5 is like trying to hang on to a fish: it just wiggles out of your hands, jumps back into the ocean, and off it goes, likely never to be seen (or caught) again!

One possibility that may subconsciously lure the 5 (or be a predestined course) is to become well known and respected, whether within their own community via owning successful businesses or holding high-ranking positions, or, indeed, throughout the world for any of a million reasons. It is the only number to hold such a possibility, to attract media attention as a result of specific actions or talents. This attention can easily result in fame and even infamy; it depends on the reason for the attention in the first place. Granted, this is a rare possibility, but fame does occur and the more 5s in the chart, the higher the potential. Many celebrities of today and yesteryear carry prominent 5s in their analysis charts (Oprah, Jay Leno, Angelina Jolie, Nicole Kidman, Katharine Hepburn, and Charlton Heston, to name but a few). In the case of multi 5s, to expect a domestic, normal type of life may not be even remotely realistic

until the 5 is well into and perhaps beyond middle age. There is a chance that, with age, the 5 will mellow, but that would likely only be presented in the type of challenge or excitement they engage in. Quite frankly, most 5s like their lives exactly as they are, thank you very much.

I find both of the Major Arcana tarot cards that contain the 5 energy to be very interesting in that both serve to provide balance: one of them, the Hierophant (5), is usually regarded as a powerful and sometimes religious figure who exerts tremendous influence over a large group of people. He can be read as the saving grace: the one who provides proper law and tradition in order to maintain and sustain control over the various characters and personalities under his domain. As mentioned, one of the redeeming factors of this number energy is its natural balance point, or the ability to maintain order through chaos, and the Hierophant acts as the speaker of the house—he leads the masses and lays down divine order to counterbalance chaos.

The second Major Arcana tarot card that totals to 5 is Temperance (14), which refers to the need for balance as well, but while the Hierophant is for the masses, Temperance holds a more intimate and personal message: it is aimed at the individual and usually points to the need to restore balance in one's own life. It references moderation (especially after sensory overload), healing, and taking time out to connect with Spirit. This

can be seen as an indication of a spiritual awakening that will result in a smoother progression and attitude in general. This card is very philosophical and its message is gentle yet firm: it says regroup and rethink one's actions and habits before all balance is lost.

Both Temperance and the Hierophant offer calm in the face of potential chaos and firmly support the meanings of the number 5, just from different angles.

On a personal note, I have noticed in my numerical travels that some combinations of numbers share certain qualities, and, consequently, those qualities become magnified. The numbers 5 and 3 are two such numbers. If you should run across someone with these energies as totals for their names, or in a variety of placements in a chart, you will likely find that you will rarely see these people and when you do, it will only be for a short time and will come with no assurances of a next occurrence. The combined energy of the ever-active and somewhat carefree 3 with the thrill-seeking and independent 5 can make for unreliable bedfellows (for instance, the domestic-loving 6 might not find a 5/3 a good match). However, if you are looking for someone to share your free climb up a mountain or to race bulls with you in Spain, the 5/3 would make an excellent choice in companions. Just make sure you have everything you need (and I do mean everything) to survive by yourself if need be. Through no fault of their own, the 5/3 is not one of the most dependable energies known to man. Exciting, yes. Boring, no. Committed … well, maybe to making it to the airport on time.

Multi 5 Values

Excessive 5 values will produce a confusing energy for anyone who cannot relate to an intense desire for freedom, and this freedom will be reflected in all areas of life. Multi 5s are notorious for changing jobs or careers, relationships (and sexual partners), locations, and interests. These are indeed free spirits who all but loathe normal, routine, and predictable situations and circumstances. Since the 5 is also ruled by the senses and anything that can alter reality, the risk of becoming involved in the use of drugs or alcohol or any number of alternative sensory-overload methods is accentuated. The main pull for this vibration is to attain freedom in any way possible.

Obviously, the high-volume 5 is not the best bet for a romantic partner; for if you are looking for a solid and reliable presence, the 5 can be there in body but be miles away in spirit. Perhaps a better choice would be the 4.

A Chart with No 5 Values

A personality without 5 values in their read may find their life and its components rather restricting and even boring. Few changes and little stimulation can create an underlying dissatisfaction with the quality of life. On the other hand, no 5 values can be seen as a relatively calm and peaceful existence, but one that lacks in adventure and sensory expression: it really depends on the person involved. To someone who prefers tranquility, no 5 vibrations will be seen as a blessing indeed.

Traditional Meanings

An average 5 can be described as charming, sensual, adaptable, social, entertaining, compassionate, curious, very artistic, adventurous, thrill-seeking, ever-changing, enticing, fascinating, sexy, and dramatic. They can also be negatively described as irresponsible, unreliable, inconsiderate, flighty, deceitful, disloyal, unfaithful, self-centered, restless, addictive, noncommittal, and frustrated.

Words that Total to Number 5

A few words that conceptualize and total to the 5 energy and point to the body, its abilities, and ultimate freedom are birth, heal, health, body, evolve, excitement, crazy, sexy, entice, end, finish, coffin, priest, and God.

Lifepath for the Number 5

This Lifepath is one of "expect the unexpected." The number 5 energy thrives on freedom above all else and therefore the life can reflect constant change—people, places, and things come in and out of the life on a consistent basis. Since it is also, thankfully, one of the most adaptable numbers in the scale, it is able to move from one situation to another with relative ease (although it dislikes closed or controlled environments). The 5 personality is usually quite attractive to others because of its ever-changing circumstances, connections, charm, and communication skills. The 5 is best suited to self-employment and its talents lie in the area of creativity and any form of artistic communication. However, because of its non-conformist tendencies, this vibration can also experience periodic financial ups and downs, but these will even out once the talent is found and the time dedicated to perfecting it.

Challenge for the Number 5

The challenge for the number 5 is to honor their free spirit while avoiding the temptations of stimulants such as alcohol and drugs, or anything that feeds the senses. The focus of the 5 is on themselves and, as a result, they may need to learn to consider the emotional scars left on those who are inadvertently left behind because of their transitory nature.

Their challenge also involves setting down roots and learning to commit, whether that involves a relationship or a goal. The 5 can succeed beyond its expectations if it focuses on one thing and sticks to it.

Quirky Phrase to Remember the 5 By
5 Nurses X-ray Harry's Eye
This should help you remember that the number 5 represents the letters N, X, H, and E.

Number Six (6): Domestic Love

Let's surmise that the teenager belonging to our Lone Man and Woman has spent a few months disappearing from the house in the dead of night, hanging out with less-than-desirable friends, partying until the sun comes up, arguing with everyone about everything, wearing strange clothes, and sporting green hair. Let's say that this teenager has also fallen in love and has found this love to be unrequited.

What do you think this poor, heartbroken young person will do? Where will this person want to be? Anyone who is in pain will want to return to the place and to the people who make them feel cared for and loved—they will want to go home.

And that is what the 6 is all about—returning to the fold, flying back to the nest, seeking a port in the storm—it is the vibration of warmth and security, and above all, safety.

The most attractive element for our lovesick and overly stimulated teen is the comfort that is offered by the familiar arms of family, especially the mother, which is why I feel this number as more feminine than male. This vibration is usually only fully appreciated after various outside adventures have prompted retreat. Here is where our teen knows that acceptance is not an issue nor is trust, or rather, the lack of it. The 6 accommodates and encourages the different desires, daring, personalities, and dreams of its family members while also providing a consistently calm place to ground and center after losses, failures, or traumas.

The 6 energy has everything to do with love, as it is ruled by Venus and is representative of the Nurturer, or the Parent who is often regarded as a solid and dependable pillar of the community. Here is the energy of caring, of domesticity, and of gentleness. This is the true domain of the 6: it is the protected harbor into which one may retreat, it is the safe place to hide. In the dedicated 6, one will find the homemaker, protector, nurturer, and peace-keeper, whose main interest is in providing a secure and balanced home, one that is based in love.

This love can and does extend to things of beauty. The 6 truly appreciates the brush strokes in a painting, the hours of talent poured into a sculpture, the elegant lines of a home or a car, and an almost natural by-product of this appreciation of beauty promotes a sense of pride in their own appearance. The 6 will always try to look their best.

A person with several 6 values in their chart is usually quite loving and lovable, sensitive, kind, humanitarian, and compassionate and requires a calm and serene atmosphere, although these intense leanings can easily cross the line into interference and over-involvement. The 6 is also artistic, musically inclined, and rather conventional, and is the responsible provider or caretaker. If this multi-layered harmony is endangered by lies, betrayal, or deceit, the 6 can turn on a dime and become withdrawn, self-righteous, and seriously passive-aggressive. Worst-case scenarios present clingy, insecure, accusatory, self-pitying whiners who, at peak performance, can make you want to toss your tacos. In such an event, it may well be advisable to re-establish harmony as soon as possible—genuinely, of course. In general, this should be fairly easy, as the 6 is a truly gentle person who dislikes discord and only reacts negatively when they feel used, neglected, or threatened. (Similar to the 2, which is a component of the 6.)

The Major Arcana tarot card of the Lovers (6) speaks for itself. Its number pertains to love, sex, trust, family, and happy homes. However, there is another level to this card and it is one of choice: do we go home to safety, or do we take the hand of the adventurer? This particular image illustrates how strongly body language can speak—the woman, who stands beside the Tree of Life (complete with a serpent, which she is almost touching—symbolism easily recognizable as temptation), reaches out her hand to the man, but he is not receptive; his eyes are downcast, one hand pulled back behind his thigh while the other splays open as if to say, "wait, I am not quite sure about this." While they are both naked, they are not touching or joining, nor do they look as though they might. However, we do not know; the decision has not yet been made. So while this card refers to intimate actions and even fruitful procreations, it can also point to illicit affairs and emotionally damaging or destructive relationships, intimate or otherwise (although the choice will often have an element of love of some kind within its structure). The choice belongs to the participants and it boils down to stay in the safe zone, or take the hand offered.

On the other hand, we have the Major Arcana tarot card of the Devil (15). He is the actuality, the materialization of the temptation I mentioned earlier, and portrays the negative side of the 6, which is found not in an actual devil, but rather within the human body, mind, and soul. This is the card of negative desires or *forces* (1), which manifest as thoughts, habits, decisions, and actions, like succumbing to the lure of drugs, alcohol, extramarital affairs, and of all kinds of other sensory-based stimulants (5), and the *changes* that follow, which can include everything from broken trust to the devastation of relationships, homes, marriages, and lives. This 15/6 speaks to the potential *loss* of domestic security, tranquility, and safety. The thing about this card and its message is that it *also* concerns choice—have a look at the chains around the necks of these two figures. In other illustrations, these chains are pictured as easily removable (this deck portrays the couple as more bound than others, but their chains are still relatively loose), which suggests that with a little bit of work, one or both could escape if they truly wanted to. The Devil does not keep them bound: they themselves do. Two alternatives are on offer here: remain confined and chained and face the consequences, or break the habit (chain) using whichever means necessary to return to a place of safety and security. Since the 6 often concerns relationships and love, chances are good that any damage done will ultimately core down to some*thing* that is loved (a drug, a job, or even a hobby— almost anything can fall under this heading) versus some-*one* who is loved (a mistress, wife, sibling, or anyone else). Therein lies the challenge and the choice.

So while the 6 is a loving and nourishing essence, it also carries, like all other number essences, a dark side. The Lovers and the Devil symbolize this quite well.

Multi 6 Values

Repetitive-6 values can be an interesting occurrence—this will either be someone who would literally give you a kidney or someone who will make you regret ever accepting it. The multi 6 is overflowing with good will and good intentions, however, this overload of love can easily morph into an overly sensitive, moody, and guilt-inducing personality.

The multi 6 can also manifest as someone who feels the need to control the family and all of its inner and outer dealings (especially true if the odd 8 pops up as well). This 6 can impose their will and expectations upon others without considering what might be best for those within the family structure. This would translate into someone who has the genuine interests of the family and community at heart, but who only sees their own ideas as viable because they are reputedly based on love for all concerned. Understandably, this can and does lead to misunderstandings and can even create distance between family members.

In a domestic situation, the multi 6 can point to someone who is overly concerned with their family and its inner workings to the point of interference and even obsessiveness. The most negative aspects of the multi 6 will show as a loss of individual interests and outside connections—the world usually shrinks to the world of the home and its members, and emotional suffocation can be experienced by all involved.

A Chart with No 6 Values

A personality who lacks any 6 values in their chart is rarely overly concerned with white picket fences and the traditional family unit. This is not an energy that wishes to be tied down in the domestic sense, although there may well be strong evidence of community ties and involvement. The opposite type of lacking 6 energy often has a block of sorts concerning the traditional family unit that usually roots back to childhood. This can cause a disinterest in pursuing domestic issues or partnerships. On the other hand, it could well be that belonging to a family or even having one is not part of the individual's intended goals and lessons this time around. The other numbers and letters in the chart will comment further on this.

Traditional Meanings

A positive 6 can be described as the following: loving, kind, gentle, romantic, empathic, compassionate, forgiving, home and community oriented, loyal, and nurturing. On the flip side, the embattled 6 can become moody, withdrawn, passive-aggressive, manipulative, secretive, smothering, needy, and temperamental.

Words that Total to Number 6

The following words total to a 6 energy and reflect the essence of home, family, and community: live, homes, garage, couch, sleep, mom, son, daughters, baby, cry, compassion, loyal, summer, artist, society, and church.

Lifepath of the Number 6

The Lifepath of the 6 involves nurturing family, friends, and community. As such, its primary meaning involves love—of a person or a group, a home or an area, an idea or ideal. The 6 is loyal and upstanding and is attracted to things of beauty, which means they appreciate the luxuries of life but do not obsess over having them. However, they are usually conscious of their appearance and present themselves in the best light possible. Proper yet charming, the 6 is generally a calm and gentle person who is respected within their social circle and much loved in the home.

Another level of the Lifepath 6 involves removing barriers that present blocks to attaining domestic bliss. Sometimes the lesson for the Lifepath 6, like all others, can involve *becoming the essence of the number,* or working on opening a path thereto.

Challenge for the Number 6

The challenge for the number 6 is to expand their world from one of home to one of community. This number energy is one of Universal love and the challenge involves the Family of Man rather than one man's family. The work of the 6 should reflect this connection. The 6 is also warned against allowing their sense of identity to merge with that of their family or job. They need to be personally aware of their own power and individuality and work to not disappear into *any* unit, be that family or otherwise.

Quirky Phrase to Remember the 6 By

6 Voluptuous Union Workers

This should help you remember that number 6 is valued by the letters V, U, and W.

Number Seven (7): The Brain—Logic vs. Spirit

Upon returning to our Lone Man family a few years later, we find our teenager has become a young adult who is now somewhat older and, hopefully, wiser. The free-for-all experimentation of the 5 phase and the regrouping of the 6 phase has allowed time for thought and even for some level of planning: the number 7 speaks to the power of the brain. As our teenager passes into adulthood, childish thought patterns are replaced by more mature ones. This is the time during which our young person will begin to formulate ideas and use the power of the intellect and intuition to guide future decisions and to define future directions.

Should you find this number in a key spot or two, know that you are ruled by your *brain*: the enigmatic 7 primarily concerns using our thought processes to realize true wisdom (or, perfect thoughts), which can traditionally only be realized one way and that is through direct and varied life experiences that are given deep, intellectual, objective, and, eventually, spiritual thought. This number essence is also very intriguing: it is the protected number of the occult (that which is not seen and needs to be investigated in order to be understood) and holds incredible power and potential, but only if its power is acknowledged, honored, respected, and gratefully and graciously *used*. The number 7 rules the consciousness and is composed of two separate and distinct schools of thought: the practical logic of the scientist in a lab and the abstract aura of the metaphysician in a forest. The idea here is to grow beyond the parameters of logic to embrace that which may seem, upon first glance, rather illogical or arcane (and includes anything beyond the parameters of normal, like numerology, for example), but is actually part of the overall truths upon which wisdom is based, and for this reason, I feel this number is both feminine and masculine: its logic feels male while its mystique feels feminine.

Silence can play a large part in the life of the 7, as, for the most part, thoughts are inner vibrations and involve plenty of good old-fashioned thinking, reminiscing, and rumination. The facts of daily existence are part of this process, but so too is the contemplation of what lies *beyond* the parameters of daily existence: some 7s will investigate this question while others will not. Therein lies the challenge for the distinguished 7—to think or not to think about the world of spirit and what might exist alongside us or await us beyond this physical reality. However, while most 7s are either one type or the other, the brain-driven, intellectual, and logical 7 is most common, and will often remain unenlightened unless an event or highly influential person provokes a metamorphosis or an epiphany (or they are born under one of the water signs of the zodiac, especially Cancer and Pisces, which would leave them naturally open to metaphysical exploration), and as such, they will walk this Earth seeking (logical) perfection in the self and in others. This energy can also find it very difficult to disassociate itself from the past—to release bygone experiences or memories.

The personality of the 7 is one of striving, of seeking, and of living logical perfection. They are industrious students, excellent educators, keen scientists, talented computer programmers, respected nurses or doctors, and exceptional lawyers, and will usually excel in any position of authority, responsibility, and trust. They present themselves as in control, secure, and at ease. The reality beneath the act is that the 7 is constantly analyzing, dissecting, judging, re-arranging, and fixing, as their brain is in constant motion and, like a computer, scientifically and judiciously oriented. It justifies its actions by holding fast to the belief that it is truly trying to do the logical, best, and proper thing for all concerned in any given situation. However, despite this genuine desire to help, emotions are often kept under strict guard, a condition that places restrictions upon open displays of affection. Logical 7 energies are not overly tactile, nor are they overly emotional.

The 7 who lives primarily inside its own head may walk a fine, stressful line between maintaining their dignity and reserve, while trying to ignore a sense of emotional imbalance that results from their reclusive and perfection-ist tendencies. This can result in what I call a heartblock—a deep, silent unhappiness that can become toxic over time and lead to all kinds of physical ailments, and fairly seri-ous ones, at that. The undeveloped number 7 can become world-weary, jaded, disillusioned, and if there have been significant failures at establishing close, personal friend-ships or relationships, they may well find themselves alone in their impeccable home and life. The multi 7 especially can find that over time they have built a wall, one which effectively blocks both the way in and the way out. As dif-ficult as this may be to understand, many 7s feel safe in this self-imposed prison. To them, it represents protection and order, and since each person has his or her own path to follow, this is often exactly what the reserved 7 is destined to do, and no amount of advice or coaxing will (or should) make it otherwise. (Indeed, it is inadvisable to interfere in another's Lifepath or assigned lessons. We all create the sit-uations for the manifestation of circumstances required to teach us the very things we are here to learn.)

The resilience of this type of 7 is actually quite remark-able—it relies on facts and tangible evidence to gauge future actions and can become a force to be reckoned with, but it will only come into its true potential once the mind opens wide enough to allow the entry of spiritual and metaphysical data.

The magick of the 7 and the dismal outcome of ignor-ing or misusing its gifts are equal in power. Anyone who is under the influence of this vibration and accepts and grows into its magickal properties will experience magickal occurrences and revelations. Those who choose to ignore and subjugate this natural process will likely experience a sense of dissatisfaction, or of having missed something, and sometimes this feeling can be quite intense.

In a nutshell, the lesson or challenge inherent in this energy is for the holder to apply their considerable brain power, data processing, and analytical acumen to the investigation of the unscientific. It is a challenge many restrained holders of the name number 7 will find difficult to meet, yet it is as easy as picking up a spiritually based book and opening up to its contents.

Consequently, there are two types of 7s running around. Type one appears very together, yet is also distant. Closer inspection can reveal a level of expectation that may come across as critical and even judgmental, yet there is an open friendliness, and often many social avenues and connections. This energy will be difficult to get close to on a personal level but will be an exceptional worker, highly responsible, social, intelligent, and articulate, and will appear in control of themselves and their situations. This type of 7 is hard to get a handle on; they do not open up emotionally very often.

Type two will be the antithesis of type one and may even appear very strange upon first meeting. This 7 may seem eccentric, different, or "not all there," which is to say that they are, indeed, not all here. This energy is open to other dimensions, interests, lifestyles, belief systems, and the many forms of artistic expression, but shares the intellect of the rational 7. An open 7 may be involved in metaphysical pursuits, healing and alternate spiritual and health quests or forms of dramatic or artistic expression, all of which can make for a fascinating and appealing personality.

This number energy has mystical and occult connections and connotations. Its metaphysical power is fairly common knowledge, even among those who do not know they believe—after all, how many times have you seen folks sitting before the one-armed bandits that litter casinos, just praying for those precious 7s to drop down to the pay line, one after the other? When the bells whistle and the lights flash and the winner walks away, he or she feels touched by luck, even if the payout was in pennies.

The 7 is an odd energy. It can work wonders, or it can work disasters. Its darker side can involve scary, weird, downright strange and eerie occurrences. It holds a kind of peculiar power, which can swing either way depending upon the energies affecting it. Its negative or undeveloped side also has a propensity to be connected to unfortunate events. For instance, Norma Jean Baker was a 7, and despite a name change (Marilyn Monroe, which totals to Master Number 11 and carries the potential for either a very positive or a very negative outcome), she did not escape the negative side of the fickle 7. Neither did John Belushi or Cleopatra. Extremely negative 7 energies include Adolf Hitler, Theodore Robert Bundy, David Berkowitz, and Gary Ridgway.

Abraham Lincoln and Christopher Columbus are great examples of the positive 7 energy and what it is capable of creating or achieving.

We have all heard the saying "from the mouths of babes" and experienced a wry recognition of the often-uncomfortable truths an innocent child will speak. Some may also have heard the notion that all information gathered and experiences had by a child until the age of 7 will dictate the adult he or she becomes. A young child is a clear and open channel and conduit who radiates and receives pure truth, intuition, and wisdom and has not yet learned about doubt, betrayal, or fear; he or she trusts and believes everyone and everything. In the eyes of a child, we can see the beauty of pure wisdom and untroubled understanding. (In fact, the word "child" is a number 16/7.)

The child as I just described is the perfect example of a developed 7: a clean and unclouded openness that thirsts for knowledge and receives it just as eagerly. We have all seen such children (Mattie Stepanek, a young poet and peacemaker, born on the 17th day of the 7th month and whose domestic energy was 7) and understand their rarity. Rarer still would be to find such an open channel in an adult.

The wise 7 would honor and investigate the other side of reality. It is mysterious, electric, and powerful, and will never truly be understood by man, but it can be accepted and respected in a logical way by anyone, and once something is truly understood, its gifts come into play and the intuitive and spiritual side of the logical 7 awakens.

Number 7 contains the seeds of both absolute positive and absolute negative, much as a child can grow to be one or the other. For the 7, the key is to attempt to view the world through the eyes of innocence, without fear, doubt, or ridicule.

Here are some interesting sayings, or facts, about this number. We are all familiar with the idea that God made the world, then rested on the 7th day. We gaze in wonder upon the 7 colors of the rainbow, work on balancing the 7 chakra centers in our bodies, look forward to certain of the 7 days in a week, and enjoy trying to express ourselves using the 7 notes in the scale on a piano. We cross the 7 seas and search the skies for that elusive 7th heaven, but are more likely feeling the 7-year itch even as we catalog the 7 deadly sins and count how many of the 7 virtues we may still have. Or not. And then we break a mirror and speculate for just a moment about the 7 years of bad luck often attached to such an event. Speaking of luck (good or bad), those familiar with knot magick will know that 7 knots are used for spellbinding and that incantations are often repeated 7 times. I suppose the hidden perfection of this vibration would be most clearly delineated in the pure gold intention of the alchemist—a goal involving 7 metals. Suffice it to say that this energy is one great-big mystery which holds wonders, revelations, puzzles, riddles, tests, and rewards, and this is supported by the fact that almost all cultures view it as the number of perfection and as having connewctions to higher levels of perception and consciousness. The 7 is the total of all there is: the 3 of the heavens (the Holy Trinity) and the 4 of the Earth (the 4 directions, seasons, and elements), and as such, anything is possible.

If you have one or two of these number energies anywhere in your chart, please do yourself a huge favor (if you have not already done so) and begin to acknowledge and pay some mind to your third eye. There is another world right in front of you that you have perhaps seen but not registered. If that concept seems rather odd, consider this— the best way to hide something is to do so in plain sight. Once pointed out, however, it is impossible to "unsee" and a whole new dimension unfolds.

If you are unsure of how to start, visit your local library, metaphysical store, or intuitive reader. In the last two cases, please rely on your intuition to guide you to the right place or person. (In layman's terms, "trust your gut.")

While one would not necessarily immediately connect the Major Arcana tarot card of the Chariot (7) to logical thought, it is accurately represented. If one looks carefully at the sphinxes (one black and the other white, to reflect positive and negative forces) who will lead the Chariot, it is clear that instead of facing us straight on, each is headed in a slightly outward direction, which means that any forward movement will result in a stalemate: neither creature will move. The failure of intent goes back to incomplete thinking—the route and vehicle were not prepared, which means the brain was not fully engaged. Any action must be backed up by rational planning (especially when there is a vehicle involved). So this message is asking us to *think*, to use our *brains*, literally.

Another aspect to the Chariot is that it was used in ancient battle situations—and a large part of winning was in *intuiting* the enemy's next move and *planning* a counter move. Hence, the Chariot points to the combined use of the intuition and the intellect (the two sides of the 7) as being the most effective methods toward achieving success. Therefore, the Chariot is making a specific request and that is to put the brain into gear.

The Major Arcana tarot card of the Tower (16) can appear somewhat intimidating in that it pictures an exploding tower, flames, bodies falling, and lightning flashing. Not surprisingly, it indicates that all is not as it appears to be and that disruption and upheaval are occurring or imminent. Since the sub number 16 indicates the force of love, it is usually reflective of family, close connections, and intimate dealings that essentially "blow up."

And how does this connect to the brain-ruled number 7? The outer circumstances are the result of inner thoughts; the presence of misguided or wrong thinking has successfully (until now) covered the truth of the situation. These thought patterns involve lying to the self, explaining away that which does not fit, chastising the self for doubting, out-talking the intuition, and generally avoiding reality (and reality checks). The truth has been submersed and ignored for so long that sudden revelations can cause life-changing explosions and the destruction of what we had previously "lived with." However, there is always a positive (even in a negative), and in this case, the Tower allows toxic energies to burn up and blow away, leaving a calm, if drained, feeling of peace in its wake. From there, a new life can be built. So while this card may appear to have nothing to do with the brain and everything to do with the devastation of relationships and things and people and even places we thought we loved, the reality of this message is "your brain knew all of this and tried to tell you—you just wouldn't listen."

Both cards testify to the power of the brain and of its thoughts, and the positive and negative repercussions these can carry.

Multi 7 Values

In the case of many 7s in a chart, any affront, real or imagined, will force this number personality to withdraw in an effort to protect themselves. Although highly intelligent, the multi 7 can become so protective and unapproachable that close and open relationships can become impossible to instigate or maintain, and existing ones can become extremely uncomfortable. It is for this regrettable reason that many "set" 7s will find themselves alone in the long run (however, it is never too late, as the saying goes, to learn something new). Their emotions are often buried under so much logic and so many protective layers that any uncontrolled feelings can cause intense confusion, anger, and defensiveness, which is a great reason to steer clear of this kind of vibration.

Plenty of 7 values can also be read as an active prod towards opening the mind enough to evaluate the merit of alternative topics. A brilliant mind is one that is truly open to all.

A Chart with No 7 Values

A person who shows no 7 values in their name read does not usually assign major importance to scientific logic; in fact, the absence of this energy can be viewed as a good thing, as this number energy can sometimes be quite restrictive in terms of spiritual development. The struggle, after all, is mostly about opening the psyche enough to allow the possibility of other, more "out there" thoughts to enter.

The lack of the number 7 energy indicates normal thought processes and an awareness that is accepting of, but not overly interested in, the world of metaphysics and spirituality.

Traditional Meanings

Some of the positive descriptives of the 7 include intelligent, dignified, efficient, reliable, calm, studious, investigative, discriminating, resilient, conversant, and capable. On the flip side, some negatives include distant, aloof, critical, judgmental, manipulative, argumentative, proud, angry, and even abusive.

Words that Total to Number 7

Here are some interesting words that total to 7 and illustrate both the elements of esoteric mystery and the practical art of education: intuition, mystic, child, dreams, ghosts, Ouija board, hell, numerology, science, scientific, intelligence, supervisor, teacher, and studious.

Lifepath for the Number 7

The essence of the number 7 Lifepath can be a difficult one. Like the brain has two halves, so too does this Lifepath. The goal is to combine these two halves into one happily functioning unit. The logical and pragmatic 7 may find their life limited in many ways; they will tend to be somewhat reticent in nature although there can be a disguised interest in the other half of existence that is often not pursued. This would fit in with maintaining a dignified, reserved, logical, and pragmatic front—rarely do others truly understand the hows and whys of this person's thoughts or emotions. The other 7 Lifepath involves active investigation of the unseen, the mysterious, and the unconventional, and often takes the form of someone others may view as slightly eccentric or different. For both types of 7, the goal is the same: the logical 7 must embrace the metaphysical half while the metaphysical 7 must embrace the logical half—this will result in the creation of a whole being. This number's goal is to seek the knowledge and truth behind everything; therefore there can be no exceptions. The bigger picture contains *all* aspects (whether seen or not seen), and true understanding of who or what forms this bigger picture can only be accomplished once the two halves have merged only then does "perfection" of thought manifest.

Challenge for the Number 7

Although the typical 7 is deeply thoughtful and contemplative, they often lack the openness that allows emotional and physical intimacy with others. This is the key lesson: to be open enough to allow others into their emotional space and to show genuine affection in both actions and words. The 7 must remove their coat of armor and risk being vulnerable—a challenge some will find almost impossible to meet.

Quirky Phrase to Remember the 7 By
7 (the land of) OZ
This should help you remember that the number 7 represents the letters O and Z.

The Number Eight (8): Balance—Matter vs. Spirit

We have now advanced even further along the path of the Lone Man family: pursuant to the thought-intensive phase of the 7, information, lessons, and conclusions have accumulated and growth has occurred. Life experiences have rounded out their individual and collective worlds, and one of the realizations along the way becomes common to the entire family. That realization concerns the limits of our reality, for beyond it lies the unknown, the unseen, and death itself. Contemplation of these and other mysteries leads to a new understanding—a confusing one at times, but now they see that the material world upon which they had based their entire existence is only a fraction of the truth. They understand that there is more to this world than the eye can see and, as a result, their physical surroundings take on a unique new light. The material world and their place in it is now of as equal import as the spiritual world and their place in it. What they *cannot* see or touch becomes as real to them as what they *can* see and touch. One has become as real as the other. They are now poised to attain perfect existential balance, which is the final form a developed 8 will take.

Anyone walking around carrying the 8 energy has at their disposal a vast amount of incredible power; although it can materialize in differing forms One person may run their domestic abode with a strict hand and prefer that his or her surroundings and the people in it are always impeccable, understated, and perfectly presentable. Breakfast, lunch, and dinner are at the same time every day, and bedtime is at the same time every evening (no one would even think to argue). The family is run similar to a classroom or, in severe cases, a military academy, and there is no doubt in anyone's mind who is in charge.

Another 8 may manifest as the president and owner of his own company who may be rich and successful but lacks respect and affection from and for his employees: in fact, they may actively dislike him and go out of their way to avoid him. This type of 8 is dedicated to controlling every aspect of his business life and those in it, and will not tolerate anything less than perfection and respect from those around him. He is not emotional, does not offer praises or raises, rarely smiles, does not want to hear complaints (even if they are valid) and is, in general, a pain-in-the-you-know-what kind of boss. This man lacks compassion and understanding for others, and his only concern is the bottom line: how much money he is making and how he can make more.

Either personality exists and each reflects the 8 in its own way, but the main issue around these types of energies is *control*, which is why I tend to assign this powerful and dominant number masculine energies, although in a perfect world, every number would be both.

The 8 is formed by two zeros, or ciphers, one atop the other, and represents the *lemniscate*, or symbol of perfect balance (imagine the 8 tipped onto its side and you will see this symbol), which is echoed in the elementals of yin and yang, masculine/feminine, and "as above, so below." Its symbol is found on several tarot cards, such as the Magician, Strength, and the World. (I often connect the lemniscate to the pattern described in the air by the wand of an orchestra conductor as he leads his musicians; they create perfect pitch, perfect timing, and perfect harmony. If the music is hypnotic in nature, he also creates perfect balance in the souls or spirits of the listeners.)

If both circles are of the same size, it indicates equality: the developed 8 holds the same intensity of regard for the material Earth plane as for the spiritual, unseen plane. (An interesting note: if you look in an old book, the 8 is represented with a larger "O" on the bottom and a smaller "o" on the top. This would be symbolic of the tendency of most 8 energies to focus on the material world: money, control, power, gain, and success here on this Earth, as represented by the lower "o." The spiritual aspect of existence is of less significance: the smaller "o" on the top is reflective of this.)

As with the 7, the 8 is rarely found as fully developed. Often, the draw of materialism can trap this vibration into being interested only in that which they can see and touch and own: security comes in the form of cold hard cash, possessions, and positions of authority and respect, which would explain why many executives, presidents, lawyers, judges, and other authority figures carry 8 energies.

These individuals are generally rational, resourceful, organized, ambitious, unemotional, publicly undemonstrative, and not overtly interested in the spiritual or metaphysical side of life. This is not to say that all 8s are atheistic or agnostic; some will attend church regularly or donate to charities; but the undeveloped 8 does often lacks true humanitarian emotion and wears a façade complete with overcoat, sunshades, and hat.

The true nature of the power 8 is rarely revealed: it is as good as the (undeveloped) 7 at cover-ups. The lessons of the 7 play a large role here: if the brain has not been enlightened by Spirit, the 8 will starve from a lack of philosophic food.

Here is a seemingly contradictory fact about the 8—beneath its camouflage and bravado, the 8 is actually very shy. It prefers to control its surroundings and the content of its life because it is afraid of failure or the loss of control; one of the greatest fears of the average 8 is suffering through the loss of prestige and power. This will manifest as deep feelings of insecurity, which will most definitely not show. The heart of the 8 often feels misunderstood, alone, and lonely and has historically been called upon to suffer great tragedies, losses, sorrows, and sometimes humiliations. The reason for this is simple: the 8 vibration must learn to use the power inherent in this energy to benefit humanity, and said power must be used in simple, honest, and spiritual ways. The following gives you an idea of why I call the 8 highly complex.

The symbol of the cipher (circle) holds all. In the case of the 8, two ciphers are connected, which will naturally intensify the power of the following description. The 0, or zero, is the alpha and the omega. Its shape can be seen in the form of the double DNA helix and in the interlocking serpents of the symbol of medicine. It is the ouroboros—the snake eating its tail. It is the inside and the outside. Its symbols form the circles inside the Flower of Life. It is the "in utero" and the pregnant woman. It is the beginning and the

end: life and death. It is both ends of the magickally revealing telescope. It is the shape of a coin and the string of zeros
that increase its value. It is the roundness of the moon that
reflects the life-giving and glowing circle of the sun.

If this multifaceted and downright exhilarating power is
used for personal gain (especially at the expense of others),
without the balance of spiritual awareness, it will provide
one hell of a karmic kickback. The power of the ego is massive, and as the old adage says: the bigger they are, the harder
they fall. The 8 may well suffer repeated professional and personal downfalls until they get the message, the core of which
revolves around the ability to feel *compassion* for others, an
emotion the 8 will only ever truly know after they themselves
have undergone considerable hardship and heartache.

In business, it may be fine and good, even desirable, to
have one or two of these powerhouse energies in your corner as an ally. However, if you dislike the tiniest hint of a
materialistic, power-oriented controller in your mate, you
may want to keep looking. And counting.

If, by some stroke of lovely fortune, you have attracted
into your life (or even have developed into) a positive, fully
developed 8, you are one blessed person, indeed. The true
8 is an advertisement for positivity: spiritually awake and
aware, loving and balanced, fair in all its dealings, wealthy
yet humble, generous to a fault (without expecting anything in return), unassuming yet highly intelligent, a creative genius, an attentive and devoted and unselfish lover,
friend, son, brother, or father, and a person we would all
love to have as a political leader. Enough said?

As a matter of interest, here are but a few examples of
the pure power held in an 8 name: John F. Kennedy, Martin

Luther King, Paul Allen (Microsoft co-founder), and President Barack Obama. Barack totals to an 11, which suggests an imaginative, sensitive, intuitive, and sympathetic personality, while Obama totals to a 15/6, or the loving, caring, nurturing aspect of a parent, or a safe haven with community overtones. The "O" of Obama further suggests an openness, a potential leap forward in progress, and when his entire name is combined, he reads as a 17/8: a leader who is tuned in to the people around him and also to himself but who may also struggle against both arcane powers and his own mental directions (7). Remember that the 8, while being one of the most powerful numbers in terms of achievements and so on, is also susceptible to complete and utter loss of balance. The combination of the 11 and the 6 do, however, point to a President who can and truly does *imagine* a perfect and loving world. The question is whether he will be able to attain the world-wide balance this would require. There is little doubt that he leans towards the positive 8—one who is spiritually and materialistically balanced—however, the Master 11 in his name energies can also forecast a certain dreamlike quality to his visions, which is in conflict with the control and authority of the 8.

The sheer power of this number energy is loaded into the Major Arcana tarot card of Strength (8). At the core, its meanings center around authority and control; however, Strength talks about having the courage and resolve to acknowledge and calm one's *own* inner beasts, thereby gaining control over personal emotions and reactions. So while this image shows a lady ostensibly calming the lion, this message actually refers to controlling the self: both through attaining high levels of self-acceptance, faith, peace, and compassion within the soul, and by being able to calm others as a result. This is why the young lady pictured here is able to place her hand near the mouth of the lion and not have it removed for her. She is balanced in body, mind, and spirit and knows no fear, which is shown in the lemniscate floating above her head. This lack of fear and her inner serenity is sensed by the lion she strokes and affects him accordingly.

On another level of strength stands the Major Arcana Tarot card of the Star (17), and its message is similar to

Strength: to achieve ideal balance and the gift of serenity and acceptance. However, there is another level to this vibration. The old chant from childhood might help explain it: "star light, star bright, first star that I've seen tonight, I wish I may I wish I might have this wish I wish tonight." The sub message of this card is that once complete symmetry between the spiritual and material worlds is reached, thoughts and dreams can become real. In a way, this card connects to the Law of Attraction in that how thoughts are formed and projected can dictate your circumstances, surroundings, and even the events of your life. This card is representative of the *actuality* of reaching a place of acceptance and perfect balance, which is shown in the woman's stance—one knee is firmly planted on the grass, while the other foot rests in the water. Further, she carries two jugs of equal size and is pouring water both onto the land and into the water... poetry in motion. The perfect balance between matter (the earth) and purity of spirit (the water) has been reached and is being tended by the woman. Realizing that the worlds of spirit and materialism are equal in strength often ushers in a time of dreams coming true; the focus of the "force of the brain" (17) points this out quite clearly.

The two examples of 8 energies are quite different, as you can see. However, both refer to personal strength and how it can affect and improve life.

Multi 8 Values

In the event of multiple 8 values in a read, chances are good that power and control will be important factors in the life of the holder. Material possessions, career success, respect, and authority will be strong motivators, but consideration of the meaning of life is not often found in the top ten of the priority list. One of the aforementioned pitfalls that this type of 8 energy can encounter is failure on a recurring basis. Hence, the realization that there is another reality beyond this material one is almost necessary before the 8 will find lasting success. However, this observation is not cast in stone: there are positively developed 8 energies (those who truly feel compassion for others and also regard the spiritual side of life as intrinsic to existence on the material plane), and those people will find lasting and meaningful success in their lives in which materialism has a place, but one which is not considered the be-all and end-all of life. Rather, these kinds of 8 energies will use their success and status to assist others in meaningful and on-going ways.

A Chart with No 8 Values
A personality who shows no 8 values in their read is normally a soul who is not concerned with amassing power or material wealth, nor in holding positions of authority for the personal purpose of satisfying the ego. Someone who lacks the 8 energy is often fairly easy-going and takes great pleasure in the surprises and gifts life offers, but can also find themselves drifting without a definitive purpose or direction.

Traditional Meanings
The usual terms used to describe the average 8 include determined, tenacious, focused, intelligent, powerful, inventive, organized, successful, adaptable, generous, charming, and inspiring. A few negatives for the 8 are almost predictable and they are controlling, unemotional, egomaniacal, judgmental, critical, condescending, secretive, materialistic, and sometimes abusive.

Words that Total to an 8
These words all total to 8 and refer to success or the different aspects of balance: dictator, oath, logic, tenacious, success, organized, freedom, life, community, planet, earth, airplane, abstain, guilt, psychotic, and grave.

Lifepath for the Number 8

The average 8 will be attracted to power, money, and success and will often find themselves in positions of authority and influence. This number energy is willing to do the work required to achieve status and respect. Focused on progress and responsibility, the 8 can experience success in various areas and generally is very self-confident and goal-oriented. If the 8 learns its lessons regarding compassion and sharing, the sky is the limit in terms of power amassed and material gain accumulated.

Challenge for the Number 8

This powerful number is challenged to accept the existence of another realm that cannot be seen yet holds supreme power and control over life. Simply put, they must come to understand that they are not, after all, the ultimate "boss." The 8 is challenged to develop compassion and to maintain humility so that it may come into perfect balance and thereby realize lasting success, both spiritually and materially. If the spiritual side of life is ignored, the 8 can find themselves in repetitive cycles that involve dramatic gains and losses.

Quirky Phrase to Remember the 8 By

8 Fair Politicians

This should help you to remember that the number 8 represents the letters F and P.

The Number Nine (9): Endings and Beginnings

Have you ever met an old lady or man (I am referring to someone who is over 90) who just seems so kind, gentle, sweet, wise, and lovable that you want to take them home and place them in a rocking chair in front of your fireplace? I have. Maybe once or twice. These are the relatively rare folks who have learned the lessons of their lives, accepted and integrated them, and who are now ready to move on. They radiate an inner peace and tolerance, which is the energy we respond to as it reflects the peace we all wish for ourselves. This number's nature is magickal and its power revered by the ancients. The 9 is considered sacred, as it is the highest level of spiritual awareness attainable before reaching Master Numbers and is the end of one set of lessons and the beginning of another. These rare people seem to understand this cycle and are in the process of both releasing and anticipating—they will finally discover what lies beyond for themselves.

Let us now visit with our Lone Man family once again. The original structure of the family unit has ended. The young parents are now old and their child has become an adult and has begun a family as well: one family form is ending while another has already begun. On another level lies the understanding of the parents that one phase of life is ending and another has yet to begin: they will shortly leave the confines of their physical bodies and embark on a new and unique adventure which, as yet, remains a mystery, but one which does not frighten them. Once the parents have passed, their child will begin yet another phase of existence—one that no longer includes his parents.

Again, the number 9 is all about endings and beginnings and is considered a hallowed number, similar to the 7, but for different reasons. The 9 encompasses all of the lessons held in the prior number energies of 1 through 8 and is also the embodiment of purity in creation (9 is the triple 3, Triad, or 3x3—in fact, any multiplication of this digit will always begin and end with the number 9). This is the completion that leads to the doorway of the number 10.

Ideally, the 9 is highly developed, compassionate, spiritual, creative, empathic, unselfish, intuitive, and motivated by brotherly love. These qualities can be illustrated with the use of one name and whether one is religious or not is beside the point—it is the simple calculation of the name in question that is significantly illuminating. Jesus totals to a (18) 9. Christ totals to a (18) 9. The two names together total to a (36) 9. Again, religion aside, this person is purported to have been gentle, kind, forgiving, and benevolent while demonstrating unconditional compassion and offering lessons in truth and love. Further, this man seemed to be connected to a Higher Power. He knew what would befall him (intuitively and psychically), seemed to possess mystical powers (turning water into wine and one loaf of bread into enough to feed hundreds, and even walking on water—all carry an element of magick) and lived by divine laws. The two 18s speak to the "force of control and balance in all things," while the 36 speaks to the "activity and thought of nurturing and love." Both fit the overall description, or energy, of the man. Jesus also has a distinct beginning, despite already being an adult, and a distinct ending. (Two other examples of the 9 energy are John Wayne [18/9 x 2] and Elvis Presley [18/9 and 27/9]: both were regarded as soulful and benevolent men.)

The truly developed 9 has indeed incorporated all of the difficult lessons inherent in the experiences of 1 through 8 and understands that there is a higher power at work and that this knowledge is to be shared without reservation. It is for these reasons that the number 9 is assigned no letters and thus presents another of the major differences between the simplified Pythagorean method of numerology and the Chaldean (or original) method of numerology.

The number 9 personality has likely survived some harsh life lessons, which can range from abuse to poverty to all points in between. This makes sense when one considers that the tougher the lessons (moving through "grades" 1 through 8), the harder the homework. These are sympathetic, sensitive, and romantic people who have often endured great hardship and pain; if they assimilate and learn the lessons held within such negativity, they can become great artists, healers, counselors, spiritual leaders, writers, speakers, teachers—and many other positions that are aimed at assisting, inspiring, or motivating others. This number energy feels both feminine and masculine to me, as pain and hardship and the desire to assist knows no sex.

Unfortunately, the 9 is prone to depression if unenlightened, misunderstood, ridiculed, abused, or betrayed, which can, in turn, lead to escapist tendencies such as those offered by the use of drugs and alcohol. While the 9 is liable to sudden, unexpected outbursts of temper, these are rare, as they are normally extremely patient or simply passive. This passivity can also lead to financial instability, as the 9 is not generally overly concerned with the materialistic side of life, and therefore money is not a prime concern. It is almost as if the 9 knows through its faith that all will be there as *needed,* which by definition means exactly that, what is needed will be there, but extra may not be. It is a complicated energy but one that is compelling and sometimes even slightly hypnotic.

The 9 will do well working on their own in some form of artistic, spiritual, intuitive, or healing/helping field and makes a loving (if slightly perplexing) romantic partner. To the developed 9, the search for spiritual truth will be paramount and can result in shifts in interests, focus, and growth in general, which can create rifts between partners, especially if one is not on the same path as the other. Remember, the 9 heralds completion followed by new beginnings.

The 9 finds trust the most difficult issue to come to terms with, as this has usually been violated regularly during formative years. The 9 may be open and loving and all of those wonderful things and yet still be stuck when it comes to trusting someone or something implicitly; often actions and time are involved in order to gain that trust.

However, once it has been earned, the 9 will return that trust unerringly and their loyalty will be unwavering.

The mystical energy of this number essence is represented by the Major Arcana tarot card of the Hermit (9), which revolves around beginnings and endings and the roads taken or not taken. The Hermit is a loner: by choice, he removes himself from (or ends) his involvement with the normal trappings of life and society and withdraws to begin consideration of his own spirit and how it connects to universal energies. In this image, he is depicted as traversing a rather barren landscape while holding a lantern to illuminate his path (which is a metaphor for his soul's journey), while in others, he is shown as living in a tall tower on a distant hill, where he devotes himself to introspection and the search for metaphysical and spiritual knowledge. No matter where the Hermit is found, he is the ideal example of ending one connection (with the material and with society) and beginning another (with himself and Universe).

Another Major Arcana tarot card that carries the 9 energy is the Moon (18). This card also illustrates the theme of beginnings and endings: the moon itself appears and disappears with regularity but is never really gone, as it is tied to the Sun for life. Further, as it is illustrative of our journey from point A to point B (or life and death), it also shows the various distractions (beginnings and endings) we must deal with along the way: in this illustration,

the dogs seem poised to provide at least some of these distractions and even obstacles (it depends how friendly they are). The Moon is illuminating and shadow-casting at the same time; therefore its connections to the intuition and psychic impressions is emphasized—another main aspect to the sensitive 9 energy. This card clearly shows the start of the long road that passes through two columns (positive and negative experiences and reality versus illusion) that we all have to travel if we wish to find out what lies at its end.

Both of these card energies highlight the mysterious and spiritual tones of the empathic and compassionate 9 energy; even the symbols of a solitary robed figure and a round, luminescent moon (which looks suspiciously like the Sun, the Moon's "mother") speak to these energies with understated eloquence.

Multi 9 Values

A personality who shows many 9 values in their names may find the theme of starting and stopping, ending and beginning, trying and failing, and having and losing quite tedious and can, indeed, become prone to giving up. However, the nature of the 9 forces new beginnings, so despite setbacks, this vibration will eventually try again. Many 9 values also point to a strong possibility that abuse or difficult and trying life experiences have formed and shaped their expectations as adults, but the compassion that is part and parcel of this essence allows progress to continue, even after considerable and repetitive delays.

A Chart with No 9 Values

A personality who shows no 9 values in their chart is often rather closed to certain esoteric or spiritual ideas (such as the possibility of life after death) and might even believe that this life is all there is; that once it's over, it's over. No rebirth, no second chances, no reincarnation, no judgment. In such cases, spiritual, metaphysical, and mystical investigations are not usually considered worthy of pursuit. Of course, this is a general observation; much depends on the other energies in the chart.

Traditional Meanings

The number 9 is very easy-going and is often described as intuitive, empathic, helpful, imaginative, thoughtful, creative/artistic, intriguing, inquisitive, gentle, romantic, sensitive, and spiritual. On the other hand, a negative 9 (one who seeks escape) can be lacking in self-esteem and confidence, unfocused, aimless, addictive, and wasteful—and is one of those unfortunate number essences that might even consider "ending it all," one of the more permanent methods of escape, but not one recommended, for the door of reincarnation awaits.

Words that Total to Number 9

Think of the following words, which all total to the number 9, involve a beginning or an ending or both: night, dark, war, scream, trauma, rain, education, family, heaven, and kiss.

Lifepath for the Number 9

The Lifepath of a 9 is perhaps one of the most difficult. Their depth of feeling, empathy, imagination, and inner musings can make functioning in a regular job something of a challenge. Since the content of a 9 life is subject to a theme of ongoing endings and beginnings, changing jobs, locations, relationships, and interests (among other things), the 9 can be quite puzzling to others. To make matters even more complicated, the Lifepath of the 9 typically involves committing to explorations of the *other* side of life—the unknown and mysterious. Overall, this energy is illusive and private and will withdraw rather than have to explain or justify itself. The best bet for a 9 Lifepath is to honor their calling (the direction their intuition is telling them to go), which will more often than not be found in areas that concern assisting others or expressing themselves, whether artistically or verbally. Number 9 is highly creative and talented; they make exceptional artists or thespians, for example. One of the challenges for the 9 is to take the time to try out painting or singing or writing for anything they are drawn to will provide the most rewarding results.

If you are a number 9 Lifepath, do not expect your life to be like others. You are a unique entity with unique talents: you are challenged to overcome feelings of doubt; understand that everything happened as it was intended and to just do it, whatever "'it" might be for you.

Challenge for the Number 9

The challenge for the 9 is to relax into their knowledge and path as spiritual students and teachers, and above all, to live as much as possible by the divine laws. It is to accept difficult personal and often formative experiences as pivotal and necessary to spiritual growth and that pursuit of material possessions and positions of supreme authority are actually toxic to their spiritual progress. This does not mean a 9 cannot have and enjoy material and financial success, just that becoming too attached to the images connected thereto can be damaging to their psyche. "Fame is fleeting even as life itself" would likely be one saying readily understood by a successful 9.

Quirky Phrase to Remember the 9 By
There are no letters for 9.

This is the end of the regular 1 through 9 number scale; however, there are a few more numbers that are worthy of mention because of their intrinsic power or unusual histories.

Number Ten (10): The Turning Point

The number 10 is not part of the Chaldean chart; however, like the zero, I wanted to include it, as it sits in a class by itself and is deserving of special mention. This energy is a combination of the Original Force of the number 1 and the infinite and potent possibilities inherent in the 0. Put the two together, and you have a brand new start. This indicates a returning to the beginning, but in a different way, on a different level.

This is the number of completion (of the scale 1–9), perfection (10 is used to illustrate the perfect woman), and a turning point (1 to 10 now becomes 11 to 20, 21 to 30, 31 to 40, and so on).

Rebirth, second chances, rising to the challenge, and new purposes are all highlighted with the appearance of a 10. In a person's name or as their date of birth, 10 indicates that at some point in the holder's life, they will undergo a transformation or rebirth, and will often have the ability to create or do something unique that will become noticed by others and may well serve to assist humanity on either a large or a small scale. The potential is there to be used or ignored. That will be up to the holder.

The 10 is a unique vibration that gives the 0, or cipher, a point of focus (number 1), and this point will be an original, creative, and singular one. Since the 1 is already a force to be reckoned with, imagine the power the 0 adds to it.

Along with new beginnings, the 10 also brings endings that must be experienced and accepted (despite sometimes being quite negative and difficult) before the new phase kicks in. The number 10 is also tied to the number 10 card of the Tarot, the Wheel of Fortune, which points to coming change. One situation will end and another will begin; the endings involved in this process can be negative, but the beginnings are usually positive in tone.

Number Twelve (12): Completion of a Cycle

The number 12 is found in so many places and demonstrates so many complete collections that it deserves mention here as well. Its theme of a complete unit can be seen in the 12 apostles, 12 signs of the zodiac, 12 hours in a day and night, 12 inches in a foot, 12 months in a year, and 12 grades in school. Interestingly, a child is considered a teenager (and by definition, no longer a child) once the 12th year has passed. The sense of fullness, of having come full circle, and of culmination is held in the feeling of this number energy—and that another level lies beyond it (which is another interesting number all on its own: number 13). This is also the aim of the 12th tarot card of the Hanged Man: the young man has actually deliberately hung himself upside down so that he may have both time and an altered vantage point from which to consider something—to slow down enough to contemplate what has been done and to decide upon his next step, which intimates that one phase has ended and another will begin. Once he gets down, that is.

Should you have a few such numbers in your chart, and specifically in your Lifepath, chances are good that you are here to act as a *finisher* of some kind. You might be the one who is destined to tie up loose ends (whether they be real or imagined), to complete something begun long ago, or to provide mankind with answers to questions long standing. The 12 suggests unification and groups; its energy can manifest in so many ways, it would be impossible to define all of them. Overall, this number is considered a positive one and seems to imply that a next level is to come. (Ronald Reagan began and completed his film career and began his political step-up all the way to the presidency. He then went on to create a new level for Germany as one united country. Mary Magdalene, on the other hand, saw the completion of one phase of life for her leader and the beginning of the faith that his death birthed. Both were 12 energies, experienced in different ways and different times.)

And there is also the chance that something will occur in this lifetime that is necessary to balance out actions or deeds that were either carried out in this incarnation or a past one. Look out for that karmic 13!

Number Thirteen (13): Lucky or Not? (The Karmic Debt Club)

So what *does* happen to the completion of the 12 if something is added? Apparently, it tips the scales. The reputation of the 13 is tied into the balance of the 12 and what occurs when that extra 1 is added (and I'm sure the 13th card in the tarot—Death—doesn't help matters).

Do you see a number 13 anywhere in your chart? If so, you are a card-carrying member of what I call the Karmic Debt Club. Do not panic. I, for one, consider the number 13 to be a *lucky* number, despite the theme of negative karma that is commonly associated with its essence. Unless you were an exceedingly frightful youngster during your formative years, chances are good that debt incurred in *this* life will become due and payable in the next. Consequently, the majority of payback in this *life* was likely incurred in the last.

Having said that, a perfect example of payment exacted in *this* lifetime appears to be fairly straightforward when one considers the trial of O. J. Simpson (whose name, oddly enough, totals to sub number 12) for armed robbery and kidnapping, which stemmed from an incident on September 13, 2007, in Las Vegas. To make a long story short, Simpson was convicted of all 12 charges on October 3, 2008 (10 + 3 =13), exactly 13 years *to the day* after he had been found not guilty in the deaths of his wife, Nicole Brown Simpson, and her friend Ronald Goldman. However, I still believe the number 13 to be a lucky number in that it holds the possibility of a fresh start. A new beginning. A clean slate and the chance to start over. This is even true for Mr. Simpson. Transformations can occur anywhere, even in jail.

Traditionally, the number 13 has been associated with bad luck. Superstitions and hocus-pocus. Witches flying around on broomsticks and stirring their cauldrons, urban legends, and dark and stormy Friday nights. A fairly typical ("black") witch's coven consists of 13 members. The 13th member, by the way, is purported to be the Devil himself. (No, I do not believe in the Devil: however, I certainly recognize the existence of destructive energy, which can also be called evil. Did you ever notice that the word Devil is composed of a Doorway to "evil"? And that "evil" reversed is "live"?)

While number 13 in and of itself is not unlucky, as its energies translate into the "force" (1) of "activity" (3), and total to the firm and foundational 4 that provides a secure base from which to operate, it is still subject to instability if the base is built on sand or if the energies are used for destructive purposes.

The history and legend of the number 13 certainly does manifest itself in an assortment of weird and illogical ways. We have all noticed various and sundry buildings with no room, level, floor, or door number 13, which is also nowhere to be found in some offices, airport gates, hotels, parking lots, letter slots, and street addresses. My favorite absurdity is the absence of an elevator button for the 13th floor. I once lived on the 13th floor of a high-rise and it irked me every time I pushed the 14th floor button. You can call it 12 or you can call it 14, but it is still the 13th floor. It is impossible to count from 12 to 14. Trust me—I'm a numerologist. It cannot be done. It's as if by erasing the number, the architect expects us to accept the absence of part of a physical structure . . . a rather funny response by society to the superstition with which this number is regarded.

The most infamous shadow ever cast over the number 13 came in the form of Judas as he joined the Last Supper and followed up by not only betraying Jesus, but by losing his own life in the process. He was the addition to the completeness of the number 12, who swung the energy into the negative.

King Philip of France (total name and term: 13/4) is also responsible for the suspicion with which 13 is viewed. On Friday, October 13, 1307, the king ordered the arrest and torture of the then-revered Knights Templar. His charges of heresy were apparently primarily based in greed (the king needed to pay off his considerable debts, and the knights were not only wealthy, they were also in tight with the papacy and popular with the people). After this massive arrest, the knights were so heinously tortured that some confessed to sins they had not committed. Later, when some Templars recanted, they were burned at the stake. Jacques De Molay was the last known Grand Master to have been so tortured. It is said that as he burned, he issued an invitation to both Philip and Pope Clement V to join him within a year. Accordingly, both men died within one year (this, and the 13th member of the Last Supper probably combined somewhere along the line to form yet another superstition, which says that the 13th guest at a dinner party will die within a year). All of this resulted in Friday the 13th being declared an evil day, one to be mindful of, and even now, millions of people actually stay home on Friday the 13th.

Friday's association with the 13th and negativity in general was cemented by a variety of links. Public hangings were usually conducted on Fridays and carried out at structures consisting of (reportedly) 13 stairs. Eve's offer of an apple to Adam, the Great Flood, and the crucifixion of Jesus are all purported to have occurred on a Friday.

In marked contrast, the ancient Egyptians revered and respected the number 13. To them, this number was holy and referred to eternity. The Egyptians believed that ascension involved a ladder to Heaven that consisted of 13 rungs; this being the final step taken in order to reach immortality, which, of course, was much desired and therefore worth the work required to get there. This last view is the most reflective of my own feelings about the essence of the number 13: its presence indicates the need to settle one's dues, no matter how difficult, before that final step up the ladder can be taken. This is an almost-perfect example of finding the positive in the negative. By clearing old debt, we are able to move on and up and into spiritual cleanliness, rebirth, and enlightenment.

This karma is a welcome explanation for those age-old questions asked by millions of people on a daily basis: "Why is this happening to me?" or "What did I do to deserve this?" Knowing that you are clearing your slate and preparing for a fresh start somehow makes it easier to bear. And keep in mind that all things pass; this should make the repayment or atonement period easier to get through—not much, perhaps, but a little. It's like being in a long, dark tunnel for a long, dark time and suddenly seeing a light in the distance. The light is hope and an indication that there *is* an end to any bleak situation you may find yourself in. It is also the motivation to keep you moving, for it is a given that by placing one foot in front of the other, you *will* reach the light. It's inevitable. Just keep going.

It was hard for me to accept the reality of my own karmic debt when I recognized and accepted that my Daily and Domestic Names, Lifepath sub number, and Extended Connection numbers had more than a few 13s strewn about (Heather A. Lagan is composed of 13 letters, my first two names are composed of 13 letters, my social security number totals to 13, and my childhood address of 4405 totals to 13), but this realization also began to shed light on the possible answers as to why my life was the way it was—and what I could do to fix it, but it was a slow process.

Over the years, I had found myself repeatedly stuck in very destructive situations and relationships until I slowly began to isolate and recognize patterns, or cycles. And I do mean slowly, but once I opened the door, the light of understanding gradually illuminated my spirit. I have fairly recently passed the half-century mark, and it is only now, after many years of reading, researching, and listening to others and just being quiet within myself, that I can say I am beginning to truly understand the infinite connections between all things: actions and reactions, causes and effects, and the Law of the Universe that binds all things and people together and counts all of its infinitesimal parts as indispensable to the whole. A section of this law decrees that whatever ye sow, ye shall reap, and that is what karma is all about.

The term karma (which totals to 10/1, or Original Force) comes from Sanskrit and means "to do." To me, karma feels like seeds that are planted and almost forgotten until some time later, when they seem to grow overnight. Depending on what is planted, the results will be positive or negative, as in what you plant will grow, what you plan is known (the idea is as bad as the deed... even *seriously considering* having an affair creates almost the same karma as having one), and everything you do or say comes back to you eventually—except the really bad things come back quicker, even in this lifetime. Look at O. J.: his deed was done in this lifetime and karma bit him almost instantly.

Buddhists believe that karma is continual and is carried over from past lives and simultaneously created in current ones and comes in positive and negative forms. While we obviously have no control over debt already accrued, we most certainly do have control over karma that we create in *this* lifetime, at least as adults. Since all experiences originate in a Cosmic classroom of sorts and we are all students, we will experience failure, but that does not mean we quit school: we simply repeat the course (or experience) and pay attention this time. All anyone really needs to do, whether in class or trying to create good karma, is to make the effort, to at least *try* to be as honest as one can be at any given moment and to try to do whatever is at hand the right way. That is the key... to *try*. Being successful is not as important as making a genuine effort. Acknowledging and accepting that all experiences are but lessons seems to relieve some of the tension we may feel when stuck hanging upside down on the metaphorical roller coaster of life—especially when it is temporarily stalled.

As a matter of interest, here are a few name energies carrying the negative 13 vibe: Lizzie Borden, Napoleon Bonaparte, Andrew Cunanan (responsible for the deaths of 5 people, most notably Gianni Versace on July 15 [7+6=13], 1997), and Phil Spector, the once-great songwriter who was indicted (on November 20, 2003: add the 11th month to the 2 and you have 13) in the murder of actress Lana Clarkson. Twice tried, he was finally found guilty of second-degree murder.

On the other hand, Thomas Edison must have amassed some pretty good karma; he brought light to our darkness. Franklin Delano Roosevelt must have as well—not only did he bring hope back to his people, he is also responsible for the oft-repeated phrase "the only thing we have to fear is fear itself" (First Inaugural Address, March 4, 1933).

Master Numbers

Master Numbers are the only combination of digits that are not added together. If the numbers 1 through 9 theoretically represent grade and high school, then Master Numbers represent college and university. Master Numbers that carry the most weight will appear as Whole, Total, Daily, or Life-path numbers, and the more in one name, the stronger the potential for accessing and using this elevated energy. Lesser Masters can also be found sitting side by side in the content of a name, an address, or a phone number, in which case they should also be taken into account when analyzing the energy. For example, any name that holds double C, G, S, or L values will show double 3 values and can indicate subtle connections to the Master 33 energy. For example, my sister Claudia has CL in her main name, and she does indeed illustrate the qualities of Master Sacrifice—she will place others' interests and concerns over her own, has a great big heart, and is giving and forgiving, nurturing, and nonjudgmental. This rule of thumb will hold true for any numbers that repeat themselves this way—their character will reflect a lesser version of the Master Number represented.

Master Numbers are unique. The numbers 11, 22, 33, 44, and so on offer to take us to a much higher place of learning and participation, or to a much lower place of destruction and malfeasance: such is the power held within.

These double-digit, double-energy numbers are highly developed vibrations that carry extraordinary potential for achievement and legacy (which is only overshadowed by the knowledge that the flip side of the Master Numbers is also extraordinary, but in an extremely negative way). To fully develop, or "come into," the full power of a Master, a person would generally require time, experience, and maturity before being equipped to handle such high voltage in a productive and positive way (most step into their power as middle-aged adults, and some never do). Students of the Masters are grown people who have experienced much of what life has to offer, or has thrown at them, including pain, loss, and sorrow; it is only after having direct knowledge of the negatives that the positives are truly appreciated and respected. Masters will be prone to meditating, practicing divination, investigating metaphysical subjects, attending spiritual meetings, and/or altering their lifestyles in accordance with their spiritual awakenings and pursuits.

Of course, mortal beings cannot consistently operate at such high-vibration levels for too long, and sometimes, this energy is completely denied and submerged by the name holder (which is often the time this energy will turn, like sour milk, and become the exact opposite energy from that which was intended). In either case, the 11 can and will revert to the softer 2, the 22 will revert to the grounded 4, and the 33 will mellow into the loving 6. Although Masters run from 11 to 99, their occurrence is practically non-existent above the number 44 (as in a Whole or Total Name Number). I have only come across a few 44s and 55s in all my years of calculating names, and if I ever see anything higher, I would probably spend the next few hours trying to find a mistake in addition that doesn't exist. In other words, chances are slim to none that you will ever come across, for example, a 77 as a final sub or as a Total, Daily, or Whole Name Number.

Master Number 11: Intuitive Imager

The positive 11 radiates a silent and introspective magnetism that tends to attract others. Ruled by a highly developed intuitive mind and psychic introspection, the Master 11 is very aware and sensitive, and is as prone to daydreaming as they are to actualizing. Known as the visionary, the 11 has within the power to manifest, that is, to focus upon that which they desire until it becomes reality, often without realizing they have done so. In fact, the 11 lives in theory—they are not overly concerned with materialism or worldly gain, which can be a bit of a hindrance in this goal-oriented society. They are highly artistic and imaginative and can use these talents to create impressive works of art that can involve paint, words, musical notes, or even illusive and fascinating sleight-of-hand displays.

All of these qualities are perfectly illustrated in the name of Harry Houdini. He was a double 11, which means Harry and Houdini both add up individually to 11 and combine to form the Master Architect 22, an energy that, essentially, takes the visionary magick of the Master Psychic 11 and makes it real, in a manner of speaking. In fact, Houdini's real name was Weisz, which also totals to Master 22. Despite a name adaptation, he still carried the same energy he was born with. (Fittingly enough, Harry died on Halloween, 1926, the night when the "veils" between the living and the dead are rumored to be their thinnest. He did promise his wife that he would, if he could, get a message to her from the other side, which never happened, or perhaps Mrs. Houdini chose to keep it to herself.) Harry created something out of nothing; he tricked the mind and the eye and did it with grace and mystery. Perhaps his energies and story may give you an idea of the keys the Master 11 holds and some of the secret places those keys may unlock.

The talents of the Master 11 are not limited to creation in the artistic sense: here also is the inventor, the scientist, the original thinker in any field of endeavor. Hence, the Master 11 is the one who thinks or images in an unusual or unique way, and this can take the form of the scholar, the scientist and the philosopher, the teacher, the lawyer, the judge, the priest, the doctor, the spiritual motivator, or just the daydreamer. These traits can become so developed that the Master 11 can almost inadvertently attract global attention, which is to say some will, and have, become venerated leaders upon the worldly stage.

To offer a more succinct profile of an 11 you may well recognize as someone you know, here are some of an illuminated 11's main characteristics. Master 11, when in high operation, will be very approachable, friendly, warm, genuine, and welcoming, although one may sense a bit of mystery around them (and if they are pursuing an odd or unusual subject or lifestyle, they can be downright mesmerizing). Master 11 adapts well to any situation they are dropped into and are able to adjust their behavior to match the behavior of others. A true 11 is always creative in some form or another: they will be painters, writers, actors, inventors, singers, and often leaders in some form within their community. Sensitive and romantic, the 11 longs for love, not only for themselves, but also for the world. They are often employed in a healing or counseling field, and a great many of them are involved in the fields, of paranormal, holistic, and metaphysical arts.

The number 11 Major Arcana card is Justice, which is all about fair play and doing the right thing, both on the Earth plane and on the spiritual plane. It is balance achieved through mediation and meditation, and its premise is based on the lack of illusion or that which is hidden. It is the exposition of truth, and that is what a genuine 11 is all about— justice and truth. (It is also what Harry Houdini wished to accomplish: *belief* in the truth of what the eye sees.)

When the 11 is low on energy, it will function as a 2, which is gentle, loving, domestic, and kind. As the 2, it will be surrounded by loyal friends and maintain a variety of interests and connections through business or art.

The drawback to the highly charged, activated, or special numbers are their negative sides. If I have managed to convey the strength of the number 11, it should come as no surprise that such power, used without respect or understanding or even with deliberate maliciousness, can produce atrocious and malevolent results. Here is the charming psychopath who masks his intent with smooth grace and hideous pretense. The beauty and purity of the positive 11 is the scale by which the ugliness and impurity of the negative 11 is weighed. Unfortunately, although this is true for all numbers, it is most especially true for the stronger Masters. Since everything has an equal and opposite side and the measure of that power is reflected by its original, the intensity of the positive energies will be equal to the intensity of the negative energies.

If you are involved in any way with an 11 and are picking up very wrong vibes, red flags are waving furiously, and your intuition is screaming at you, in all seriousness, *run*— don't walk—to the nearest exit. These energies are bad news and, depending on how advanced, can range from just plain weird to downright dangerous. To tie this up with a not-so-pretty bow, here are but a few name energies that total to a negative 11: Genghis Khan, Aileen Wuornos (the first female serial killer as documented in the film *Monster*), Jack the Ripper, Karla Homolka, and Charles Manson.

The 11 can also manifest in a variety of eerie, connective ways. Sometimes the energy carries an untimely end (Marilyn Monroe, James Dean, Marvin Gaye) or creates an atmosphere of surreal mystery (Alfred Hitchcock) or startling discovery (Einstein). It is the number of celluloid magick and knowledge as reflected in the names Michael Moore, Sharon Stone, and George Clooney, to name but a few.

It is also the number of combined forces. Imagine the physical form or body aligning with an unseen but powerful belief or desire. All of the following 11 Masters "joined" with their beliefs in such strong ways that they actually became part of our history: George Washington was the first President of the United States; Florence Nightingale became the first nurse to actually tend to the wounded British soldiers during the Crimean War (1854–56); Mother Teresa gave her life to Love (or God as some people preferred to call it), opened the first Home for the Dying (Hospice) in Calcutta, and was awarded the Nobel Peace Prize in 1979; Margaret Hilda Thatcher became the first woman Prime Minister of the United Kingdom; Martin Luther King Jr. became the youngest man to ever receive the Nobel

Peace Prize (1964) and became the figurehead of all those who "have a dream" and often conversed with John Fitzgerald Kennedy, who became the first Catholic president and the youngest (at the time) president ever elected to office. He is also the author of a famous saying: "Ask not what your country can do for you, ask what you can do for your country." As mentioned, there is a certain mystique and myth attached to the 11 energy, and these people illustrate and honor it quite well.

Multi 11 Values

Anyone who boasts a number of Master 11 values in their name often has a splendid imagination, can be viewed as a visionary, and is often involved in spiritual or metaphysical pursuits. However, the presence of numerous 11s can also point to someone who needs to *acknowledge and incorporate* the unusual leanings of the 11 into their daily lives. Experimentation in artistic expression, dramatic writings, or paranormal topics is strongly suggested as a method helpful in focusing the "third eye," which is part and parcel of learning to use the gifts of the 11.

On the other hand, if the multi 11 in question is overly involved with the esoteric world, it could be that basic functions and responsibilities are ignored and more attention needs to be paid to the realities of living.

Lifepath for the Number 11
(also see Lifepath Number 2)

As the first Master Number, this Lifepath is all about honoring the intuition and seeking and absorbing all manner of esoteric knowledge as required to function at a higher level of spirituality. Ever the enthusiast, especially about the mysteries of life, this number energy is very empathic, idealistic, romantic, and nurturing, and is perfectly suited to teaching and inspiring others. This is, in fact, its direction—to leave some manner of an imprint on the psyche of man, even in a small way. The Master 11 who chooses to follow their intuitive leanings will lead anything but a normal life, as indicated in the examples given above. Although their contributions may not be quite as large, they will be valued, noticed, and treasured nonetheless.

Challenges for the Number 11

This vibration is very susceptible to the world of the imagination and the arcane and can easily become withdrawn and separated from society, family, and friends. Although its natural propensity is to lead and educate, its deep thoughts can leave it vulnerable to anything that offers sensory stimulation or a temporary escape from the heaviness of this reality. The 11 must learn to accept (and release) their often negative experiences of youth as necessary developments to the inner self and to step into their roles as spiritual beings and leaders in order to successfully complete their work on this earth plane.

Master Number 22: The Builder

This Master is the elder sibling to the 11; however, where the 11 is the prophetic dreamer and idealistic sensitive who uses their gift of words to inspire and lead, the 22 has the motivation to take the dreams, visions, and words of the 11 and transpose them into objects that one can touch, see, and relate to as material objects. This energy not only lives by the divine laws, they are able to work within those laws to create material legacies and amass incredible wealth and possessions here on this Earth plane. While the 11 is content to work from their head (read imagination) and heart (read emotions, psychic impressions, and intuition), the 22 works with their intellect, communication, and building skills. Their need to produce tangible results is the strongest motivator for this electric force, and it will reach out to the people in a large way—seeking to touch as many as possible with its undertakings.

The positive 22 will create homes for the less fortunate, build centers for the elderly and fashion extensions for hospitals, begin charities, and so on. The desire to aid is genuine, as is the hope of connecting with humanity at a core level. While I may be focusing on actual buildings to illustrate the central feeling of the 22, they can also accomplish the expansion of mass awareness through song, the written word, dramatic presentations, films, and a myriad of other outlets. The doctor who pioneers the latest medical breakthrough, the lawyer who fights for the underdog, and the volunteer who collects donations for the less fortunate or homeless are all likely to be under the influence of the 22. Whether the 22 is found running around in a business suit, riding shotgun in a beat-up pickup, or clutching a battered briefcase to their ripped sweatshirt, make no mistake, the developed and dedicated 22 is not generally concerned with *how* it gets done, just that it gets done. If they do find themselves wearing an expensive get-up, driving a Lexus, and sprouting a variety of technical gadgets from their various body parts, rest assured, those things mean exactly nothing to the 22. They are a means to an end. At home, a 22 might wear jeans and a T-shirt and meditate by the fireplace or the open window (as with all Masters, the 22 has down-times and functions as a grounded and responsible 4 when not "on"). After meditation, the 22/4 is very likely to go pull some weeds, take out the garbage, do the laundry, scrub the toilet, and vacuum the hairballs from under the couch.

The character of the positive 22 is cheerful, progressive, outgoing, and open-minded. This energy is willing to try anything if the outcome looks at all helpful to others. Charming, intelligent, and spiritually cultured, the 22 is highly social and adept at connecting with "higher ups," yet in an unobtrusive and humble way. As mentioned, the 22 will likely become wealthy if they stay on the straight and narrow, but risks losing it all should they it allow themselves to be sidetracked down a dark and twisting alley.

There is one very important warning attached to the 22. As they hold the power to gain and collect massive amounts of money, power, prestige, and material possessions, it is fairly obvious that a very real possibility is the threat for slip-sliding down the slope of ego and greed and losing their grip on the divine laws and light they are living by. In this worst case scenario, the wealth and power that has been attained can lead to intense boredom and inspire a craving, a search for *more*. More excitement, more something. When one has everything or can buy anything (or anyone) the heart desires, one becomes susceptible to the "I am untouchable" syndrome. The laws are forgotten and the light goes out. Moral and ethical misbehavior or lack of judgment is the principal caveat attached to the errant 22. Essentially, whatever the reason might be, the 22 can lose their way or balance and, sometimes, their life.

One major example of such an apparent loss of balance is characterized by the unfortunate case of Michael Jackson. Prior to his untimely death in 2009 (which totals to an 11, by the way), Jackson experienced the results of intense Master 22 energies when allegations were made (but never proven) that fit in with the above warning.

Mr. Jackson came into this life on the 11th day of August, 1958, carrying a golden gift (or some would say heavy load) from Universe: his Total Name Number is a Master 55, which refers to Fairness and Judgment. His Daily Name is a double 22, which totals to a Master 44; it carries the theme and responsibility of being or becoming a Master Healer, which he most definitely had the ability to do through his music. However, the flip sides of all of these Master Numbers can create massive meltdowns and very negative consequences.

One cannot dismiss history or the presence of these powerful numerical repetitions and their messages, positive or not. The numbers are incapable of lying. And the fact of the matter is that Michael Jackson's life and career *were* negatively impacted by allegations of immoral conduct, which is an unambiguous example of the exact warnings attached to the powerful 22. His untimely passing also fits in with the earth-shaking vibrations of the flip side of the Master 44—two side-by-side foundational 4 values can and will create massive earthquakes that are capable of destroying careers, reputations, and even lives.

While there are obviously darker shades to all Master Numbers, the number 22 can be the light shining in the darkness as well: Moses and Buddha both total to Master 22.

An interesting conclusion to the Tarot connection is that the cards depicting major life events (Major Arcana) common to mankind number 22, which is reduced to the number 4—the base or foundation for all of mankind to build upon. So while the message of the 22 Major Arcana is to build and create, it also points out the need to anchor yourself very securely on the way up and to never forget to check the quality of your foundations.

Multi 22 Values

A read that shows several Master 22 values is screaming for the realization of a dream—it points to a potent level of achievement that is perhaps dormant in the name holder. Master 22 has the ability to create large legacies, to build empires, to make a big difference. The message of multiple 22 energies is to *go after the dream*—it can become reality.

On the negative side, the presence of multi 22 values can also be indicative of the potential breach of ethics that was mentioned earlier—this person may need to come down off their pedestal (or be knocked off) before they will understand that power does not excuse bad behavior.

Lifepath for the Master Number 22
(also see Lifepath Number 4)

The Master Number 22 Lifepath points to all roads of manifestation: this number can move the world of imagination into the tangible world of reality. Focus will fall on large projects or important advancements that will tend to benefit larger groups of people or even the Earth itself. The 22 is capable of amassing material wealth and of rising to almost meteoric heights and should pursue its dreams with complete devotion and even controlled abandon.

Challenges for the Master Number 22

This Master is called to be aware of excesses. Having too much of everything can lead to boredom and, thus, a need for stimulation. Moral and ethical guideposts are to be observed and obeyed. If they are ignored, the 22 will crash from the heights of that which it has built, often with catastrophic results.

Master Number 33: The Leader

While you will come across the occasional 33, they are relatively atypical and are often undeveloped. A positive 33 is completely concerned with activities that connect in some way to love. It is the highest level of the love vibration and joins the spiritualist, the monk, and the priest: one who serves many. It is the "teacher of teachers" and is connected to the 6, which is ruled by Venus, the planet of love. The two 3s combined refer to the activity and thoughts of one that influences the activity and thoughts of many. Here we have one voice, one person, who is the faith-filled leader of a flock, in whatever form this may take. This leader must make the required sacrifices of the traditional home and family: the *people* are their focus, their love, their family, and their world. They are private, yes, but their main reason for being is to help others stand in the light of love. They live for God and spirit and to spread the word of faith and positive action and thought. Should you be fortunate enough to know a positive 33, you will find they are selfless and giving, honest to a fault, and display the courage of the lion, yet without the roar and scary teeth. The 33 will be difficult to know on a casual, personal level (unless they are functioning as their sub energy of nurturing 6), as there is absolutely nothing casual about them and they are for the masses, not for the mundane or meaningless or trivial. These are energies that will be honored and respected: genuine revolutionaries who speak an age-old truth.

Some negative possibilities for the 33 include taking on too much worldly responsibility and therefore feeling burdened to the point of becoming depressed and ineffective. The 33's goal is to deliver their gift to humanity, and their greatest fear is the inability to either carry this weight or to complete the delivery of said gifts.

Another negative attached to the 33 is obviously manifested in spiritual leaders who are not what or who they appear to be, or those who become insufferable martyrs for their cause. At the other end of the scale, here follows a perfect example of the inherent sacrifice present in the mission of a true Master 33: religion aside, Jesus was a teacher and messenger of pure love and faith who was put to death, or sacrificed for and by the people, at the age of 33.

As a force alone, the 33 is impressive. Take the scope of the World Wide Web, which totals to Master 33 (Master 22+7+4=33): this computer grid does indeed deliver a gift to the world, to the masses. That said, it also shows the potential for intensely negative energies that are particular to Master Numbers. Its damaging, dangerous, and ugly side is separating people from their money, children from their parents, and social contact from many lives (consider that its Cornerstone energies are WWW or 666). It is as though this gift holds within a sacrifice of ethics, safety, and basic goodness, but it is the hand of the user that defines the path of the knife.

Lifepath of the Master Number 33
(also See Lifepath Number 6)

Here we are getting into a more direct manifestation of the spiritual Lifepath— someone with this energy will often find themselves feeling apart from others in that they are on a different level of development. They can feel alone, segregated, and misunderstood. Often seen as a Master Teacher, the fully developed 33 will usually be called upon to sacrifice a personal life (spouse, children, home of their own) in order to fulfill their destiny as a teacher of spiritual truths and of unconditional love, although they will likely travel in order to share their knowledge; they will also be quite alone. Someone who does not know a 33 personally may mistakenly label them as distant and even arrogant.

Challenges for the Master Number 33

The challenge for the Master 33 involves a deep insecurity that is never shared with others. As they are often placed in positions of reverence or supreme respect, any perceived personal failings will be kept to themselves. These inner emotions can easily lead to a sense of despondency and reliance on substances that can become addictive. The pure 33 must learn to transcend their own personal desires and lifestyles in order to learn and teach their lesson of unconditional love.

Multi 33 Values

Anything above Master 33 is relatively rare, and several in one chart is rarer still. If this is the case, the name holder is likely to be fairly lonely in that the frequency of the Master Numbers is elevated above the regular, or normal, number scale. Anyone under its influence can find interacting with others in an intimate and personal way quite challenging. After all, the 33 is more concerned with the bigger picture than with the individual components. If several 33 Masters are indicated and the bearer is a developed spirit, then the potentialities here are limitless; this is someone who could easily impact the world in some way.

Master Number 44: The Healer

This Master could be compared to the Giant Doctor in the Sky. It is the Master Healer/Therapist, the one who, ideally, rights all the wrongs within the human race, or the spirit body of mankind. This energy would have the ability to affect the mental and psychological states of massive amounts of people. The manner in which this would be accomplished would vary—it could be through words, medicine, actions—the list is endless and open to the imagination. The point here is that the positive 44 would be able to reach out on a fundamental, base level to the emotional core of society and effect positive change—a Healer who offers therapy to the masses. As we all know, such a leader is a rare find, indeed. Hopefully, we won't destroy such energy when the positive 44 does make an appearance. (Or it won't destroy itself.)

Along the same vein, a negative 44 would not be an energy anyone would enjoy being associated with. The shaking of the foundations of the two 4s would create chaos—a treacherous and destructive energy that would undermine a basic belief system and result in a collapse of hope. The negative 44 would inevitably stumble and fall, which, of course, would feel like an earthquake in the world of the 44 in question and in the worlds of those who admire him or her. The fall of a potential Leader and Healer would obviously cause considerable disillusionment among the people, as well. (See Master 22, Michael Jackson: his double 22s total to Master 44.)

Master 55: The Genius

This energy is beyond intelligent. It is the perfect blend of fair judgment and authority. Justice and genius. Intellectus perfectus. This energy rides along the crest of changes and fame, but it is also the balanced and neutral number 5 doubled, which suggests a world of ideas and intellect that are transformed into their most positive and beneficial forms for mankind. Ideally, of course. One of the very few Master 55 energies I have come across is Queen Elizabeth (22+33=55). Another is Michael Joseph Jackson.

Master 66: Crazy Love

Fecund and fertile, this Master unites all aspects of creation into one pure energy. It is like a laser beam of creativity—under its rays sprout pregnant women, trees heavy with fruit, growth and greenery, and massive brainstorms and epiphanies. This feels like true love and creation gone wild but in an organized, focused manner.

Master 77: Cosmic Consciousness

Perfect union of logic and metaphysical truths is the realm of the Master 77 and results in complete balance in the brain and in the consciousness. In fact, some would call this essence the Divine consciousness: pure and clean thought and pure and clean manifestation of those thoughts. This is the brain of all things operating in *perfect* harmony.

Master 88: Success

This is the absolutely unpolluted blend of true humility with pure, raw power. This is the lemniscate (see number 8), the yin/yang, the infinity symbol; it is the 2 circles of the 8 matching one another to 0 degrees of difference. Master 88 is absolute universal understanding and perfect balance in all things.

Master 99: Fulfillment

I am convinced that this one would only be encountered upon reaching the other side. This number is the only one of the Masters that reduces back to its form number (9+9=18=9) and carries energies and knowledge that I believe we can only access once we have left this Earth plane. Fulfillment, then, only comes when one leaves, or is about to leave, this plane of existence. One would have to be dead, or close enough to knock on its door, to truly be able to say, but I have heard and seen enough to know that folks who *know* and *accept* that they are dying are somehow at peace and even eager to get going. Funny, but there you have it. What waits for you and me, to my way of thinking, is complete truth, unlimited knowledge, and clarity so fine, so delicate that it feels as though it could shatter with a whisper. It is something that you, dear reader, may have already experienced, albeit perhaps only occasionally.

Everyone has moments of sudden understanding, sudden epiphanies; weird moments of clear knowledge. Remember an instant when something clicked into place, when you suddenly "got it"? Can you remember that feeling? That sheer understanding, that split-second flash of recognition is the element of which I speak: the Truth. In the case of the Master 99 it is ongoing and perpetual. The truth revealed, one degree at a time, yet simultaneously. Each truth immediately becomes part of your spirit, which absorbs and expands until all facets of truth are exposed and assimilated.

> *... originality exists in every individual because each of us differs from the others. We are all primary numbers divisible only by ourselves ...*
> —Jean Guitton (1901–1999)

four

The Letters

Each letter of our twenty-six-letter alphabet, in its upper-case form, is a character unto itself. Each reveals something about itself simply by its appearance, or the way it stands and its shape. If you think of the letters as made up of individual stick figures or symbolic shapes and look at each letter with an open eye, you will uncover another layer in the mystery, another layer to the onion. The letter H, for example, always looked like a ladder (minus a few rungs) to me. But if you stack a few of these on top of each other ... there it is! And, indeed, its primary meaning is exactly that: a ladder that one can choose to climb up or down, and up is preferable.

Much like reading the symbols on tarot cards, whichever way you choose to relate to a letter or number is the right way for *you* and will stick in your mind, which will, in turn, assist you in memorizing meanings. So if the O reminds you of the Sun, so be it. All that matters is that it works for *you.*

The following section contains the meanings of the letters and discusses the specific characteristics of each symbol. Special attention should be paid to the letters that come up as your Cornerstone(s), for they will carry stronger meanings for each particular name. So if your name is Sharon, the S will be a strong influence over the entire name. If, on the other hand, your name is Sasha, the S will double in intensity due to the Cornerstone and an additional S energy. If your name is Sharon Sasha Samson, the S will coil around your energy like a snake. Which is not necessarily a bad thing; it depends on how you choose to use this overload of S energy. It is always a personal decision.

Also, like anything else, everything has a light and a dark side, which I do not shy away from describing. You will know which meanings are yours and which are not.

Words are alive. Cut them and they bleed…
—Ralph Waldo Emerson (1803–1882)

A (Value of 1): The Alone Survivor

Obviously, A is the first letter of the alphabet and shares much of the same qualities as the number 1, which is also its value. Traditional meanings of the letter A point to beginners, go-getters, loners, and the pioneering, "Original Force" from which all else emanates. It represents the first breath, the first action, the first word. The A is very much about the self, or ego, and it is also very much Alone.

In ancient symbolism, the A represents the pointed phallus: it is creation and self-survival in its purest form. Sometimes the A personality will come across as arrogant, self-absorbed, aggressive, ostentatious, and egocentric, yet their primary function is to survive and prevail, which can, in turn, create a short temper and ignorance on many levels. This limitation can manifest as frustration or anger, a lack of social skills and tact, and a variety of projects begun and left unfinished. The A is generally an energy that expects and looks for immediate results. Their emotional level is not well developed, as they do not focus on *feelings*, but rather on activities, investigations, accomplishments, and success. This does not mean that the A does not *feel*, simply that they are very self-contained and controlled. Emotions are given very little consideration in their pursuit for advancement; the A is, after all, at the starter's gate, so to speak (A and number 1 both hold first place in their respective energy fields). Neither of these starter energies are familiar with (theoretically) mingling and blending with other energies in a productive and positive way, so the consequent lack of social and interactive ability is almost to be expected. However, it is easy enough to remedy the situation for those of us who sport a few A energies—all it takes is a little bit of focus and a moment of thought before opening the mouth or taking action.

This is a strong vibration and holds a deep reservoir of endurance, perseverance, and tenacity; the A is the most likely of all letters to keep on keeping on. They are also very instinctual; they listen to that voice from inside as it guides the survival, but open acknowledgement of the mystery of the *intuition* is not likely to be made.

In worst case scenarios, the A can also be read as sheer force, as in an abuse of power or control. Since the A is such a strong force on its own, people who have high levels of this energy in their names can be found at either end of the spectrum: as the giver or the receiver. In other words, someone with a few As in their name could just as easily be the Abused as the Abuser. No other letter in the alphabet has this potential, and it is simply due to the A forming the initial entry point for all the energy to follow: the A blasts open the path, therefore its potential for over-the-top force is emphasized.

In best case scenarios, the A will represent someone who is driven, focused, even-natured, progressive both materially and spiritually, open to new ideas, and admirable in their desire to succeed.

Traditional Descriptions

Typical descriptions of an average A energy include original, ambitious, determined, focused, driven, creative, progressive, energetic, and curious. Extreme 1 energy can create personalities who are self-absorbed, unfeeling, tactless, vain, aggressive, abusive, cruel, critical, and proud.

Cornerstones

The following words all hold an Original Force in their first letter: Alphabet, Astrology, Air, Alive, Anger, Ancestor, Ambition, Aggression, Actor, Artist, and Atomic.

As a Current Energy Phase

This 1-year period involves new starts. These can manifest as winning a promotion, getting that job, starting a new and exciting project, going back to school or simply coming into a strong sense of identity and knowledge of what is wanted or required in life. This is not an *emotional* beginning; rather it is a logical, practical, or educational one. This may also be a year to be very aware of whom or what one becomes involved with as these connections may have negative kickbacks, especially if the intuition is ignored.

B (Value of 2): Blending and Bonding

B refers to the place of birth, or of a hidden place where unseen energies bubble—unspoken words, thoughts, ideas, plans. It is a place of germination and gestation and, ultimately, expulsion. A perfect example of this would be the brain. An idea materializes, solidifies into a plan and manifests as action. (Someone decides to build a new home. The idea solidifies into a drawing on paper, which in turn is handed to the architect and, finally, the builder. A *thought* has led to the construction of something we can touch and perceive as real.) The B also points to balance: as above, so below. (The house has to be balanced and its numbers correct; if the degrees or angles are off by just the slightest amount, it could very easily collapse.) Like the façade of a house, Bs tend to present a particular front—one is not quite sure what is really going on within the building, or in the pregnant lady's belly (again a process where numbers form the essence of creation as cells split and multiply again and again until there are billions of them that bond and blossom until a baby is fully formed).

The B appears calm, peaceful, domestic, gentle, and warm. It is, appropriately, ruled by the number 2, which is duality: two sides or features to one object or subject. In this case, the inner versus the outer or the one versus the other. Since the average B's tender and often frustrating emotions are held inside and require a tremendous amount of trust to share, regular outbursts can be expected, not necessarily of anger, although that would certainly occur should the B feel unappreciated, taken for granted or used. The B seeks blissful and blessed relationships, which can lead the blind B into extremely intense and even obsessive relationships. Impulsiveness can intervene or interfere in an otherwise serene lifestyle. In other words, the B is somewhat reticent by nature, so the chances of the dam breaking or being breeched is not inconceivable.

Anyone who carries the B as a Cornerstone must learn to express emotional truths and to voice opinions, a difficult lesson because the B is primarily the peacemaker and will therefore hesitate to introduce elements that can result in conflict or tension. The B will often put up with things just to avoid confrontation, which will come anyway. Once the patience of the B has been tested to the limit, be prepared to run because an explosive B is not a pretty sight. But because the B is primarily about balance and bonding, these explosions pass quickly. Once the emotions are expressed and the anger is out, the B will settle back down into the role of the peacemaker.

Traditional Descriptions

Typical descriptions of the B include domestic, even-natured, soft-spoken, helpful, concerned, faithful, loyal, and loving. Less positive traits appear as being secretive, withholding, uncommunicative, impulsive, explosive, and overly emotional/needy.

Cornerstones

The following words all show an inner or hidden quality: Baby, Body, Belief, Biology, and Bubble, or an explosion outward like Birth, Boom, Bang, Bomb, and Burp.

As a Current Energy Phase

The realm of relationships is highlighted during this two-year period, although the B energy can refer to both unions and separations. The main point is the duality; the B either is no longer alone or is once again alone. This can manifest as marriage, divorce, forming business partnerships, joining clubs—anything that has to do with more than one person and is new to the Lifepath.

C (Value of 3): Communication in All Its Forms

Ah, the open mouth! Among many other qualities or characteristics, the prime traditional meaning for the C is communication in all its forms, the most obvious and readily available being the mouth. The C *is* a great big open mouth and is the creator of all forms of communication, be that words issuing forth, or creation issuing forth in the form of painting, song, sculpture, or dance—anything that expresses what lies within. The C is a giant conduit—for magick, entertainment, and activity and, since it is ruled by the ever-active number 3, the C tends to say what is on their mind (or tongue) without too much hesitation; therefore the C is known for its honesty or blunt manner of speaking. This character trait can easily offend others, which is puzzling to the C, as they truly believe that they are speaking the truth for the good of others. The brain and the mouth seem to be directly linked and sometimes operate without a filter—what is thought can be spoken almost as quickly. As the C is also highly creative, success may come through the pursuit of the combination of words and art. The C also responds instantly and naturally to anything of beauty and prefers to present themselves in the best light possible and to surround themselves with articles or energies containing and reflecting beauty and creativity as well. The beauty of cash and the power it holds is also among the C's attractors, as it is the call to travel and to see (C) as much beauty as possible.

The conversational C creates great teachers, parents, and community-oriented individuals. Some are memorable in that they take the art of communication, which can be translated via music, art, magick, drama, or entertainment of any kind to a whole new level: Criss Angel (illusionist), Edgar Cayce (prophet), John Cleese (actor), Julia Child (chef), and Confucius (Chinese philosopher) are but a few examples.

The C untethered brings to mind the saying "loose lips sink ships," which is my delicate way of saying that while the C is nothing if not brutally honest, they can also be prone to gossip. The C is like the child of the alphabet: they speak their truth and then run away to play. The C is innocent;

they respond to gentleness, truth, and creativity, and they love all things that reflect this innocence and beauty.

The C also likes to eat. It is, after all, an open mouth.

Traditional Descriptions
Typical descriptions attached to the C include communicative, creative, honest, even-natured, adaptable, active, and charming. More negative traits include the potential to be authoritarian, argumentative, blunt or rude, scattered, stubborn, and insensitive.

Cornerstones
The following words all follow the lines of Communication: Call, Chat, Cry, Chant, Choir, Criticism, Confess, Camera, and Computer.

As a Current Energy Phase
This will translate into a three-year period of creativity and communication and can take the shape of bringing new life into existence (a child, for example) or beginning a creative/intellectual project. Vocal sharing is highlighted; sometimes this is a warning against giving away too much of the self or talking too much. Some might join a choir, go back to school, begin journaling, or take painting lessons. This period is one of activity, creativity, community, and open communication.

D (Value of 4): The Open or Closed Door
The D is probably the most unyielding energy in the alphabet, springing from the fact that it is representative of a closed door. Its challenge is knowledge versus

ignorance, and its dilemma is whether to open the door or leave it closed. The D needs to *see* to believe, but because it is ruled by the very firm and foundational number 4, it is also against the nature of the D to open up and thereby risk exposure to the unknown or uninvited. The desire *does* exist to see what lies on the other side, but it is difficult for the D to release itself from the essence of its being so the door often remains closed. It is not too hard to imagine a dim room beyond that door that would be gloomy, limited, and dull. The D needs to open its door, let the sunshine in, and break with routine. The D is intelligent but scientifically inclined, which would explain why they need to see, touch, and experience anything out of the norm before they will believe, and even then, the D will have countless reasonable explanations as to why this thing (whatever it may be) is not possible, or is not what it appears to be. Frustrating? Oh yes, the D certainly can be that. At the same time, the D has an admirable (if annoying) ability to discern the truths of opposing points of view; they are able to debate issues from different angles at the same time. The D's keen sense of logic, honesty, methodical thought processes, and firm grip on reality gives them the honor of being able to see both sides at once and each as clearly. These qualities make the D, understandably, an excellent employee or manager/owner and the influence of the reliable, dependable, and hard-working 4 cements the deal.

Due to its resistance to change in general, the D may also find it difficult to consult a Doctor when physical symptoms arise and may therefore suffer Dis-ease, or niggling, ongoing heath issues, which are usually the result of unaddressed emotional issues (which is true for all people who suffer dis-ease; something in the life, past or present, has remained unchallenged for too long and has become physically toxic).

The main message concerning the D is that its chief adversary is boredom. It must question its boundaries and explore outside its normally closed door and extricate itself, at least periodically, from the ho-hum routine and repetitiveness of a rather limited lifestyle and belief system.

The D holds so many keys and yet rarely investigates which key opens which portal. The D's very deep sense of limitation often keeps them stuck in one place—theoretically, physically, or both. Two or more Ds in a name reveals a strong element of immobility, which can keep the D from investigating anything other than their own interests, which is a great pity, as the only thing they are "closed" to is knowledge. As mentioned, the average D needs to see before they believe, but if they *could* see, they would believe. This is the challenge for the D: to remain ignorant of sights unseen, or to open up to significant revelations held in different "rooms," or even in the expanse of the world lying right outside their own front doors.

I must add here that some D people are perfectly happy living within a small and unchallenged world—they feel quite secure there. Any attempt to widen their horizons or drag them out of their safe place will meet with a resistance the likes of which you have never seen. Stubbornness is one of the D energy's finest attributes, which, depending on the circumstances, can be a good thing or a bad thing.

Traditional Descriptions

Some traits of the D include being sensible, faithful, tenacious, practical, hard-working, dedicated, methodical, and honest. Negative sides of the D include being dishonest, stubborn, mean-spirited, obsessive, uninspired, inactive, pessimistic, restless, and bored.

Cornerstones

All of these words relate to the Doorways that separate one place or state from another and encompass two different sides or elements: Death, Divorce, Disease, Dream, Dungeon, Deep, Distant, Divide, Double, Devil, and Dumb.

As a Current Energy Phase

This four-year period holds the key to advancement and growth. Opportunities are presented, secrets are revealed, mysteries are afoot, and the norm is being challenged. During this time, the D has the opportunity to gain knowledge, try new things, and spread their wings. Alternately, the stubborn streak will intensify as the D digs in their heels and dogmatically resists and resents anything new, unique and/or spiritually oriented. This can also be, more mundanely, a period of hard work, a nose-to-the-grindstone type of energy that is laying the foundations for a business, a home, or even a relationship.

E (Value of 5): Energy in All Its Forms

While the D is one of the most immovable energies, the E is the most energetic. It is traditionally ruled by enthusiasm, and holds within a pure energy that is open to expansion. Its connection to energy is evident in the ratio of $E=mc^2$, which is Einstein's theory that matter and energy are really the same thing. It is also the mathematical basis for the first atomic bomb. The E's ruler is number 5, which relates to freedom, communication, independence, authority, the senses, and change. If one looks at the actual construction of the E, it reaches forward with three limbs: the top arm represents the brain; the middle, the soul/heart; and the bottom, physical action. It is the most forward letter in the alphabet, meaning its energy centers on the future. The E personality is also impulsiveness at its finest, and they will often commit themselves completely and entirely to various (and perhaps questionable) causes, sometimes without sufficient forethought or consideration. They are receptive to all and, as such, the E is governed by their open mouth, heart, and mind, which brings up the next point.

The E is susceptible to excessive behaviors when it comes to their sensory sensitivity, and therein lies a warning concerning the potential for overindulgence in anything that feeds those senses—be it food, alcohol, drugs, too many sexual partners, and/or taking unnecessary risks in order to satisfy possible cravings for excitement and stimulation. *Everything* is contained in the E: good, bad, and in between. One example of this concept of the E holding everything is to be found in the word and idea of our Mother Earth. She is everything. Without her, we are nothing; we cease to exist.

The average E would make a fantastic singer, orator, teacher, student (who is often interested in the occult or unusual), leader, politician, or actor, and is extraordinarily progressive and curious. The more 5 values and/or E energies in a name, the more likely it is that the holder will be drawn to unusual elements and attracted to extremes, adventures, and sensual, or "of the senses," stimulation. The unrestrained and multiple E can easily become overwhelmed by their own search for excitement, which can translate into nervous or scattered energies, explosions of temper, restlessness, and lack of focus on basic issues, such as relationships. An unadulterated E can become both trying and tiring. This type of extreme energy is hard to turn off: they are the chatterbox, the nervous fiddler, the bouncing-off-the-walls personality. On occasion, especially when excited, the E is an energy that can be difficult to be around for extended periods of time. Fortunately, the E is usually softened or toned down by letters surrounding it. Usually. If not, get ready for an exceptionally eager extrovert who might drain you like water from a bathtub.

The normal manifestation of the E is someone who is nonjudgmental, supportive of others, easy to be around, and usually very sensitive to the deeper dimensions of the senses—as in hearing the individual instruments in the band, seeing the face in an abstract painting, feeling each thread in the silken cloth, smelling the sea in the wind, and tasting the essence of the only bay leaf in the spaghetti sauce, and is also naturally receptive to the sixth sense, or intuition. The average E is generally happy, for this energy is aware of the possibilities of life and knows that opportunities abound, just waiting to be discovered.

Last, but not certainly not least, the E is very affectionate, whimsical, loving, and sensually oriented. The E is also a potentially exciting intimate partner; the E puts the exotic and erotic into sEx.

Traditional Descriptions

Typical descriptions attached to the E include energetic, eager, positive, curious, open-minded, social, active, sensual, and adventurous. On the flip side, the E can also become careless, addicted, overbearing, unfocused, temperamental, restless, and self-absorbed.

Cornerstones

These are a great set of Cornerstone examples ... the E is Effortless in its Expression: Energy, Eager, Enthusiasm, Extend, Electricity, Excite, Exotic, Excess, Euphoria, Explode, Evil, Eon, Era ... the list is almost Endless.

As a Current Energy Phase

The five-year reign of the E offers many options. It can become a time of indulging the senses (perhaps negatively, as in addictions) or of seeking independence and freedom. When under this influence, the E/5 person can often find themselves swept along in a sequence of events, chosen or otherwise. It can represent an unstable and ever-changing time in relationships, jobs, homes, and life in general. If, however, the E follows an A, for example, this can be indicative of a new project, job, relationship, or "start," and the enthusiasm generated by same. The E holds excitement, travel, new endeavors, success, and new faces and places, and its energy is anything but boring.

F (Value of 8): Family and Cerebral Power

The F holds similar energy to the E, minus the progressive action of the feet, or lower extension. Without its feet, the F tends to fall flat on its face should it go against its grounded and foundational nature and try to flee, for example. It is dependable and forward thinking but is fairly fixed.

Cerebrally driven, the F personality is ruled by their logical brain waves and their mouth (like the E, this energy is open in head area). To say the F is governed by intellectually superior thought processes would be to say that ducks like water. The F is a composed and authoritative letter, which is fitting, as it is ruled by the usually controlling 8. It is a reclusive energy, not an active one and, as a result, needs a calm, quiet ambiance in which to think and rest. While the F's choice is to express or not express, the F will not readily reveal their deepest thoughts; but when they *are* motivated to speak, they will invariably share something of value and will express it eloquently and sometimes, forcefully. Their opinions are fixed and when angered, their choice of words will be fierce and fine-tuned, come fast and furious, and run the gamut from frank to final. The F's supportive numerical value of 8 lends the F its strict, often inflexible aspect, which they use to maintain their odd penchant for periods of silence while considering all points of view or information available on any given subject or situation. Since it is, as mentioned, influenced by the leftover energies of the E, the F can occasionally explode vocally with such velocity that walls and knees may shake, but their bark is worse than their bite. While more in control of themselves than the E, the F is also a fast-moving, flowing, and forward-reaching vocal letter energy, and can often be quite funny.

The F makes a solid parent, good teacher, lawyer, doctor, researcher, scientist, or anything related to the necessary use of the intellect to form conclusions and then to share those conclusions with others. They also provide well for their family as responsibility, fidelity, and fortitude are amongst their guiding Traditionals; therefore, the F would make a good spouse or parent figure.

Traditional Descriptions

Typical descriptions for the F include the following: intellectual, responsible, loyal, dependable, humorous, expressive, faithful, domestic, controlled, and calm. Some more negative qualities include impersonal, impulsive, opinionated, critical, judgmental, inflexible, argumentative, and temperamental.

Cornerstones

The following words all point to open and flowing thought processes and the firmer aspects of established energy patterns: Fast, Fantastic, Furious, Fierce, Faith, Fertile, Friendship, Family, Father, and Federation.

As a Current Energy Phase

The F covers an eight-year period during which time one may find oneself under the control of a father, parental, boss, or authority figure or may *be* that father, parental, boss, or authority figure. It may also appear as a phase of learning, studying, and/or carrying familial or business responsibility. This is a rather rigid energy that can be relieved by vocal expression, but that is a choice only the F can make. As a result, the F is usually silent or talkative and morose or funny, or can alternate between the two.

G (Value of 3): Guardian of Secrets

The G is similar to the C, except the open communication of the C now has a "hand" covering its mouth, which effectively blocks the expression of inner thoughts and emotions; it is a protective, secretive, and silent energy. Because of the energy of the active number 3 value that supports the G, this person may appear to be extremely physically and/ or mentally active, involved, outgoing, and social, when in reality, they are rather quiet and shy. The G is known to flee from sticky situations (which can be core to self-confidence and self-esteem issues), ignore problems, react impulsively, and attempt to avoid involvement in situations that may require vulnerability or honest revelation. However, not to paint a bleak picture, the G turns in on themselves; they are engaged in an inner search, a balance between body, mind, and spirit. They are spiritual, self-searching, analytical, self-critical, deeply thoughtful, and reflective. The presence of a G in a name, especially as the Cornerstone, often indicates a past or present negative situation, such as some form of abuse or even a secret that can cause the G to pull away, to withdraw or withhold. (Any word ending in a G holds the essence of the word, e.g., "holding.") The inwardness of the G, their withholding and protectiveness, can and does lead to emotional toxicity and dis-ease that often sources back to the wounds that caused withdrawal in the first place. The G fears exposure and will go out of its way to avoid being found out. Their secret can involve anything—from just being genuinely shy to deliberately hiding something that makes them feel different (being gay, or feeling "geeky" perhaps), which they may have carried since formative years.

The G is sensitive, has good intentions, is very intro-spective, and is generally calm and gentle in nature. It is hard to get to know a true G, as they can be superficial in some ways, which is to say that there is much more going on within than is reflected without.

Another possibility for the G is not so pleasant. This can refer to an energy that is just plain untrustworthy. The secretiveness becomes deceit, the guardedness becomes deviousness, and the gentleness becomes disingenuous. This type of obviously negative G energy will hide their true selves and motives, will lie easily and be focused only on their own gain and progress. There are plenty of these types of G energies around, but the majority, thankfully, are more of the former description than the latter.

One way of telling them apart, aside from surrounding letters, numeric influences, and your own intuitive sense, is that the positive G will often offer you spontaneous hugs or share something personal with you when you least expect it.

Traditional Descriptions

Typical descriptions of the average G include gentle, social, calm, nurturing, spiritual, seeking, active, reflective, charm-ing, and helpful. More negative manifestations of the G essence include being suspicious, overly-idealistic, antiso-cial, moody, irrational, and manipulative.

Cornerstones

The following words all illustrate hidden or inner types of energies: God, Ghost, Gone, Gravity, Grudge, Gut, Giggle, Glutton, Gambler, Greed, and Gas.

As a Current Energy Phase

The three-year cycle of the G may manifest as a time to keep secrets—whether by choice or by necessity. It can also be a time of secrets revealed, again, by choice or by necessity, although a third party could also play a part here. A clandestine relationship or an event or a habit (addiction or abuse) could fall into both categories. Alternately, the G energy could present a time of soul searching, spiritual awakening, or a time of healing after surgery, a divorce, a death, or any other type of trauma.

H (Value of 5): Ladder of Hope

While the letter H is sometimes imaged as an open or closed window, I prefer the alternate symbol of the ladder—one that will take you up to Heaven or down to Hell. It is a potent letter, or ladder, offering a choice to reach up for the stars and success, or to sink into the underground of negativity, gloominess, toxic behaviors, and harmful habits or beliefs. A worst-case scenario for the downstairs H is addiction and self-destructive tendencies. Valued by the 5, which seeks freedom, independence, change, and sensory stimulation, the H is susceptible to curiosity about the world of the senses and often takes a trip, sometimes in the hopes of escape, down the ladder where they remain, or hide, until they choose to attempt to rise up from the depths. The choice for the H is obviously not a difficult one to make. It is to reach up. To climb and keep climbing until there is as much distance between the base of the ladder and themselves as possible.

I know a lot about this particular letter, as my first name is Heather. I *did* go down the ladder; I *know* the cold, hard floors of the basement; however, I have two H values in my name and one of my trips through its energy phase finally took me up the rungs. I will not say the trip was without slippage, but ultimately, I have reached the upper rungs of my ladder and am still climbing. I can almost see Heaven from here.

The H/5 is all about success and failure. It is about the ups and the downs of life and how well the H is able to hold on during the ride. As a cornerstone, the H will either reflect someone who will give up or someone who will, repeatedly if required, fight back and struggle for purchase. If progress is made up the ladder, the H can eventually become spiritually enlightened, wise, respected, loved, and successful.

What is available to the H is achievement, success, and status. What is also available to the H is failure, addiction, and loss.

It truly is a choice between Heaven and Hell, which all of Humanity faces.

The balanced H is friendly, fun to be around, quite intelligent, and values freedom and independence while assimilating change and experiences with relative ease. An H who is passionate about something and overcomes the temptations residing at the base of the ladder is perfectly capable of going up the ladder and acquiring spiritual and material wealth. The H also has a splendid sense of humor, is nurturing and empathic, and is partial to good music, food, drink, and art in any form. The heart of the H is not easily reached. However, when the H does fall (down the ladder?) in love, it is heavily and heartily—and often hope-lessly. The H is the type who will carry a torch for years, long after the person loved is no longer in the picture.

The H is ruled by the senses and is susceptible to hurt feelings, insecurities, and strong emotions. If someone should shake the ladder until the H loses its grip, so to speak, the risk of depression, backsliding, and reversal of gained ground is always possible. Possible but likely not lasting, for the H builds and maintains solid friendships and is rarely without support and encouragement.

One of the original meanings for the symbol H is that of the "cultivator of the field of spiritual growth," and their instinct is to construct a firm foundation for the base of their ladder to rest upon. The H will, almost unknowingly, do just that during the course of their lifetime, particularly if the H is a Cornerstone, the result being that once the H has embarked upon their journey, they are rarely down for long. The trick is to get going, keep climbing, and not succumb to inertia brought on by disillusionment and disappointment.

Traditional Descriptions

Typical descriptions of the H are independent, private, helpful, compassionate, intuitive, spiritual, gregarious, and humorous. The darker aspects of the H can include depression, lack of motivation, aimlessness, addictive tendencies, irresponsibility, arrogance, and stubbornness.

Cornerstones

This letter energy speaks its essences quite clearly—it's either up or down or two opposite elements, as the following words depict: High, Height, Heaven, Hope, Helicopter,

Hemisphere, Harmony, Happy, Hazard, Hate, Hysteria, Heat, Harm, Hurt, and Hell.

As a Current Energy Phase

The five-year phase of the H involves several major life choices, and these choices impact all areas of the life of the name holder. The essential choice is simple, yet is a difficult one to make. It is mainly concerned with the spiritual, and centers around questions involving personal values and belief systems—there is potentially serious emotional chaos here, and the challenge is to find the strength to *overcome* and to reach *up*. Hope over humiliation, heal over hurt. It is to choose the positive over the negative: it is "going for it" versus settling; having faith versus having another drink, or donut, or pill. It is accepting or turning down the challenge. It means hanging in there when your arms are so tired they feel like overcooked pasta strings. This is the time to take the risk on the positive side. Take a deep breath, plant your feet, and try one rung at a time. If you are afraid of heights, have faith. You will not fall, and even if you do, God will catch you.

I (Value of 1): Intuition or God's Gift

This is the symbol of the human being in original, ancient pictorials. It is the way we refer to ourselves as beings, but its specific reference is to the connective communication (Intuition) between God and Man, but is also the separation between the two: it speaks of man's ego as in "I want" and "I need." Its energy is at once personal and collective, as in Include.

I have the highest respect for this particular letter, as it represents the genuine unification of all to a higher power. The I represents the gift of intuition, which speaks as that "gut feeling" or the phrase "I *knew* that was going to happen." Generally, the subject would have had a bad feeling about something or someone but repeatedly ignored their intuition. I think of it as a telephone. A little, tiny red one that sits in the middle of my stomach and from which a thin, red cord climbs inexorably, endlessly, up into the skies. At the other end of my phone is my Creator. Or, my Universal "Dad." He is my protector and advisor and calls me when something is amiss. My phone rings and produces a "funny feeling." This sensation can be experienced other ways as well, but whatever way it comes, it rings your bell to communicate important information to you. I think of the intuition primarily as a warning system, although it can guide you to incredibly positive things, too.

Ruled by the unstoppable number 1, this is a letter that equals very strong intuitive energy (even the word that defines this energy has three Is within its form, one of which is a Cornerstone) and is open to new ideas, progressive in thought and deed, intelligent, spiritual, and objective. Those with several of these letter energies in their name could make talented artists, musicians, lyricists, spiritual guides, priests, social workers, or therapists. (Did you happen to notice all of the I values in the occupations I just listed?)

Where the number 1 is focused on itself and its own survival and gain, the letter I is a world apart in that it speaks of spirituality. It is tied to reproduction, creation, God, and man, and its ultimate purpose is to reignite the spark of the candle that leads us home—think of the candle in the window, guiding all to safety, and the safety is to be found in spiritual awareness. The I/1 is representative of the awakening; the understanding that there is much more to the existence of mankind than mankind realizes. This realization is underscored by the Original Force energy of the number 1.

Traditional Descriptions

Typical descriptives that are attached to the I include original, open-minded, approachable, creative, intellectual, selfless, and intuitive, while the more negative side can appear as impatient, egocentric, selfish, close-minded, and a my-way-or-the-highway kind of mentality.

Cornerstones

The following words all picture something that starts or originates from the inside: Imagination, Instinct, Intuition, Illusion, Insight, Immune, Ignite, Intelligence, and Intellect.

As a Current Energy Phase

The one-year period of the letter I is a highly charged period of increased intuitive activity. This is the time and opportunity to listen to your own gut feelings. Dreams may become stronger and the sense of déjà vu may occur more frequently. There may be something of importance, a message of sorts that is trying to make itself known to you, but most definitely, this is a wake-up call, which is designed to awaken you to your own inner knowing or sixth sense.

J (Value of 1): Judgment

Here is one of the more straightforward and occasionally rather harsh letters in our alphabet. It is fairly direct in its message; it holds on to the past as a reference point for its future, which one can readily see from its aesthetic structure: its bottom leg reaches back into the past. For this reason, it is often found that the J (especially when found as a Cornerstone) will have experienced something rather destructive or, at the very least, quite negative at some point in their early lives and spend a lot of thought and energy either remembering the event or occurrence in question or trying to suppress it. The J tends to live in the past, or at least, they have a difficult time living fully in the present. Slights, snide words, or real or imagined critiques are not soon let go—the J is not one to forgive and forget so easily. It may *say* it does, but the inner truth is a different story.

The J is the jury of your peers, the judge from your nastiest dream, and the jailer from your worst nightmare. The extremely negative J is capable of holding on to inner anger and justifying it for quite some time. On the other hand, they can also be fair and balanced as they weigh actions versus reactions and causes versus effects, as the J learns from its past experiences. The J then tries to protect itself from any undesirable situations repeating themselves.

The J is valued by the number 1, hence they are very self-reliant, able to survive on their own, ego centered, and will rarely ask for or accept help, even when they might need it. Not naturally demonstrative, the J appears non-emotional (although they will indicate affections through their actions) and in control of themselves and circumstances. This combination helps J energies become natural leaders, authority figures, and persons in positions of control—the J energy does indeed create good judges, jury members, lawyers, or any other member within the justice system. They are also excellent teachers, doctors, politicians, bankers, or power brokers. The J likes to be in control of themselves at all times and they are almost incapable of letting their true feelings and insecurities show, especially in social situations. They are outstanding actors who seldom play themselves. The lesson of the J is to marry the past with the present, or to learn the lessons and then let the past go.

Of course, the intensity of the J is affected by the energies, or letters, around it and is often tendered by surrounding energies. These ambient energies often give the J a chance to be objective about its experiences, and hopefully a sense of humor has a chance to develop. Although there are certainly some J energies whose sense of identity is tempered by softer energies, they will still hold true on some level to the above-mentioned characteristics, but may reflect a joyous, jubilant, jocular disposition, which is sometimes a juxtaposition of their true self.

Traditional Descriptions

The J is usually focused, determined, efficient, meticulous, disciplined, logical, and self-reliant. The negative side of the J can produce someone who is tense, reserved, superior, critical, judgmental, severe, unforgiving, unemotional, and even cruel.

Cornerstones

The following words all hold a link to history (or a point of origin) within their framework: Justice, Jealous, Judge, Jettison, Jump, Jail, Join, Jackknife, Jet, and Javelin.

As a Current Energy Phase

The J covers a 1-year period that involves something from the past becoming an issue in the present. This can be a person from the past returning with some unfinished business in their briefcase, memories resurfacing, or an old pattern rearing its ugly head. This can manifest as problems in a relationship or job, or can involve the legal system, lawyers, and contracts. This is not generally a loving time; rather, it may involve anger, frustration, sorrow, or battles. It is also, obviously, a great opportunity for self-growth through self-knowledge. Although dealing with a past issue can be uncomfortable, it also brings with it the opportunity to adjust or correct previous errors in judgment or actions.

K (Value of 2): Kaleidoscopic Knowledge

Unlike the J, the K has little or nothing to do with the past. It is open to anything and will try everything at least once since it is reaching forward to gain new experiences and new knowledge. That is one of the strongest traditional meanings attached to the K: the endless drive for knowledge of anything spiritual, intuitive, or progressive in nature. The structure of the K shows an arm reaching up with an open palm, which is connected to both the offering and the receiving of gifts. If you think about a kaleidoscope and visualize the brilliant shards of vibrant colors endlessly clicking from one pattern to the next, you might have a vague idea of the inside energy of the positively developed K. It is a special letter—one that holds its own, almost-mystical element, which, if accessed and used, is quite beautiful and esoteric.

Since it is ruled by the number 2, the K is easy to be with, kind, full of interesting ideas, and curious about almost everything. The K looks only to the future; they have no ties to the past other than what they learned there, which means the K is not one to hold grudges or remain angry for extended periods. In fact, the K will release the past with admirable ease. They love good music as music calms the soul; they are compassionate and interesting to observe in that the K is not a typical everyday energy. It may even be an unusual experience to kiss a K! In a good way, I mean.

The K steps into its power with its palm up—it is at once holding opportunities and gifts out for others and accepting them from Universe. The K is the Spiritual Seeker, the one who thirsts for knowledge such as that held in the awakened Kundalini (which in Sanskrit refers to the coiled serpent or snake at the base of the human spine—its awakening is thought to represent a higher state of consciousness). The developed K follows their natural path, much as a King assumes the throne. I have to add here that Kings have been known for their extravagance, which illustrates the warning attached to the K/2: beware of squandering unexpected windfalls, or anticipating a windfall that hasn't blown in yet and spending it anyway. Could be a bit of a downer when the windfall bites the dust and the K is left holding the bills.

Aside from that, the K is a good friend, who will often come up with unique solutions to problems, present off-beat ideas, enjoy attending rather unusual social events, and motivate others to try something new. The K can have many paramours for they will seek until they find the "right one." This may take awhile, for the K will not settle—they will keep searching until they have found the perfect "other" to complete the number 2 they are ruled by.

Traditional Descriptions
The K can be described as experimental, progressive, curious, outgoing, social, generous, unique, forgiving, adaptable, and kind. More negative manifestations include inconsiderate, hard, moody, sneaky, manipulative, overbearing, unpredictable, and selfish.

Cornerstones
The following words all point to new levels reached or unusual elements: Karma, Knowledge, Key, Kinetic, Kevlar, Kilowatt, Kinky, King, Kangaroo, Kidnap, and Kill.

As a Current Energy Phase
The 2-year period of the K brings with it originality and sparkles with new concepts, ideas, actions, relationships, jobs, and a myriad of other potentialities. The spiritual aspect of the K can result in the awakening of the Kundalini, which in turn results in a new spiritual outlook, new attention to the health of the physical body, and new hobbies or interests being undertaken. The K phase brings with it refreshment, a sense of renewal, and a resurgence of curiosity and ideas.

L (Value of 3): Loving Hand

The L represents an outstretched arm, one reaching out to help, to assist, to motivate, to guide, and to guard. It is connected to *lamed* in Hebrew (which connects to a "prod" that gently moved oxen forward, rather like a "tail lift") and refers to the Life Force and, in particular, the procreation of the species. Therefore, it also rules sensual and sexual expression and, when combined with its numerical influence of 3, the activity inherent in the L/3 could lead the innocent aspect of the L, or its "seeking love" aspect, into situations more to do with lust, impulsiveness, or obsession than love.

The L is also an upside-down 7, which explains the L's overall interest in the metaphysical and openness to the psychic world. The L carries a strong belief or sense that there is something more to this world than our eyes see and is also very idealistic, positive, romantic, sensitive, compassionate, motivated, and cheerful. The Lusty Lungs of the L can even translate into song: more than the occasional L is a closet, shower, or car singer, and some have even made it their career (LeAnn Rimes, Lenny Kravitz, Lena Horne, and Linda Ronstadt, to name but a few).

The positively developed L is an upbeat energy, likes to help, falls in love wholeheartedly (often repeatedly and helplessly), and is a loyal and true friend. However, cross an L and watch out. Any breach in trust or moral or ethical guidelines is almost unforgivable and you will watch the serene L disappear in front of your eyes. Silence will descend, the air will chill, and frost will appear in the L's eyes as thick as frost on your windshield. You will be out in the cold. For how long depends on the seriousness of the transgression. Luckily, the L cannot hold a grudge terribly long.

Traditional Descriptions
The L can be described as spiritual, loving, peaceful, compassionate, receptive, motivational, eloquent, empathic, passionate, and helpful. A negative L energy can produce someone who is obsessive, intrusive, interfering, frustrated, insecure, depressed, and addictive.

Cornerstones
The following words all illustrate a forward, helpful, or loving aspect: Leader, Lawyer, Laser, Learn, Lend, Lasting, Light, Laudable, Laugh, Lust, Live, and Love.

As a Current Energy Phase
The 3-year period of the L is one of emotional fulfillment or emotional pain, depending on the letter before it and energies surrounding it. The L can refer to becoming involved romantically, socially, or in self-improvement regimes such as yoga, diet, and exercise. The L also offers the opportunity for spiritual growth and personal education, be this in the form of scholastic or artistic pursuits, volunteering time to those less fortunate, or aiding and assisting in some way. This time is spent on the self, another, others, or all three. It is a time of love in all its forms.

M (Value of 4): Mute Cover
Spread the legs of this character and double it and one has what resembles a Mountain range. The M shows ups and

downs, heights and valleys. It is above and below; the surface and the depths.

Curiously, the M is the only letter in the alphabet that is pronounced with the lips together or mouth closed. It represents that which is mute, unspoken, deep, or unseen. Its closest tie is to water (it is an upside-down W); many M energies love scuba diving, swimming, and fishing, or are otherwise enamored of H_2O. Picture a marine robotic engineer living alone on a houseboat and you will have a good idea of the M energies. Those connections to water, which rule emotions, and its inherent muteness make emotional openness a difficult, if not impossible, task for the strong M. In other words, the M has a hard time expressing honest and intimate emotions. However, since the governing of emotions ties in with the responsible, dependable, reliable, and logical number 4, this energy is a natural in terms of running a business or a home (marriage), for that matter. Although the M sometimes forgets the nature of the two is completely different and, as a result, can succeed at one and fail repeatedly at the other. The challenge for the M is similar to the D (both are ruled by 4), which is to open up. In the M's case, it would mean emotionally. If the M is not able or willing to disclose inner thoughts and feelings occasionally, these unexpressed emotions will naturally build up, pressurize, and eventually erupt, surprising anyone around into silence themselves.

The M is closely connected to the W in that they are similar, although reversed, images of each other. The difference between the two is that the M energy is centered in the valley at its base and middle of the M, while the W's point of view is from the top, or peak of the mountain in its center. One is most certainly a brighter place to be sitting than the other.

The M is appears to be a rock, from the outside, at least. It is in control, solid and dependable and is attractive from the point of view of a potential partner, in business or otherwise. There is much hidden under the veneer of the M. Consider that a volcano could sit inside any mountain you should care to look at; one may not be able to *see* it, but that does not mean it is not *there*. There are deep emotions kept under wraps: the M is very intense and profoundly vulnerable, which explains why it hides—fear of rejection, humiliation, and pain. It is actually a tender energy that is, due to past circumstances, used to shielding and protecting itself. This urge also extends to those the M loves... this energy is one of the strongest in the familial-protection department.

Traditional Descriptions
The M is usually seen as in control, administrative, authoritarian, intelligent, efficient, determined, loyal, domestic, and factual. Negative characteristics can include judgmental, condemning, defensive, uncommunicative, uncooperative, withdrawn, arrogant, tactless, and critical.

Cornerstones
The following words all connect to a concealed activity: Marine, Marsh, Mountain, Marriage, Mind, Magick, Mystic, Mask, and Mystery.

As a Current Energy Phase
The 4-year period of the M is an odd one. There is a silence in the air, an immobility. Yet it is also a safe time—a time

ruled by proper logic and responsibility. This could be a marriage, the formation of a family, or the acquisition of a steady (boring?) job, but one that pays the bills. It is a time of unspoken thoughts and feelings. I read this period as one of stillness and practicality. Not a bad place to be, but one that would demand release after 4 years.

N (Value of 5): Natural Energy Filter

I find the N a curious letter. I am not sure exactly why, but I do. Maybe it is the normal, naturally balanced energy which emanates from it which seems at odds with its numeric value of 5 that represents constant change, keen awareness of the senses, freedom, and open communication. The neutrality and balance of the N is further diversified when one considers that it contains two joined 7s lying sideways (which makes it inordinately intuitive and open to mysteries) *and* that it retains its exact shape when turned upside down. The N is like an electrical charge—it comes from somewhere and is going somewhere. The energy of the N travels up the left limb, down the corridor, and up into space, so to speak. Imagine the two legs gripped and pulled apart into a shape like a bolt of lightning, similar to the Z. There is constant energy flowing straight through the letter, almost a direct connection to the next movement or occurrence or event; yet it somehow remains on an even keel. One thing flows into another and the N adapts.

One of the challenges for this letter also sits within the world of the senses, and the understanding and incorporation of the intuition, the additional sense. Since acceptance of this sixth sense has the potential to turn the world of perceived senses on its ear, the main goal of the N involves keeping everything balanced, or normal. The N spreads a soothing balm over unexpected or disruptive vibrations.

The N person is generally a happy character. They are calm, rational, and neutral. They are open to new experiences and enjoy unique people and places. Being under the influence of the 5 makes the holder prone to seeking excitement and experiencing changes, which would translate into someone who loves to travel rather than live an entire life in one place. The N changes jobs, partners, and interests with regularity, but does it all smoothly and with a certain grace. When they do settle down for a bit, they prefer to be in a position of authority (whether in a job, home, or relationship) that affords plenty of room to move. The N does well in almost any career, as they are highly adaptable and can adjust to new situations quite easily; however, they must learn to accept day-to-day routines in order to experience complete success.

In relationships, again, the N is adaptable and will attract many potential suitors and has a good chance of marrying an almost-perfect mate. The N is nothing if not balanced and will instinctively recognize their match.

Traditional Descriptions

Typical descriptives that are attached to the N are calm, balanced, candid, receptive, accepting, adventurous, diplomatic, charming, and attractive. The negative side of the N can create someone who is self-indulgent, irresponsible, addictive, materialistic, and shallow.

Cornerstones

The following words all connect to a flow of energy that alters one state of being or place to another: Noose, Nirvana, Neutral, Naked, Nourish, Nuclear, Nurture, Numb, and Nervous.

As a Current Energy Phase

Going with the flow would describe the 5-year span of the N. Changes abound, travel is probable, the senses are peaked, communication is highlighted, and freedom is necessary; it all requires maintaining an inner calm through possibly chaotic circumstances. This is a time of activity, yet, paradoxically, it is also a time of quiet adjustment. Marriages, divorces, public recognition, relocations, births of babies and businesses, deals made or lost, deaths and other endings all tie into the elements of change. The N phase seems to carry its very own guardian angel as a sense of peace accompanies its presence throughout this phase, chaotic or otherwise.

O (Value of 7): Open to All

The O is so vast in its potential meanings that it is almost impossible to express its breadth with mere words. It represents the All-Seeing Eye, which sounds like a rather omnipotent energy, and alludes to the intuitive and spiritual quality of this obscure letter energy.

The O also refers to the actual eyeballs in our heads: how and what we see and how that is interpreted. Further, it relates to infinity as it is a cipher, and it adds strength to that which comes before it (for example, 3 people versus 3,000 people). It holds all and yet is empty. The O is also the open mouth and rules that which comes out of it. Hence, it also relates to verbal flow as in talking, whispering, yelling—any form of oration and all things utterable—or unutterable, for that matter.

The O is ruled by the magickal number 7, which is brain-focused and involves a choice of science (material-ism and reality) versus metaphysical (spirituality and eso-teric) study. The O is of a seeking origin and can represent an opening, portal, or door to another dimension or realm of understanding.

This energy can fall victim to frustration and outbursts of anger as a result of not understanding the vastness of its interests and potential. This is, truly, the all-or-nothing let-ter. The scope of the values and possibilities in the O make it one of those letters that is rarely fully developed—par-tially perhaps, but not quite all the way. Should you run into someone who has a few Os in their name and, assum-ing these are even marginally developed O energies, you will find some of the following characteristics: charming, adaptable, conversant, intelligent, confident, social, intui-tive, investigative, curious, and fun to be around. The more common form of this energy, however, is more focused on the struggle between frustration/anger and objectivity: think of it as being either trapped inside the O, or being on the outside, free. Open book: closed book. Open shutter: closed shutter (as in camera lens or window covers). That's the O. The energy can either get through or it can't—a condition quite similar to the D (door) energy, yet so very, very different.

A further aspect of the O is that it has a choice we have already seen in other letters: sensual versus spiritual growth, and intellectual versus metaphysical pursuits. The only way for the O to come into their own is to understand that objectivity and wisdom are their most valuable tools. Should this happen, the magickal will combine with the almost Omnipotent to unleash Power Supreme. For one symbol to hold so very many meanings and potentialities is somewhat difficult to grasp. The O is just such a fascinating energy; it seems to hold the beginning and the ending of everything in its form. Like Alpha and Omega.

An O energy will be engaging, open, entertaining, opulent, and mysterious. Their interests will range from the sublime to the ridiculous, the intellectual to the mundane, the intangible to the concrete. This character may be difficult to keep up with at times, as their curiosity and desire to know is sometimes all-encompassing and can leave others feeling rather left out or on the "outside" looking in.

By contrast, an O can live on the inside of the circle and live a life of sheer frustration due to feeling trapped by boundaries, which they have chosen themselves. This type of O energy will be ornery, opposing, oppressive, obtuse, oblivious, odd, opinionated, or just plain obnoxious.

Some O energies that illustrate the vast potentialities of this letter energy include Obama, Oprah, the Osmonds, the Osbournes, and the (Wizard of) Oz.

Traditional Descriptions
Typical descriptives attached to the O include articulate, adaptable, friendly, honorable, intellectual, curious, open-minded, intuitive, powerful, and creative. A trapped or

frustrated O energy can come across as arrogant, opinion-ated, stagnant, stubborn, conceited, irritable, overbearing, angry, secretive, and bossy.

Cornerstones

The following words all suggest the power and breadth the O covers: Origin, Omnipotent, Ocean, Orbit, Olympic, Opposites, Occult, Ominous, Obese, Ordeal, Obituary, and Old.

As a Current Energy Phase

The 7-year span of the O can be an eye-opener. Since the 7 rules the brain and will involve either logic or spirit and often both, it can contain an abundance of almost anything you can imagine. The O will either free or imprison; it will offer a variety of paths. Openings appear and it is up to the individual whether these openings are viewed as obstacles or opportunities. It is a time of expansion, of looking at things from a different point of view, of investigating for-eign ideas and ideals and of integrating this knowledge with that which is already known. Habits, beliefs, routines, emotions, and spiritual bases are all up for possible review and revision.

P (Value of 8): Pensive Intellect

Similar to the F, the P is highly intelligent, intellectual, and analytical. However, there is a major difference between the two. While the F is open to communication, the P is closed. Much of the constant brainstorming is done in silence and is an ongoing process during which the P analyzes, weighs, and finally forms a decision or verdict, which is only occasionally expressed or pronounced. This expression will often take the form of explosive yet controlled criticism or anger.

Valued by the 8, the P is the one in control of itself and others, the ultimate authoritarian, the leader—consider the term "president." The P will do all in its power to persevere under pressure. Their personal goal is to present a perfect and pleasing performance and persona.

However, while they are so busy creating and sustaining a picture of perfection, the P is likely to entirely miss the lesson of its numerical teacher, which is to learn to balance Earth power with spiritual knowledge. The P needs to learn to think (ironically) before they speak, for the words that come, unchecked, from their mouth tend to be blunt even if intended to help. But more than that, they need to learn to use their thoughts in a less structured and disciplined manner, thus allowing spirit to enter the mind and heart.

It is a curiosity that while the P's world is one of thoughts, words, and contemplation of information processed through the brain, their main weakness is ineffectiveness when communicating. The P can sometimes suffer from a superiority complex, which is a direct influence from the controlling 8, and thus often finds it difficult to express themselves without passing judgment or offering what they see as constructive criticism. Another lesson for the P: to expand their insatiable appetite for data to include compassion for the less fortunate and acceptance of differing lifestyles and opinions. While the P demands perfection of themselves, their expectations of others is often excessive, unrealistic, and demanding, and too often results in separations of all kinds. The P needs to soften itself, find the liberating balance in the positive 8 they are ruled by, and look more to faith than to fact.

Romantically, the P must learn also to differentiate possessiveness from love and marriage from partnerships (as in business partners), for never the twain shall meet. Until this is accomplished, the P will find perplexity to be a constant companion in their search for love.

Traditional Descriptions

The P is often described as intellectual, focused, moral, controlled, goal-oriented, reliable, honest, and loyal. In negative form, the P can be opinionated, stubborn, uncommunicative, possessive, dictatorial, curt, and in extreme cases, psychotic.

Cornerstones

The following words all illustrate the closed or deep source of the P and include Philosophy, Pregnant, Pause, Pensive, Portal, Power, Panic, and Paralyze.

As a Current Energy Phase

The 8-year reign of the P is not usually a particularly liberating time. Its energy is one of being confined, either by being locked in thought patterns, lacking emotional release or being caught in a situation from which there is seemingly no escape. Prison, if you will. This prison can be one of one's own making, or it can transpire through marriage to an inappropriate partner, or by being under contract to something or someone that one discovers too late is not working out as hoped or planned. There is a need for emotional release—to free the psyche from pain and paralysis.

The key to releasing this pressure is in the holder's hand, and it is up to them to use it.

Q (Value of 1): Quirky Energy

Here is yet another highly curious letter. Its pictorial history includes images of a monkey with a "tail," a head with a "neck," and an O with a "leg," although its main reference is to the base of the brain. One connection is the French "queue," which originates with the Latin for "tail" (which is exactly what a group of people in a line look like). It holds many of the positive potentials of the O, but is now balanced by the tail which primarily results in its ability to laugh at itself as the tail "tickles" the base of the brain. Some sources suggest the tail of the Q represents O x 2, which refers to the sign of infinity, the lemniscate.

While the O is ruled by the thought-filled 7, the Q carries a value of 1, which gives it focus, ambition, and energy. It also represents an eye, as in the Third Eye or vision on a more psychic level. The Q personality is very outgoing; they see things differently, have an incredibly vast imagination, are original, quick thinkers, and are open to all, which means the Q may just as easily become enthralled by the nonsensical as the conventional.

Another curious, however purely mechanical aspect to this energy is that the letter u follows most words beginning with Q. There is seemingly no real reason for this anomaly other than the sound is fairly guttural (ancients wrote the sound of the Q as "Cw"), and it lends itself to few other vibrations. Alphabetical evolution now allows us to visit the "Queen" instead of the "Cwen." Upon further introspection, perhaps therein lies the closest to the truth about the Q: Queen. I believe that most Queens were or are, indeed, slightly eccentric and their lifestyles definitely differ from those of the average citizen. Their traditional role in life almost guarantees that they will view daily existence from a particular vantage point. They will see life differently, experience life differently, and live each day in a unique and unusual way. This description seems to illustrate the overall essence of the Q ... even if one is not a Queen.

Most Qs are found to be quirky in one way or another. They are original energies and deeper than they might first appear. Kind of like quicksand: make sure you do not prejudge the unconventional Q. You might find yourself stuck in a nasty situation with a sinking feeling in the pit of your stomach.

Traditional Descriptions

Common character traits for the Q include objective, curious, original, creative, humorous, imaginative, intuitive, and sometimes, eccentric. A negative Q can be egocentric, aimless, sarcastic, unreasonable, arrogant, and just plain odd.

Cornerstones

The following words all have to do with a base or particular origin: Quagmire, Quake, Quest, Question, Quote, Quick, and Quench.

As a Current Energy Phase

It is perhaps a good thing that the reign of the Q lasts only 1 year or one may have to be quarantined! This is an odd letter and its affects can be just as odd. There is humor present as well as bizarre occurrences, out-of-the-ordinary situations, revelations, and questions. This will most likely be one of the queerest energies to pass through in the entire alphabet, but it is not negative—merely uniquely quirky.

R (Value of 2): Reaching for a Higher Level

Here we have the pent-up energy of the P, combined with progress as the foot moves forward (lower right extension). The R is restrained, yet forward moving. It reconciles caution with optimism and may indicate travels along a rough road requiring resilience and faith.

The R is quite mysterious and reticent, and its energy seems to be one of challenge and gain after several losses: this energy centers around testing and repeating. The experience of the R phase is a period of time during which either all hell breaks loose in one form or another or past experiences with the R phase now present rewards and riches. The R is all about tests given and lessons learned, but its core subject is really quite simple. It is the test of right and wrong (notice the R sound to both words) and the voice of intuition that provides the answers, whether listened to or not. If said lessons have been absorbed and truly learned, then the R will present a rare chance at rebirth, complete with the ability to rewrite (or at least edit) personal history. Generally speaking, though, passages through the R must be taken a number of times before redemption is possible. During the testing times, the R is often fortunate enough, with its value of 2, to find solace and support from many friends, yet the road of the R can be a very lonely place: the lessons are often quite personal and private and involve, primarily, intimate or family relationships. The truth about the R character is that they must honestly answer questions about *their* conduct and contributions in regard to intimate and social relationships. This can be a painful run, lesson-wise, but the sooner the truth, the sooner the reward.

The R represents the Pineal gland, which is about the size of a pea and sits right in the center of the brain, between and behind the eyes. Even scientists have reluctantly agreed that there is a certain mystery surrounding the Pineal gland and it has been carefully acknowledged for its intuitive potentialities.

The R represents resurrection, rebirth, and regeneration; therefore, a new start, or a new way of "seeing" this world and Universe. Drastic measures are sometimes required to accomplish a deed of such major significance and magnitude. This energy needs to reach ahead, to resort to alternate methods, to strive, to try again. It has a moving-forward feeling to it. To illustrate, read the following words and notice the *forward motion* held within the words: rush, run, race, relay, reckless, rescue, rapid, ready, and raise. Another interesting indication of this forward energy is apparent in words with "re" as prefixes. The intimation in these words is that of receiving a second chance at something, the opportunity to do it again. For example: reactivate, renew, recreate, rehearse, reclaim, relive, resurrect, and reform.

The seeking and spiritual R experiences their tests, sees things in a new way, hears with new ears, and adjusts their existence and perceptions accordingly. Prominent Rs hold second chances and, most importantly, renewal. Upon completing a name rotation containing one or two Rs successfully, the R would revel in revival and radiant rejoicing, for the rewards and riches I mentioned earlier would be theirs to enjoy. This type of developed R, usually into their middle years, would make exceptional teachers, leaders, motivators, or writers whose humanitarianism and compassion could herald much success. If single, this is the most likely time a "ready" R will find its mate. Romantic soul mate, that is. It is also the time that the direction, the *niche*, regarding careers can finally be found.

On the other hand, the R is also known for its negative responses to repetitive tests. The R can become rebellious, rude, and filled with rage. They are reactive and unrepentant. Roar, terror, and horror are good examples of negative R energy.

Happily, these periods do pass, so don't panic, but I must add that anyone with several Rs in their name might want to consider spelling it differently, if possible (by dropping a double R, for instance). The energy of the R, while progressive, often entails seriously trying times: the R is designed for those who are willing and able to grasp the higher level of knowledge held within its structure. Major spiritual transformation is possible in the presence of the redeeming R because the holder sees themselves as they truly are, and a certain humbleness comes along with this new point of view.

Traditional Descriptions

Character traits of the R energy include progressive, tenacious, thoughtful, accepting, loyal, compassionate, forgiving, loving, and understanding. The darker side of the R can manifest as being unmotivated, passive, self-pitying, self-destructive, impatient, angry, and even abusive.

Cornerstones

The following words all hold a fresh start or show a reaching-forward type of energy: Rebirth, Reconcile, Relieve, Resurrect, Run, Race, Release, and Risk.

As a Current Energy Phase

The 2-year period of the R holds one of two distinct possibilities. Both are deeply personal and are related to the hidden truths of right and wrong actions, words, and treatments.

The first is to revisit lessons not learned and trials not completed in an effort to understand the reasons for the presence of an R in a name energy, which is, quite simply, to learn the difference between right action and wrong action, specifically around relationships. If this is the case, this 2-year transit can prove to be trying to say the least, and if it happens to be followed by an E, well, that will just emphasize this phase.

The second possibility is one of having successfully learned the differences between right and wrong action and having applied them to one's own life, specifically in relation to intimate connections. Relationships improve, as does the outlook and reaction to life in general. This phase can be extremely positive, fortunes can improve, and the future can hold many pleasant surprises; if an E follows here, blessings may be counted.

S (Value of 3): Senses of Man

Strictly ruled by the *senses* and valued by the activity of the 3, the S can be sensitive, stimulating, smart, silly, sly, sneaky, and seductive. The activity of the 3 it is ruled by takes the power of adaptability up into the brain, where the S analyzes, then down into the physical body, where the S actualizes. A strong connector here is that the senses represent the actual physical body and what it is capable of doing in this physical world. They can also point to the actual functions that occur within the body itself, and again, the idea of adaptability comes up. One of the main strengths of the S is the ability to go with the flow and to adapt to different situations, which is likely why the S is perfectly capable of telling you what you want or need to hear and then heading off to do exactly what they see fit to do for themselves. The S is overly grounded—they *rely on their senses* and how to use them to get ahead in a material world.

The S puts the snake it is symbolically connected to in the grass, the sex in sexy, and the secret in secretive. The S is charming and deceptive, although not always on purpose, this just seems to be their nature. Like the snake, the power of the S is insidious; they can be swift and stealthy and can slide right under your nose and disappear silently into the soft shadows of the sunset before you have even clued in to their presence. This energy can adapt to circumstances or change their approach, manner, timing, or entry point to line up with their intentions, which is to say that the S usually gets what they want (look at the structure of the S and you will see that it is open in the upper curve and open in the lower curve; this leaves it exposed and even vulnerable to all influences, both positive and negative). Extremely attractive to the opposite sex, this essence can easily become involved in several affairs, often with disastrous results.

While the S is pursuing their objective—be it romance, work, or anything else—the power of their natural seductiveness, grace, and charm allows the S to realize their aspirations. The S is a self-starter, a philanthropist, very active, exceptionally talented and artistic (which is sometimes ignored or undervalued), and has tremendous potential as an actor or entertainer of some type. The true S seems to sing and dance to their own tune. They do exactly as they please, when they please, and how they please. Independence is important to the S, and since they value their freedom above all and dislike orders of any kind, they are best left to work alone. The S sees what needs to be done and is capable of doing it, if they so choose.

The S/3 energy, which is a combination of charming and seductive and slick and secretive, can present an energy that is almost hypnotic—this is, without a doubt, the smooth operator of the letter energies. Again, the potency of this description will depend upon the other energies present in the name, but, generally speaking, if there is an abundance of S energies in the name of your paramour, for example, you will likely find yourself under an alluring spell or witness to the results thereof at some point. If *you* sport an abundance of the S energy, be aware of your potentials and charms and use them wisely.

Since the S relies on the senses to get what they want, their lesson should not be hard to grasp. The S (perhaps more so than any other letter energy) needs to learn that there is an additional sense to the five they use so regularly, which is, of course, the intuition, or the sixth sense. Once this is absorbed, the next step would be to acknowledge that there is more to the picture than the eye can see. The senses sex versus spirit *meta* physics. This pretty much sums up the situation for the S and anyone involved with someone with an S or two in their name.

One more tiny detail: the S is the "Symbol of $uccess." However, the S will only experience true and lasting success once they move away from the instant gratification found in the world of earthbound senses. This energy, like many others, needs to look *beyond the physical body* in order to view their true nature or soul.

Traditional Descriptions
The S person is usually energetic, social, charming, enticing, eloquent, sensual/sexual, artistic, persuasive, adaptable, imaginative, mysterious, and confident. More negative descriptives of the S can include devious, sneaky, nefarious, unfaithful, manipulative, flighty, shallow, and untrustworthy.

Cornerstones
The following words all reflect the connection to the senses: Sing, Scream, Shudder, Shriek, Scent, Sex, Sad, Shaking, Shock, Schizophrenia, and Slumber.

As a Current Energy Phase
There is a challenge present in the 3-year span of the S and it can come in the form of using every possible manner of approach in order to get some*thing* or some*where,* whether that be a person, place, or thing. There may be moral and

ethical dilemmas as well since this energy is often sensual, sexual, and self-gratifying in nature and can experience temptations or lures that can be overwheming in intensity. It can also refer to a time of awakening, again, of the additional sense, and thus can refer to the opening of the "inner ear." The challenge presented is one of mind over matter: mind in this case pertaining to spirituality and matter pertaining to the base instincts of man. This phase often presents a choice between the two.

T (Value of 4): The Plus Sign (+)

The T holds a number of important characteristics, not the least of which is its tie to the cross, and thereby religious and spiritual beliefs. Its essence is explained quite well by the plus sign (which has no connection to the Chaldean Letter T, rather it refers to the common symbol for mathematical addition as well as to obvious religious or spiritual connections): it takes that which comes before and intensifies it—the nature of the plus sign is to "add to."

The T is curious about everything. It wants to see more, know more, have more, and experience more. If it is the Cornerstone of a word, it generally hits the ground running. Think about a triathlon or a moving train. Because the T holds the energy of addition, it must have a focus, or a base from which to begin, and is fortunate to be valued by the firm and foundational number 4—a welcome, supportive element to potentially unfocused or excessive T energy. For example, if two Ts appear side by side, it is usually indicative of too much going on at the same time, of inner emotions building up, and of pressure mounting. This would translate into someone with too much going on in their life and no method or desire to release stress or simplify circumstances. The double T character will often find themselves feeling "bottled up" and frustrated for whatever reasons. If the T won't talk, they will become toxic and uneven, resulting, almost inevitably, in a toxic meltdown (not an explosion normally—the T is too quiet). A sub meaning attached to the T is the image of an umbrella: this character is quite protective of themselves and of those they love, but it can be difficult for the T to open up and reveal their thoughts and feelings. It would be a wise move for a multiple T to talk, to share, and to reveal their inner tumultuousness in regular "decompression sessions" designed to relieve stress (a word that holds the S of the senses, the "adder" of the T, the testing energy of the R, the emphasizing energy of the E, and a double dose of more senses ... the end result would read as an *overload of the senses*, which is pretty much what stress amounts to).

Names that begin with T should be aware that they will need to pick attention points and stick to them, or they will literally bounce from one subject to another, one place to another, or one person to another. Or all three.

On a more positive note, being grounded by the solid and responsible number 4 keeps the T battling the odds, keeps it going, and provides a firm foundation from which to operate. Taking this square foundation one step further, imagine that square foundation in the shape of a box, unfolded on its sides and lying flat on the surface. What do you see? The cross (or plus sign) is one of the ancient symbolic connections to the cross of Jesus and the weight of his burden. This secret letter within the foundations of the 4 is representative of the potential for higher learning, or access to spiritual truths. The T takes their responsibilities very seriously and can often feel weighed down—the opened cross box speaks to the need to unburden the self. To this end, the T really needs a partner with whom the load can be shared and spirituality explored.

If left alone for too long, this energy can become susceptible to feeling frustrated, oppressed, and incomplete. Some extremely negative behavior can be expected from a frustrated and toxic T, and the key for the T, quite simply, is to lay down the weight they carry. Atlas might be able to bear the world upon his shoulders—mere mortals cannot. The main challenge for the T is to lighten up by discarding grudges, guilts, and imagined or assumed responsibilities, which can be difficult because of the inherent stubbornness of the 4.

Traditional Descriptions

Typical descriptives include curious, investigative, protective, helpful, active, intellectual, and progressive. Negative T energies can be unfocused, unreliable, high-strung, illogical, unpredictable, scattered, and emotionally unstable.

Cornerstones

The following words all show the "additional" nature of the T quite clearly: Tall, Time, Tip, Tension, Tax, Tide, Temper, Terrible, Terror, Tornado, and Temptation.

As a Current Energy Phase

The transit of the T will depend upon whether it stands by itself, or if a letter stands before it. In the latter case, the

T will intensify the energy of the letter that comes before, like it did in "stress"; alternately, it can add to the energy of the E in Eternity, and so on. The run of the T/4 will center around responsibility and routine, however, depending upon its placement, it could indicate a time of many interests; if an E follows a T, this is pretty much guaranteed. Alternately, if the T stands as a Cornerstone (Time, Total, Tax), this indicates an energy of extension, of multiplication, of "adding to." The T is the unknown element: it may go this way, or that, it may come in or go out, it has so many potentialities that it can often be a time of unfocused energies, restlessness, and varied interests. However, the nature of this energy can also reveal unexpected surprises, which can be a good thing. Or a bad thing. Or both.

U (Value of 6): The Cup

And here we have yet another fascinating energy. Simple, yet convoluted. It is at once the cup of receptivity and the cup of limitations. Ruled by the loving number 6 and highly influenced by the "water" of emotions, this cup with its rounded base is very prone to tipping; its overall state of being relies on a delicate balance—one element that swings the wrong way can cause catastrophic emotional upset. If the U phase is encountered early in life, events during that phase will form the root for later levels of emotional equilibrium, so it may take a lot or a little into its "cup" before succumbing—it is the mess it makes afterwards that is worthy of note.

The cup is dual in nature: it is extremely sensitive and desires closeness, yet it is ill equipped to handle serious sentiment. Pictured with its two beseeching arms reaching upwards, the U will try to defend itself, building walls and defenses against its perceived weakness. This often manifests as dual personalities: two distinctly different sides to the character. One will be warm, cheerful, and loving; the other chilly, critical, and untouchable. Two sides of a coin, or, in this case, extremes of emotion. Anyone involved with a dominant and negative U may become used to feeling both loved and labeled simultaneously. An unpleasant, uncomfortable, and unhappy feeling, to be sure.

The U is also representative of a conduit or a plug. It holds the potential to change or alter energy that passes through its reaching antennae, or arms. Like the Universe, it is a series of energies coursing through channels, which have the ability to unplug and undo, or to jump start and ignite. It is a change in direction and flow. To put it simply, it is the U-turn: like turns into lust, metal into rust, and dreams into dust. It also turns winds into hurricanes, dry spells into droughts, tremors into quakes, and calm waters into tsunamis. It is the verdict of the judge, the sentence of the jury, and the finality of the undertaker. The dual nature of the U may also be depicted by an excellent public speaker who is unable to communicate on a personal level, or the individuality of the baby inside the mother who is still connected to her by virtue of the uterus and umbilical cord. There are always two sides to the U, some shown, some not. The uncommunicative U will often have an alternate outlet for their emotions like painting, yoga, tai chi, singing in a choir, or jumping out of planes.

Obviously, it is also representative of horseshoes, which are used for protection, deflection, and plain good luck. We throw them at poles in a game of the same name, and a horse is not properly attired without them.

The entry energy of the U is maintaining careful balance—it can be unsteady, uneasy, unsure, uneven, plus an unnervingly long list of other "un" words. "Un" essentially means "not." Not ready, not willing, not able. It is an unsettled vibration, resting on a precariously balanced base. However, the saving grace of this energy is its numeric ruler: the love force of the domestic 6. I suppose the luck of the horseshoe doesn't hurt, either. Together, they may offer enough positivity to the U to allow a relatively sustainable balance. However, betrayal or broken trust causes the most pain to the U energy and is the main cause of tippage—if hurt or maligned in this way, the U will topple and flow like a dam released, and the resulting flood of emotional pain could drown even an Olympic swimmer. Once emptied, however, the U regains their balance and carries on. But they do not forget.

In a nutshell, the U will show the world calm control even while masking an emotional turmoil. This turmoil will peek through the mask as spots of jumpiness, tension, and a sense of things not being as they seem.

The negative side to the U is rooted to its emotional issues—if left unexpressed for long periods, the U can seek outlets in inappropriate ways. Some ways will be relatively harmless, like going "underground" for a while. The seriously unstable and upset U can become unhinged, which is where these words come in: cruel and unusual, abusive, ugly, hurt, and murder.

Traditional Descriptions

Typical descriptives for the U include warm, calm, friendly, social, helpful, efficient, loyal, patient, and domestic. A negative U can be evasive, judgmental, duplicitous, sarcastic, distant, and secretive. I suppose it goes without saying that the U can also be emotionally unstable.

Cornerstones

The following words all show a channeling and focusing of energy: Union, University, Understanding, Universe, Umbilical, and Urban. Any words with "un" as a prefix confirm the shifting or opposing (will or won't, yes or no, left or right) energy of the U.

As a Current Energy Phase

The 6-year phase of the U is one of emotional intensity, potential instability, changes in direction, and possibly negative formative experiences. It is a time of falling in and out of love, and finding or being separated from people, places, or things that are loved. It is also a time of luck which, when combined with emotional issues, could make for a rather confusing but hopefully entertaining phase.

V (Value of 6): Victory

The V is the sign of peace and the victory salute and is connected to Venus. It is the mate to the A in that ancient symbolism regarded the A as a male, phallic energy and the V as the virginal female. As such, it also refers to the vessel that carries life.

Appropriately, it is the only letter to refer to marriage and the search for the perfect mate. Look at the V as two separate lines that have been pulled together at the base. These two lines illustrate the coming together of two people, places, or things. It is a "coming together, working together, and succeeding together" type of vibration. Similar to the U, the V is valued by the love number 6 and, because of its pointed base, it also struggles to maintain balance in emotional affairs. The difference between the U and the V is in the arms. While the U reaches up to protect, defend, and ask for help, the V reaches up in a determined and focused search for spiritual truth. (Remember the rabbit ears that used to sit atop your television? That vertical image is an ideal representation of the V seeking information, data, and messages on an ongoing basis.) This reaching up with love as its root motivator represents a desire for unity, for togetherness, and for victorious connections—something that goes beyond the connections between two people: it is larger than that. This connection, or desire for one, is what keeps the V on balance and able to connect to its emotions in a way that the U is unable. It is lifting itself up from the Earth plane in an attempt to reach higher and, as a result, the weight on its base is very light. V/6 will feel the need, if open and developed, to heed an inner voice that calls to create, or build, something of value to the people. The V will strive to achieve on an ongoing basis and will generally succeed at whatever goals they have set for themselves. The V is strongly tied to the belief that all life is sacred and, therefore, that one shalt not kill—anything or anyone for any reason. These folks are the type you will find trapping large, hairy spiders or other creepy crawlers in jars and releasing them back into the garden rather than killing them. They are truly gentle souls to whom killing is abhorrent. If their charts include power numbers that allow emotional distancing concerning matters of life and death or pain and suffering, they will make fantastic doctors, veterinarians, nurses, health-care workers, vicars, and holistic healers.

In a person, the prominent V will reflect a tireless worker, a highly intellectual, inventive, and intuitive soul with a good heart and the genuine desire to please. This energy generally mixes well with others and is usually a delight to work for or with. When the V finds its true mate, there will be no other energy that will work harder at making a marriage (or friendship) last. They are loyal, straightforward, honest, loving, forgiving, and consistent.

Of course, there is always the negative side. If the V's true calling or nature is suppressed, they will obviously feel frustrated and depressed. The V will lash out at those closest to them and voilà! The peaceful V can become verbose, vulgar, vile, vain, and even violent. They also play the victim quite well. But, overall, the V will overcome and prevail. They will emerge victorious.

Traditional Descriptions

Typical descriptives include ethical, conscientious, ambitious, fair, loyal, determined, nurturing, dedicated, and trustworthy. When undeveloped, the V can be materialistic, egocentric, selfish, vain, agnostic, unsympathetic, and unprincipled.

Cornerstones

The following words all indicate either victory or the loss of it: Verify, Validate, Veteran, Vaccine, Valor, Value, Vote, Vagrant, Vilify, Vulgar, Vigilante, and Vice.

As a Current Energy Phase

The 6-year run of the V is also one of emotional value because of the love connection of its ruler: the V/6 feels and expresses its love valiantly and visually. The V demonstrates its ruler of Venus through its values and viewpoints and its vibration is one of vigilance and victory. This is a time of sweet success, marriage, and peace.

Of course, the V can also swing the other way and become a vain, vodka-swigging vigilante who spews venom. But that's another story.

W (Value of 6): Waterworks

The W is the third and final letter energy with the numeric value of 6, or love. As with all of the 6 letters, its primary influence is water. Water is a profound symbol for emotions: we "cry us a river," dismiss disagreements as "water under the bridge," and find ourselves in "hot water" or dying to "get our feet wet." We "wait for our ship to come in" and "hold our water" until it happens. The long and the short of the W is to be found in the small mountain in its center, bracketed by a pair of arms reaching up towards the heavens for help and guidance. As its value of 6 suggests, the W pertains to the emotional highs and lows, the peaks and valleys and waxing and waning of love, hate, and every emotion in between. It is pictured beautifully in the image of a child floating peacefully in the womb. All is undisturbed and protected until Mommy's water breaks.

Because of its ups and downs and strong connections to emotions, the W can also promote a desire to escape, which can and does take the shape of addiction. The W will most likely undergo a welcome awakening at some time because of its beseeching "arms": after all, the divine power of Universe will not ignore a constant and unfailing request for assistance.

The typical W energy is very likable. They make lifelong friends, are upstanding employees and neighbors, and are loyal and true to their mates. The W's emotional aspect leaves them as susceptible to periods of happiness and wonder as they are to bouts of deep depression and worry. Their lesson is to find the small mountain in the center of the W's energy and make that home base. Day trips can be made down into the valleys and up to the peaks, but since the valleys are dark and damp and the peaks are hot and airless, the happy medium is to be found in the middle and is where the wise will be found. Which is another way of saying that a safe, warm, welcoming, and loving home is necessary for the W—they need a place that is solid and dependable into which they can withdraw.

The W is truly the water of love and their soul truly seeks the highest level they can reach while residing on this Earth plane. The wonderful thing about a balanced W is that the holder will also be refreshingly normal and down-to-earth—even through sometimes traumatic events—and they literally love the Earth. This vibration enjoys nature and will spend as much time as possible outdoors, for this revitalizes the soul.

Traditional Descriptions
Overall descriptions of the W include adaptable, caring, committed, direct, genuine, faithful, loyal, dependable, and objective. A negative W can be obsessive, uncommunicative, depressed, perplexing, distant, wishy-washy, and addictive.

Cornerstones
The following words all relate either to water, emotions, or different levels (as in up and down): Waves, Wash, Wet, Well, Wade, Whale, Wharf, Weep, Wail, Wallow, Worry, Weight, Wage, and Window.

As a Current Energy Phase
This final transit of the 6 value is the most understated of the three (U, V, W). Although it has the closest ties to water, it is also the most balanced. Emotional highs and lows abound; however, the W is protected in a way that the U and V are not. Its energy is centered in the middle of the letter in the peak between the arms, and usually feels safe, even through upheavals. This type of vibration is a more spiritual one; hence it is more *personal* than others. This phase concerns spiritual growth through physical experiences. Consequently, this transit is like riding the proverbial roller coaster of emotions—the highest of highs are paid for by the lowest of lows. But the process also affords moments of spiritual insight that help to form the deep and enduring character of the strong W.

X (Value of 5): X Factor
In the X, we find a multiple being. It symbolizes adding to, multiplying, crossing out and the end of the line. This

character can be a signature or an indication of an error in judgment or behavior; it can serve as warnings and attention symbols on a variety of products including poisons and prescription drugs (Rx). It speaks of upcoming railway crossings and wrong ways to go. It is the "X factor" or unknown quantity/quality that played a part, for example, in determining how many males versus females (X chromosomes) make up "generation X." This same X factor will dictate whether you are the right candidate for the role or the job and can also keep the dedicated mathematician scratching his head for hours ... or longer. It is the X button that closes computer screen boxes on X-rated sites. X marks the spot, tells you where you are (as in "you are here"), and reveals the locations of (supposedly) buried treasures.

On a more religious note, like its sibling T, X speaks to the cross of Jesus and refers to the name of Christ (Xmas) and cores down to as you sow, so shall you reap. Justice plays a part in the X: it will either become the cross by which we are resurrected (or given a second chance), or the cross whose weight we will have to bear.

The X breaks barriers, creates new dimensions and is open to new experiences and multiple realities (the Matrix). The X displays vulnerability by virtue of its open sides, yet it is the most perfectly balanced letter in the alphabet. It retains its shape no matter how it is turned. This reflects the influence of its numeric value of 5 which, despite being ruled by change, the senses, communication, and the need for freedom, is also steady at its core.

However, in name form the X is highly impressionable, vulnerable, changeable (due to its propensity to multiply and add on), and naturally progressive and active. Because of several somewhat-crooked Y forms within its structure, it can find making decisions a difficult prospect; there are quite a number of "hidden" forks in the road.

The X can easily become excessive, exhausted, exhilarated, exhibitionistic, or subject to many other versions of emotions or actions. Now we are into the base nature of the X, as in SEX. The X stands with its arms spread apart and seeking while its legs are held wide enough for a metaphorical truck to drive through. To say that the X is kind of interested in sensual pastimes would be like saying the ocean is kind of wet.

My take on the X is one of unexpected developments or unanticipated events and sometimes of pushing the envelope. The X holds an element of mystery, which is one of the reasons this particular letter captures my imagination and obviously entertains others as well—it could be the reason that the *X-Files* is still seen in syndication worldwide.

A person carrying the X factor will be unpredictable, fascinating, and curious about everything—this energy enjoys exploring the unknown or untried. The X is adventurous, impulsive, and prone to regretting previous actions, but the regret will be on the inside and will be caused by unhealthy alliances and deeds. This type of X will crucify themselves privately while smiling publicly.

The X is all about the road to take and the road best left untraveled. It is spiritual retribution for yielding to temptations, a difficult position for this energy as temptations excite the investigative and exploratory nature of the X.

Traditional Descriptions

Typical descriptives include adventurous, receptive, progressive, independent, artistic, nonjudgmental, curious, and magnetic. More negative X energies can be impulsive, excessive, addictive, careless, and self-destructive.

Cornerstones

All of the following words or abbreviations offer a glimpse of the rare X factor: X-ray, X-rated, XTC, XY (male chromosome), and XX (female chromosome).

As a Current Energy Phase

The 5-year span of the X leaves the holder open to anything and anyone. It is growth and expansion, although not always in positive ways or down positive paths. This is a time of enticement, of provocation, and of luring, which is directly influenced by the freedom-seeking senses of the 5. The desire to question and to take action is sometimes strong enough to overcome reservations and can lead to situations never expected. If the holder of the X is strong enough to be highly selective in their explorations, they can indeed enjoy this vibration to its fullest. The trick is to not allow the sinner without to out-shout the saint within. Due care and attention would be the order of the day during an X phase. For 5 years, of course.

Y (Value of 1): Fork in the Road

Let's pretend that you are alone and driving to Aunt Bessie's house in the country. You have only been there once when you were little and since you were positive you would not need a map (you've always been highly intuitive), you didn't bring one. You did bring your cell phone, but since Aunt Bessie is deaf and anti-social, she doesn't have a phone, but you can always call your mom. You are quickly running out of gas as you have made many false starts down many wrong roads. The sun is sinking into the horizon and what light remains shows identical fields rolling away from you in all directions, like gentle dark waves. You reach a well-defined fork in the road. The road to the left is apparently well used. The one on the right, perhaps less so. There is only one thing missing and that would be a signpost. The sun sinks even lower. The shadows grow. Your engine sputters and coughs. You try to call your mom for directions but can't get a signal on the cell. The battery light comes on, and you didn't bring your charger. You need to make a decision, and you need to make it soon. Left or right?

The Y is a change in direction. Sometimes it is a choice you voluntarily make; sometimes it is a choice or direction made for you. For example, *you* exist because of a long-ago fork in the road, or a decision made *for* you by the winners of the X/Y chromosome game your parents were engaged in playing long ago: the X placed the basic game plan on the table, but the Y threw options into the picture. The end of the game produced you.

To give you a further idea of the Y energy, the word "yesterday" is bracketed by the Y, which allows it to encompass all aspects of one direction (to the left, or past) and all aspects of the other (to the right, or into the future). If you have a Y in your name, you will likely find that you are forced or choose to change directions in your life more often than your average neighbor. The Y is also open to different ways of living and thinking and is often just as curious about the metaphysical as it is the scientific. The lesson of the Y/1 is to take the "rougher" road, or to take a risk and pursue the spiritual and creative side of life rather than the sensual and material one, a lesson which is oft repeated in the symbols of the alphabet. Luckily, the Y is also connected to intuition and psychic flashes, which can come in awfully handy if one is caught in an unusual or threatening situation.

Another (seemingly unfortunate) aspect of the Y is that it separates. In human terms, that translates into different relationships coming to an end through various means such as death (a transit marked, oddly enough, by the formation of the letter Y on the chest after an autopsy), divorce, imposed distances, or simply "losing touch." The Y can also manifest as an alternate lifestyle, chosen or imposed. This can be the eccentric loner, the psychopath living in a deserted motel, or the artist living in a psychedelic world. This can also present itself as having to live with a physical disability or dysfunction and the potential for spiritual growth that such a condition can pose.

What is likely is that someone with a Y in their name will be "different." They will either live with imposed issues that offer no choice in the lifestyle or voluntarily choose a "different" way of living or experiencing life. If you are living with or are a Cornerstone Y, expect your life to change directions fairly often. The 1 energy that supports the Y will afford a strength and determination to follow through on paths chosen or dictated, but at the end of the road, the path of the Y will show a long line of twists, turns, switchbacks, sharp corners, and might look more like a map of a country than the history of a life.

On a more mundane or "normal" level, the Y phase can herald a change in careers or a new job, moving into a new home, getting married, or the birth of a child. Remember that even within the mundane scenarios, the Y often presents the unexpected—so the above scenarios could also arrive as being fired from your job, evicted from your home, served divorce papers, or finding yourself dealing with an unexpected pregnancy. Again, because of the inestimable number 1, these changes can both be challenging and beneficial in the long run.

An ideal imagery for the two aspects or directions is demonstrated quite nicely in the contemplation of yin and yang. The two halves of the whole. The feminine and the masculine; two different entities that come together to create perfect balance. Yesterday would not exist without today. Yes would not exist without no. A year would not exist without 12 months, nor would a yard without 3 feet. One yo would not be complete without another yo (as in yo-yo,) which in and of itself incorporates opposing directions, up and down, or even left to right. An egg is not an egg without its yoke ... something that allows the development of a chick. The twisting of the body into different directions is commonly known as yoga and is designed to create a peaceful and limber body, mind, and soul.

Almost predictably, a familiar challenge is part of its energy. Which path to take? The logical, practical, safe one, or the one promising risk, mystery, and revelation? Material reality pits itself against spiritual truth once more.

Finally, the Y is also the divining rod. So if you are still sitting there in your truck, get out and find a long branch with a forked end. Hold the forked end loosely in both hands and stand at the crossroads. Aim the branch down one road, then the other. If the stick pulls downwards at any point, that is either the direction to take or the location of underground water. So, unless you are thirsty, get back in your truck and go forth and prosper.

Traditional Descriptions

Typical descriptives include intuitive, reflective, curious, pioneering, adaptable, confident, original, and intelligent. Some negatives are indecisive, timid, confused, impulsive, and aimless.

Cornerstones

All of the following words point to different directions or components: Yeast, Yacht, Yank, Yield, Yearn, Yell, Yes, Yin/Yang, Yummy, and Yucky.

As a Current Energy Phase

This 1-year transit is fairly straightforward. A decision or choice will be made. This will be a voluntary or forced choice, which has the potential to change directions and circumstances in life. This will manifest as anything from entering a convent to going to medical school to moving to Siberia. Of course, normal situations involving the Y are more common: a change in personal relationship status, a change of job or home—the point here is that this energy holds a change in lifestyle and content and if a choice is involved, the ultimate decision should be based on what the intuition dictates.

If you have one or more Y energies in your name, simply changing the Y to an I will not change your Whole Name Number as both numbers are ruled by the number 1, but it will remove the "fork in the road" essence and replace it with a highlighted intuitive sense.

Z (Value of 7): Zap!

Although it is reversed in shape, the Z always reminds me of a lightning bolt and the letter N on its side. The two letters are linked in that they are both interlocked double 7s, and both are highly intuitive and intellectually brilliant energy conduits that I often see as high voltage. In the case of the Z, which is ruled by the 7, the lightning, zigzag, electric energy connects to the mouth and what comes out of it; but, the Z is not concerned with editing itself: what comes out of its mouth is unvarnished and blunt. Z is the master of the spoken word, and it uses this mastery to hurt or heal, sometimes without deliberate intent either way. The Z can be the public speaker, the writer, the teacher, the politician, or the convincing liar. The difference between this letter and another vocal energy (C) is that the Z speaks not only when they should shut up, but they insist on speaking even after they have been *told* to shut up. The Z considers themselves the conveyer of facts (even when they are flat-out wrong), and nothing will stop the Z from having their say.

Here is an incredibly smart person who, sometimes, does not pause to think of the impact of his or her words before launching them. This person could also be perfectly suited to telling tales out of school, *in* school, or anywhere else, for that matter. Lies also come as easily as gossip to the unenlightened Z. The surrounding letters and the effects of same are emphatically important and will dictate how far any Z in question will go.

A positive Z, one who has mastered the challenge of the 7 (which is to focus on the spiritual and metaphysical as opposed to the logical and practical) will hold their audience enthralled and in awe of the words they speak and can prove hysterically funny. A negative Z, one who tends to speak strictly from the cold, hard platform of logic will hold their audience captive as well—their magnetism serves to attract and hold a basically unwilling, yet curious group of onlookers.

Because of their propensity to analyze everything in their realm, the Z also makes a great problem solver or detective. They also do extraordinarily well in scholarly and mental pursuits. Due to their analytical and controlling nature, the undeveloped or Cornerstone Z is not usually good marriage material; however, should a Z develop into the deeply spiritual person their triple 7 values offer, they will find it difficult to even *find* someone they can relate to on an intimate and esoteric level, but should it become so, this will be a union made in Heaven or somewhere nearby.

On the rather humorous side, the Z is full of zeal and zest and as a result, needs to zone out from time to time. In other words, the typical Z needs its ZZZs.

Traditional Descriptions

Typical descriptives show the positive Z as eloquent, confident, direct, humorous, quick, resourceful, investigative, and dedicated. Negative Z energy can appear as insensitive, brash, impatient, offensive, deceptive, and critical.

Cornerstones
The following words all refer to a sharp energy or a certain level of energy: Zap, Zing, Zoom, Zip, Zany, Zealous, Zen, Zero, Zenith, Zoned, and Zombie.

As a Current Energy Phase
The 7-year reign of the Z is one of intellectualized mastery of the spoken word. This is a time of scholarly pursuits, investigations into mysteries, and analytical processing. Such data-processing ability creates formidable lawyers, politicians, and detectives. The lesson for the 2 involves understanding that the words they speak and the manner in which they are spoken can be creative or destructive. The choice then becomes whether to use words as weapons or to use words as a balm for healing.

Test Yourself

All you need to do is remember these particular (and peculiar) phrases. Here's the list. Test yourself, because remembering the meanings of the numbers and which letters are connected to them is one of the more important steps in learning to read names.

Number 1: **1 A**ngry **Q**ueen **Y**ells **I**n **J**ail (1=A, Q, Y, I, J)
Number 2: **2 B**ig, **R**ed **K**isses (2=B, R, K)
Number 3: **3 G**rey **C**ats **L**ick **S**auce (3=G, C, L, S)
Number 4: **4 D**runk **M**en **T**alking (4=D, M, T)

Number 5: **5 N**urses **X**-ray **H**arry's **E**ye (5=N, X, H, E)
Number 6: **6 V**oluptuous **U**nion **W**orkers (6=V, U, W)
Number 7: **7** (the land of) **OZ** (7= O, Z)
Number 8: **8 F**air **P**oliticians (8=F, P)
Number 9: not applicable

… whatever words we utter should be chosen with care for people will hear them and be influenced by them for good or evil…

—Siddhartha Gautama, founder of Buddhism
(circa 563–483 BCE)

five

Chaldean Numerology and Today's Spiritual Seekers

Spiritual Beliefs ... Then and Now

The Chaldeans believed in the Divine power and were therefore very spiritual; much of their time was devoted to awareness of their surroundings and the communications held in all manner of daily events (something we might today refer to as observing omens and symbolism). Their task while here on Earth was to spread spiritual and metaphysical knowledge using the combined mediums of mathematics, astronomy, astrology, numerology, divination, music, medicine, and other systems we likely know nothing about. Regarded as soothsayers and prophets, the Chaldeans worshiped a God who was responsible for the "Energy Behind All Things," which was represented by the symbol of a half-moon nestled within the circle of the sun. Although their culture involved a variety of lesser gods, their supreme devotion was reserved for this one Energy God, the Sun, or, to my way of seeing it, the Source. This theme of observing, respecting, and working with energies and symbols runs through the very fabric of the legacy these ancient people left behind and is especially evident in their numerology system.

While no one can speak for these long-gone people, I think it is safe to say that the energy they honored and the spiritual practices they observed are core to the practice and gift of Chaldean numerology. I also believe they would agree with the following views and methods of tapping into the spiritual and arcane aspects of our existence.

But First, a Wake-Up Call

Do you believe that there is something more to this reality than meets the eye? Do you believe that there just might be another element at play: a power energy we cannot see, touch, smell, or hear, but one that is there nonetheless? Since you are reading this book, I would hazard a guess that you might say yes—or at least maybe. That means you are part of a growing number of people the world over who are "waking up" and realizing that there *must* be more to this life than mere existence followed by death. The concept of us as *spirits having human experiences* has taken firm root and is growing in massive leaps and bounds, which in turn has created an ever-increasing group of "students" in search of higher learning, which would make you and I classmates. Our teacher is known by many names, such as the Divine, the Source, Universe, or God; but no matter the name, the energy we seek to learn from and connect with is one and the same—that of divine wisdom, unconditional love, and unlimited knowledge.

While anyone can sign up, there are two major prerequisites for this "course," which anyone can do. One concerns your belief systems, and the other concerns who you are and what you have done. Let's look at the first one, the simplest of the two. I have found that folks either *do* believe or *don't* believe; there is rarely a gray area. Believing (or having Faith) is really not a difficult choice, but in terms of spiritual growth and education, it is an extremely important one. Without Faith or belief, you will wander through this life without an inner base or support system. Nothing will mean very much—not in a lasting way.

So the first prerequisite is that *you must be willing to accept something that you cannot see* and know that its energies are a constant in your life in one way or another and that you can tap into those energies should you choose to.

You must also have a personal history that includes elements of the following: good deeds, bad deeds, and *very* bad deeds. You must have both positive and negative qualities. You must even have one or two skeletons rattling around in your closet. Essentially, you must be a human being and possess all or some of the human foibles shared by us as a race.

Why?

Well, because the second prerequisite is *the willingness to accept yourself and all of your foibles as being perfectly intended.* This requires a complete and total concession to the idea that your life history and everything in it was and is a part of your lesson—your Lifepath—the reason you are here, and it centers around the things you are here to learn this time around, just like everyone else. Chaldean numerology teaches us that we are *not* perfect; otherwise, it would not be filled with spiritual content—messages of wisdom and personal motivation that are specifically designed for the spiritual seeker. The fact is that you must be prepared to accept that *you are not perfect and were never intended to be.*

You came here with a specific gift and armed with a type of "blueprint" (found in your name and date of birth) that lays out the overall directions you are ideally to take while here on this Earth plane. You do have, like all of us, free will and can choose your *own* direction, but it will rarely lead you to places you truly want to be; rather, it will run you in ragged circles, (mis)lead you down a variety of very pretty garden paths or maybe right into the heart of the deepest, wildest, and most savage of jungles. But the point here is that while we *do* have room to move and the parameters of our Lifepaths are loosely structured, you must be willing to follow the guideposts set up for you. But since nothing is set in stone, it is *your* choice whether you follow the path recommended, take a shortcut, or go somewhere else entirely. My suspicion, however, is again tied to the fact that you are reading this book—something deep inside of you *wants* to travel the road recommended.

It does sound appealing, right? To relax into who we really are: to completely and utterly accept ourselves as beings of both weaknesses and strengths who are *perfectly intended* and therefore free from the need to assign or burden ourselves with guilt, self-sabotage, anger, frustration, and all the other negative and prohibitive human emotions and reactions. We will, of course, still experience those moments of sheer emotion that will overwhelm us, but knowing that we are perfectly intended allows us to both succeed and fail at the same time—at anything and as often as we need to in order to learn the specific lesson attached to the specific energy occurrence.

This way of looking at things may read as overly simplistic, and perhaps it is, but once *you truly know that you are not alone*—that we are all interconnected; that there is indeed an unnamed, unknown, but very real Energy that exists beyond our understanding and that everything is just as it should be—you will naturally discover Faith as well. For me, Faith feels paternal, like a "Father" who is protecting me. I may not always fathom why certain things happen in my life, but even through the trauma and the drama, I knew that everything was happening the way it was *supposed to* and that I didn't need to know why. I just needed to have Faith that I would make it through—and I always *did* make it through, sometimes in absolutely amazing, unbelievable, and even miraculous ways … and it was, without a doubt, because of my Faith, my belief—call it what you will. All I know is that, like the Chaldean system, it works.

Don't expect things to change overnight once you have "woken up." If you are anything like me, it will take you a bit of time to perk up. I was groggy and lethargic for the longest time. In fact, it took years of learning, reading, studying, practicing, sharing, listening, and drinking lots of coffee before I could say that I was almost fully conscious. I say "almost" because there is *always* more to see, more to hear, more to learn, and more to investigate. Each day brings new revelations about the depths and heights this awakening can reach, and it will never end. And so it is for you, too. So it is for all of us.

Energy Is Everything and Everything Is Energy

The Chaldeans considered all things in, on, and beyond this Earth as forms of energy, which is the core of their numerology system. Having said that, let's pull back a little bit and zoom out into space. From a vantage point high above the Earth, we can look down and see our gorgeous blue, green, tan, and white world below us. What we are also looking at are grids; some visible, some not. One is electrical in nature and *can* be seen when the skies are dark and the Cities of Light shine, while the others are invisible. The most obvious of these is the World Wide Web. This grid holds both positive and negative ramifications: it totals to Master 33, which calls for some manner of sacrifice, and its Identity Initials are 666. Another invisible grid is formed by a series of what are known as Ley lines (straight lines that connect one sacred site to another—sites like Stonehenge, the Pyramids, the Bermuda Triangle, and Easter Island, to name but a few); it is said that where these lines intersect, an immense power source resides. Still another grid is formed by our very own collective thought patterns and emotional emissions—a concept that has been tagged with the phrase "mass consciousness," which is precisely what it is, and we all feed into it.

All that we see below us is formed by one band of material energy (slow- or fast-moving molecules) or another: these overlying or intertwining grids can be viewed as a giant energy matrix that absolutely everything is a part of. Including you.

You have undoubtedly heard of the butterfly effect. This theory says that a butterfly could flap its wings somewhere in Sweden and affect the weather systems across the world, even to the extent that it could cause a tornado in the Bahamas. It's a long and complicated story and has strong connections to measurements (and therefore, mathematics), but the point is, again, that all things are energetically interconnected, from the tiniest detail to the largest, and that includes all of us. We are all energy forms interacting with other energy forms. Therefore, our thought-form energies, especially when strong and repetitive, will carry the cumulative potential to create any type of vibration, both positive and negative. That is up to us and the thoughts and words we choose to live by. On a larger scale, these same thoughts and words form a distinct if, again, invisible, energy matrix. In order for this metaphysical grid to function at peak performance, all aspects must be similar in content, for if but one significant bug climbs into the system, it will no longer function as a perfect whole or in perfect harmony. (Think about the energies of terrorists: their vibrations are not compatible with those of peace lovers, and therefore chaos is thrown into the matrix.)

However, if your own work within this energy system is pure, you will attract only pure energies in return: you get out what you put in. Obviously, positive attracts positive and vice versa. If a butterfly's wings can theoretically affect another part of the world in a major way, then we also affect it with our own "wings," which are produced by the quality of our own thoughts, words, beliefs, and actions.

Once there is the knowledge that we as a people hold an immense potential to alter our circumstances, then the revelation must be made that this potential begins with *each of us as individuals.* When this information is absorbed and understood, the tools that become available to us all are beyond the imagination—perhaps even beyond belief at this point. But everything is possible, given enough time, information, and need. You are part of a massive, multi-faceted energy grid. This grid functions perfectly and offers exact fulfillment of your thought instructions. One might say it is similar to the linear operation of a computer system: once you understand the applications and how to download and operate them, an incredible expanse of possibilities becomes your control panel and you become the creator of your own reality. For some, this may take many years of disciplined study, commitment, and practice, while for others, it may be as simple as deciding to commit to interests already long held, scrutinized, and ruminated upon. Many of us are working with energies in different ways and investigating its uses and magickal qualities—something I think the Chaldeans would relate to, understand, approve of, and encourage.

Your Thoughts, Actions, and Words Carry Energy, Too

There is energy in every action we take, in every word we speak, and in every thought we think. And for every action, word, and thought, there is a reaction and response. Assuming these actions, words, and thoughts are positive ones, the resulting reactions and responses will also be positive.

Conversely, the opposite is also true—negative thoughts, actions, or words will produce negative energies and results. This goes to the Law of Attraction: the much-touted Law can be simplified into being truly and consistently aware of what you are thinking and saying and doing, knowing that the quality of our combined human thought energies can solidify into corresponding and perhaps worldwide consequences and circumstances.

What you pay attention to, you will draw unto you. That means more than just thinking positive or negative thoughts; the *contents* of your thoughts are important, too. Many folks think they are applying the law of attraction correctly by pleading with Universe "please, no more bills!" Here's the problem: Universe focuses on the *thing* mentioned in the request or thought, so if it is bills, Universe will comply and your mailbox will overflow with *bills*. If your focus on not "'being broke all the time," the word the Universe picks up on and responds to is "broke," and you will continue to notice moths flying out of your open wallet.

The nature of Universe is to *create,* so the structure and content of the "orders" you place (some have likened the Universe and the Law of Attraction to "placing orders" from a cosmic Catalog) is all-important and makes a huge difference in your results. In addition, there is also a difference between *wanting* and *needing,* so the most effective method of manifesting is to be motivated more by what you *need* than by what you *want.* Needs are necessary things; wants are desires that can often be based in greed or self-satisfaction (which is the voice of the ego). So, the next time you wish you didn't have so many bills, focus on the *need* for "extra cash" instead.

This connection extends to the physical condition of your body, as well. Negative and depressive thoughts materialize as ill energies, as does a thought that goes something like this: "I don't want to get cancer." Universe hears "cancer" and will attempt to give you what you've asked for, particularly if you worry or send out supportive thought patterns about it on a constant basis. (For example, for many years, my beloved Granny worried excessively about getting cancer and when, at a relatively young age, she died, cancer had taken over almost every organ in her body, almost as though she had thoroughly convinced Universe of her *need* without even realizing she had done so.)

I am sure you have seen illness referenced as dis-ease. This means there is an imbalance of thought energies that can cause a body to become off-balance, or ill-at-ease. If emotional issues are left to ripen and fester within our psyches, chances are good that this toxic and destructive energy will negatively impact our bodies and solidify into all manner of maladies. This is yet another reason to become more aware of what you are thinking and how you are energetically "programming" your body.

Your thoughts, words, and actions are "things" of substance. Becoming aware of the *types* of energies you are engaging and promoting will impact your life in direct correlation—good to good and bad to bad. Recognizing the differences, programming positivity, and "keeping the faith" can only assist in accelerating your spiritual progress and perhaps even in helping to improve the condition of your physical body as well.

Your Emotions Are Energy— and One Is Like a Weed

You know about the power of emotions, but what you might not think about is that they also carry and emit energies, and the more intense the emotion, the more intense the output. Can you remember a time when you went shopping and everyone seemed extra nice to you? Or another time when everyone seemed particularly grouchy? If you are honest with yourself, I'll bet a tiny, tinkling bell just rang somewhere in the back of your mind. The details are not important; the fact that an energy reflection took place is. Think about it further. Do you remember what kind of mood *you* were in on those days?

Energy is energy and negative or heavy emotions are amongst the strongest in the human energy matrix. So how and what you project is what you will get back. Larger pictures of events and occurrences will project more potent and lasting energy impressions—seems like a good reason to become more aware of what we are projecting, right? But that's not the main point of interest here. The one emotion we are the most afraid of is.

Of all of our feelings, fear is the most intense; it can paralyze us like deer in the headlights. While it applies to a myriad of situations, some of which are protective and positive (like being scared of that dark figure down the alley), the ones that affect us in a more intimate way are found in the fear of two specific things: success and failure. While we might fear one more openly than the other, both run head to head, consciously or subconsciously. Since success and failure are two sides of the same coin, the only way we can achieve success is by openly embracing our fear of it and all that it entails. Failure can be experienced without success but success cannot be *experienced* without failure. Put another way, if everything you ever tried worked out perfectly every time, you would have no frame of reference by which to measure your success. Failure is a required element in order to experience and appreciate true success. We are all familiar with failures, perhaps quite a few of them, but what about successes? If you are like most regular people, you have had some triumphs and victories, but major successes? How many of *those* have you had? Can you say that you are comfortable financially? Can you say that you are doing what you love? If the answer to both is yes, then more power to you, but if you are like most of us, the answer is usually no. Would you like it to be, though? Obvious answer, right?

The balance is clearly off when the overall picture is revealed. Stories about failures and lack and loss abound, but success stories are rarer, which is probably why they are celebrated when they *do* occur. There really are so many reasons for each of us to fear success that it would be literally impossible to even list them all, but one theme seems to be common and that is that once success is attained, what then? Have you ever heard the saying "you're only as good as the last part you played, book you wrote, house/car/jury you sold"? How does one "better" success? How do we do it again? How do we *sustain* it? That is one of the core reasons that many people sabotage themselves. We are not afraid of succeeding—everyone loves to win! Rather, it is the fear of *what happens afterwards* that keeps us from getting there. To my way of thinking, success is what it is. Once it is gained, it is never lost, it simply moves into the past. And looking forward with inward eyes will reveal the next signpost, so it's really just another stop along the way.

Yet even with the best of intentions, fear is not an easy emotion to weed out. It often has extremely deep roots that are almost impossible to completely remove, kind of like dandelions—where you pull one out, three more sprout. So it is a bit of a struggle to gain control over this particular weed, but that is where having Faith that everything happens exactly as intended comes in again—as does your own acceptance that everything in this life has a purpose and that is to teach you something. So fear is just another learning curve and is therefore nothing to be afraid of.

If we can get the idea behind "**For Everything, A Reason**" and hold on to our Faith, there is no sustainable reason for fear. The certainty of knowing we are connected to a higher element calms the mind and the soul—knowing that you are doing exactly the right thing at any time dilutes the fear of the unknown. And that is what fear is all about: the unknown. Fear is ego based, as in being afraid of not having enough or of losing what we *do* have—money, good health, good looks, work, love—you name it. Once we understand that we are *not* our bodies, we are *spirits residing therein* and that this world and its inhabitants are similar to students in a rather large classroom, we can learn to relax and await the arrival of the next teacher and the next lesson.

> *… the only thing we have to fear is fear itself.*
> —Franklin Delano Roosevelt, 1933 Inaugural Address

Believe It or Not

Equally important here is your level of belief (and this is true in all things metaphysical or spiritual): if you do not *believe* that you can tap into a source unseen, or even that there *is* one, you will not have access to its possibilities. Your ego-controlled doubt will stand solidly in your way. If you *do* feel a tickle of doubt, consider the air you are breathing this very minute. Try to touch it, taste it, hear it, see it, or smell it and you will be unable to do so. None of your senses are able to *prove* that the air exists, yet without it, you will die. Similarly, when the Sun disappears behind a moody sky or the Moon disappears from a clear one, we will swear on all we hold dear that both are still there—even though we can see neither. That is the essence of Faith—conviction on a deep gut level that *something* exists that we cannot see nor confirm with our human senses. We also know this energy is something we can connect to and that it will respond to our needs as proposed by our thoughts, words, and actions *while also knowing our true needs and supplying that which is the most beneficial for us at that time.*

As an illustration, suppose you really need a raise, and the promotion you are after would accomplish that for you. So this is the energy you have been focusing on—acing the interview and paperwork. But instead of being promoted, you are abruptly fired from your job. Wow. This would tend to create an instant skeptic, wouldn't it? But here is where keeping the faith is truly the most important thing you can do; losing it would be equal to sitting down in the middle of that long, dark tunnel I talked about before. Universe knows what you need better than you do.

Imagine this, if you will. A week or so after your firing and straight out of the blue, an unexpected job offer appears. You apply and you win the position, which turns out to pay higher than the promotion would have and more importantly, it is also the most enjoyable and rewarding job you have ever had. What you didn't know (and would have had no way of knowing) is that had you gotten the promotion, it would indeed have taken you up a few floors and to a corner office—a satellite branch of Hell. Before too long, you would have found yourself back in the unemployment lines. And you would have entirely missed out on the dream job you now have.

See how Universe gives you what you *need?* We don't have to know the whys and the wherefores, we just need to know in our hearts that we are connected and that we are protected. And that belief in the world of energy and a Higher Source is its own reward.

This is applicable to the actuality of reading the energies in your name and date of birth as well; if you do not truly absorb and believe what you are reading and hear what it is saying to you, then it will do exactly nothing for you. *Believe* what is being said to you and your life as it currently stands might just be up for review.

Follow Your Dream—It Is Your Gift

Let's just say that you are, as of today, no longer held back by fear, or at the very least, that it does not affect you as much. There is a certain wonder in that realization—a mild excitement, for you know that you have opened or cleared a blockage of sorts and the level of threat has been reduced.

You are more likely to follow your dream—to allow it to happen and to invite it in.

But what is your dream?

Look to your Soul or Inner name essences and your Lifepath for the clues if unknown. Much as my repetitious 1 and 3 Inner Soul energies point out the need for artistic expression, so will your numbers and letters speak to you. If you still aren't quite sure, go back, for the answer often lies in childhood and early youth and involves activities particularly enjoyed or something you would daydream about while simultaneously recognizing it for the dream it was *at the time.* Or it can center around an ongoing interest you had. For me, it was all about books. I loved to read every chance I had; I wrote books of poetry and almost always received a perfect score on English tests and compositions, but I did not connect for many years that maybe writing was my "thing." So finding yours may be a given or it may require a bit of digging and investigating. All it takes is a little dedication and determination ... and perhaps a bit of daydreaming.

By looking at your strongest numbers and letter values (the highest amount of each) and your Lifepath number, you should have a pretty good idea of where your strengths lie, and this observation should help trigger memories of those things you loved to do when you were a kid or young adult. If you show, for example, a high level of artistic leanings (especially numbers 1, 3, 6, 9, and Master 11 or 22) and your dream has always been to carve figures from chunks of wood, then that is your gift from Universe: the ability to create an image and bring it to life by using a simple piece of wood and a carving knife. Perhaps you are a lawyer and the idea of becoming a wood carver cracks you up—fine! Laughter is medicine for the soul. After you've quit laughing, go find yourself a piece of wood and a carving knife and some sandpaper and watch what happens, both from an emotional and a material point of view. After all, where is it written that a lawyer may not be a wood carver? Or that a lawyer may not retire to become a successful artist? Nothing is set in stone (or wood)—all things are possible. There are no rules when it comes to the forms artistic expressions can take. This holds true for any talent or predilection your particular Lifepath has gifted you with.

And how do you know if you are already using your gift? If you are, you will feel motivated to get up in the morning and eager to begin work, in whatever form it may take. You will feel peaceful and gratified and thankful. You will enjoy your existence and feel connected to something larger than yourself.

On the other hand, if you are *not* using your gift, you may feel frustrated and limited—like you are missing something. There may be a feeling of dissatisfaction or of being trapped that encompasses your entire life and circumstances. The biggest indication that you are not using it is boredom. Excruciating boredom.

The only way to find personal peace and tranquility of spirit is by *doing what comes naturally.* What I mean by that is to go where your instincts take you, to do that thing you most love to do. This can be something from long ago, something that has faded into the tapestry of your life, but is still there and can be adapted to fit into the present. Universe will literally plant it in front of you if you are truly ready and open to receive it. What is it that you loved to do? If enough thought and time is devoted to your question, the answer will come. Find your gift by being open to receiving it. And yes, I am speaking from experience.

What We All Seek and Where It's Hiding

The one thing most of us focus on, individually and as a society, is finding and experiencing love in its purest form. Sounds easy, right? But since it is the definitive reason we are all here and is central to the lessons we are still here trying to learn, obviously it is not as easy as it sounds. And it all goes back to that age-old, if banal, truth about loving oneself before being equipped to extend this gift to others. We may say we understand, but do we really? I wonder how many of us get stuck in the "loving ourselves" part? With all of our flaws, checkered pasts, and judgments passed about our histories and actions, how do we honestly grow to care about and even love ourselves enough to share pure love with others?

Again, Chaldean numerology gives us the answer: it all comes down to *accepting that we are exactly who and how the Universe intended us to be.* There are no mistakes. You are as perfect in your imperfections as I am in mine. Once that simple fact is assimilated and it is also understood that we are all teachers and students to one another, we can accept ourselves like we would another person and connect to ourselves like we would to someone we really care about. We must learn to be our own best friends and to treat ourselves with the same forgiveness and compassion that we would naturally offer to good friends... and even to strangers.

We all have the same emotions, even though some may suppress or hide them more effectively than others. We are like uncut precious gems that are here to be shaped and polished—by human interaction. Understanding that we are all "cut from the same stone" helps to remind us that we are all (as spirits having human experiences) essentially the same. We are all equal and deserve to be loved—a thought that many find easier to apply to others than to themselves, but again, anything is possible given enough Faith.

So, in order to love another, we must first accept that we are exactly who we were meant to be and that we were *intended* that way. We are perfectly designed by the Divine. Therefore, the base for unconditional love lies in self-acceptance, for it is only when we can honor, respect, and love the spirit-in-human-form beings we truly are that we become equipped to extend that clean and undemanding energy to others... and you are the starting point. *You* are the core of unconditional love, and so am I.

And yes, that is the ultimate lesson: to learn to accept, like, and eventually love your very own self. That means trusting that there is a plan for you and that there is a reason you are here. Again, this is the aim of Chaldean numerology—to help you discover your path, your strengths, your weaknesses, your talents, and your true essences. And all Chaldean roads lead to love that is wholesome and freely shared. Once this is attained and we all stand as a graduating class, our collective power is considerable.

There is much to learn and it begins with you... and me... and your neighbor... and my neighbor... and connections that continue along the grid until it encompasses all of us.

In this Cosmic School, the tools of learning can be unique, and Chaldean numerology offers all students of life a chance to perform an in-depth study of themselves and to track their spiritual growth with more understanding. Like a primer, the catalog of Chaldean numerology is designed to assist us in all areas of study and should ideally accompany each student to each class.

There are a variety of additional categories within this primer; all are designed to open our senses so that we might interact with the universal energy and hear its messages more effectively—the most powerful of which is the intuition.

Have You Ever Had a "Funny Feeling"?

Remember that time when you just had a "funny feeling" about something that you ignored, only to hear yourself say later "I *knew* that was going to happen"? It took me a long time, too, to understand that this wasn't just by chance. Somehow, I had *known* the outcome of something before it happened, or had known what the outcome would be should something be done a certain way, or at a specific time or in a particular place. My strongest intuition kicks in when someone or something dangerous or off-balance enters my personal space (not something that happens often, thankfully). There is an internal vibration that is so sharp, it feels as though my insides are actually buzzing—we all know the feeling, we just don't pay attention to it when its tone is quieter and more manageable.

The intuition (or sixth sense) is our protective sense, and all of us can hear it if we choose to. And although it is called a "sense," it is not scientifically recognized as such; nevertheless, it exists and it is real. Our traditional five senses are man-made—they consist of what our physical appendages tell our brain—but the sixth sense is "outsourced"; it is not *of* the human body. However, since it cannot be readily explained, the tendency is to dismiss it as unscientific and unproven and, therefore, essentially inconsequential. Which means it is most commonly ignored.

The intuition primarily serves as a warning system: 99 percent of the time, the message received is one concerning danger of some kind or of the need to be alert or aware, which often translates into feelings of distrust or unease that usually point to the presence of questionable energies or circumstances. This feeling can whisper through you when considering the trustworthiness of a person, the rightness of a job offer, the outcome of a certain action, or even something as mundane as not stopping at the store on the way home even though *that voice* whispered something about toilet paper—but you ignored that funny feeling—it must be wrong, right? Wrong. The intuition is never wrong. But listening too late still leaves you sitting there at home, all alone—a tad rueful and wiser perhaps, but still without a square to spare.

Learning to listen to and heed messages from our intuition is part and parcel of connecting with Universe—these messages are communications from that mysterious but very real energy and can be as rudimentary as needing toilet paper or as dramatic as a sudden and overwhelming sense of danger that screams *run* from every fiber of your being.

I often hear folks ask how one can distinguish this voice from the other voices in their heads enough to know which is the voice of intuition, and my response is that the intuition is a *feeling* more than it is a voice. It is more of a *certainty*, an instinct, a deep knowledge that is difficult to put into words. This is not centered in the brain, like a thought, or a conversation with the self—this is a "sense impression." You just *know* and it is usually something that defies explanation, but it will ultimately take the form of words or thoughts as it moves from the gut into the brain, thus the term "voice" being used to describe the *feeling*.

For instance, if you are contemplating taking a ferry over to an island and you have a bad feeling about it, go another day. If you are thinking of borrowing your sister's car to go shopping and you have a bad feeling about it, take the bus or don't go at all. If you are at a party and some young guy approaches and asks you to come downstairs with him and you have a bad feeling about it, stay right where you are. (Many moons ago, I remember receiving an invitation to attend a party on board a yacht. It was steaming hot and I was too, but something told me to turn it down, as tempting as it was. Later that night, I heard that this same yacht had smashed onto a reef and sunk, leaving all aboard floundering in the ocean until they were rescued by the Coast Guard.)

We make things more complex than they need to be: if it feels wrong, don't do it. By the same token, you must learn how to differentiate between the voices of fear and those of the intuition. Remember that fear is ego-based, whereas the voice of your intuition is a deep-seated sensation of just *knowing*. It tingles through your insides *before* it takes on a thought-form.

The intuition can also offer rare insight through, for instance, divination techniques like tarot cards, pendulums, or runes. When our thoughts are focused and our Faith is centered on that unseen element, the intuition can work wonders. While answering questions or presenting images of current energies, it can also offer unexpected and sublime messages that speak simple and sacred truths. The more you honor Divine intuition by adjusting your actions in response to warnings, the more in tune you and this sixth sense will become and the more messages you will receive. Again, time and practice are key; the ego is one huge monster with incredible shelf life, and it does not take kindly to knowledge it cannot scientifically classify. I have been working with the intuition for years and I still find myself ignoring it at times. Oddly enough, though, I am *consciously aware* of ignoring that voice ... and then of awaiting the outcome. It is like I am testing the system. Trust me when I say that those occasions were huge refresher courses for me and I even found myself laughing at the audacity of Universe, for some of the lessons were quite funny—Universe has a sense of humor, no doubt! What an exhilarating discovery that was.

Symbolism and Omens

Another element of daily life presents itself in the language of symbols that relate to the very real signs surrounding you every day. This is applicable in dreams as well as in waking life and is very simple and very personal in that what a frog means to your neighbor might not be the same as what a frog means to you. Your neighbor might view it as something to kiss in hopes of finding her prince while you might think of it as something gross and slimy that will give you warts. Very personal. Dream books can be helpful in an overall kind of way when applied to the symbols and contents of dreams, but you are the only one who can read the symbols accurately, whether they occur while in a dream or while walking down the street.

Daily symbols come in a variety of shapes and forms and styles. They can appear as cars that won't start (where were you headed?), watches that stop (has time run out for someone or something?), phone numbers that don't connect (who are you trying to reach and why?), words caught in passing (what were you thinking about?) and thousands of other things. The key is becoming conscious of them and of how they connect to things in your life, especially ones that are of particular importance at that moment.

Let's say you are strolling downtown thinking about your trip to Boise, Idaho. For whatever reason, you are worried about the hotel you just booked. Approaching you from the opposite direction are two businessmen who are chatting up a storm. You vaguely notice them and keep worrying about the hotel. As they pass you by, you catch a snippet of their conversation and they are talking about a hotel. One says to the other "it's great—you'll love it!" and their voices fade abruptly.

Do you hear the message in there for you? That is the core of symbolism: recognizing messages, wherever they might pop up, whether through conversations overheard, signs appearing in apparent answers to your unspoken questions, or odd occurrences that seem to fit into your circumstances. It is becoming aware of things around you in a whole new way. If the Universe is a giant matrix of energy, and you are a part of it, then it makes sense that a whole other level of communication exists around you and is there to assist you if you choose to hear or see its messages.

Omens are more closely connected to the intuition and occur when a funny feeling combines with something you see, hear, or experience within the parameters of your daily life and usually on a repetitive basis; read together, they present a message of something amiss.

Let's say you have been seeing someone who seems nice, but you have an underlying weird feeling about this person, like a "beware" kind of feeling. So one morning, you stop in for a coffee at your regular spot, grab a paper, and settle in for a good read. There is an article on the second page about a person who did something awful and whose picture reminds you of this person you have been seeing. Not only that, but there are other similarities between the two—same age, same career ... just a coincidence, you say (even though you don't believe in them, right?). You leave the cafe and the article becomes lost in the events of the morning.

Later, you lunch at a local deli with your buddy and there on the table, spread before you like a welcome mat, is the exact article you read that morning over coffee. Again you are struck by the similarities in the picture, but this time, you notice the name of the journalist, and the first name is the same as the person you have been seeing.

That could be called an "omen" and not an overly positive one, either. If I were you, I think I might consider a background check at this point. And I bet you wouldn't be overly surprised if you found something. Hypothetically speaking, of course.

Synchronicity

Energies that move *with* the flow of energy instead of against it will naturally experience synchronicity. Let's say you have been thinking about your aunt for a few days and finally make up your mind to call her. You haven't seen her or spoken to her in months, so there you sit, phone in hand, trying to drum up the nerve to dial her number (she always frightened you as a kid), when the phone rings. Three guesses who it is.

How is this possible? Very easily, actually—by thinking about your aunt, you were sending your thought energy waves to her; she picked them up (subconsciously) and started sending her own back to you. She might even comment that you have been on her mind a lot lately and you might think "what a coincidence" since she has also been on yours. But there *are* no coincidences. There is only energy, and when it flows in the same direction or towards the same goal and upon the same path, it produces synchronicity. You and your auntie were momentarily "in sync" with one another.

Or imagine you have been looking for a particular book, one that is out of print and therefore hard to find. You run into an old friend in one of the many bookstores you have haunted in your search and fall into an exchange about good books. You mention the one you are looking for—and he just happens to have a copy of it at home, which he will be happy to lend you. You go the short distance to his house, share a cup of coffee, and leave with the book that just hours before seemed beyond your grasp in every way. This is an example of you and Universal energies being in sync.

Ever had stuff like that happen to you? I'll bet that you can come up with at least one example from your own life. The more *aware* you become, the more synchronicity will occur and the more in tune you will begin to feel.

Déjà vu … or Reincarnation?

Have you ever had the strong feeling of having been a particular place before despite also knowing that you haven't? Perhaps you have experienced the odd sensation of having lived through a specific event or moment before? I think we all have. We call it déjà vu (from early 20th-century French meaning "already seen"), puzzle over it for a moment or two, shrug it off, and go on our way. Is this another form of sense-memory or is it something more than that?

You have undoubtedly heard of the concept that each of us travels through different incarnations, which is where the term *re*-incarnation comes in. This is a highly controversial topic, but I do find it worthy of note that despite this controversy, reincarnation does come up in almost all religious and belief systems in one way or another. Some believe it is an "end run" around God's final judgment, while others believe that only the extremely bad people must come back (to make amends). I stand with the group that believes reincarnation is an accepted element in acquiring esoteric knowledge and achieving spiritual development: how we do in this incarnation is directly related to how we will do in the next and so on ... and our performances will dictate how often we experience physical form on this Earth plane and how long it will take each of us to "graduate."

So to my way of thinking, all the information that is available to us to improve our standing is worth looking into. We have nothing to lose and potentially everything to gain by actively seeking knowledge from every "book" in our massive and ever-growing library of life. Chaldean numerology is only one such "book"—there are many others just waiting to be found. Metaphysically and spiritually speaking, knowledge is power, and, in addition to making your life more fulfilling, it might just be the ticket to attaining ultimate victory and "graduating."

six

Sample Reads

The following are sample reads on a few folks whose names you will recognize, but they are more casual and refined and are not intended to reveal everything about each person, nor could they, for the only one who will truly be able to read their own energies will be the person under analysis. Also, there is a certain level of respect that must be observed when it concerns messages from analysis: some are very personal and should only be revealed to the subject, so I have not gone down that deep in these sample reads. They are intended as structured examples of the information potentially available to you when you do your own analysis. Also, with the exception of one example, these folks are alive and well, so I have not addressed their

Current Energy Phases for reasons also having to do with respect of privacy.

Having said that, the letters and numbers *do* have over-all meanings and in reading them, we can get a general idea of prevailing energies and other things.

Apolo Anton Ohno—Olympic Speedskater

Apolo Anton Ohno reflects the strength in his name by standing as one of the most powerful and decorated American Winter Olympians of all time. He has come a noticeably long way in a relatively short time: from a lost Olympic bid while still a young teenager, Apolo has gone on to win a total of 8 Olympic medals, and all before his 28th birthday.

However, it was not always smooth skating for Apolo. He had his share of ups and downs that were serious enough to perhaps have prompted anyone with less drive and determination to throw in the towel or unlace the skates, as the case may be.

Apolo began his speedskating career while still very young, and experienced considerable victories and setbacks along the way. At 14, Apolo became the youngest athlete ever to win the US Championships. After some weight and strength issues in 1997, he failed to make the US Junior World team, yet later that same year, went on to win both gold and silver medals at the US Senior Championships. The following year saw a disappointing last-place finish in his first bid for an Olympic spot at Nagano, but he then went on to win his second US Championship in 1999. In 2000, Apolo was unable to defend his title in the same competition, yet won his first World Cup overall title in 2001 while also regaining his National title.

Controversy has never strayed far from Apolo either. In 2001, while participating in the pre-Olympic trials for short-track skating, Apolo was involved in an International Olympic Committee (IOC) dispute that centered around a questionable skate (he and a friend were suspected of throwing a race in order to ensure a spot on the six-man team for yet another friend). After enduring a three-day arbitration hearing, both were cleared of any wrongdoing. But controversy continued, this time centering around the disqualification of a leading South Korean skater for "cross-tracking" (blocking Ohno's path), which then cleared the way for a gold medal finish for Apolo. More than 16,000 angry emails actually crashed the IOC's website and subsequent death threats kept Apolo from competing in the 2003 World Cup short-track race in Korea, but again, he persevered and successfully defended his title during that same year and again in 2005. In the years that followed, Apolo continued to race and win—and also to race and lose, but he never gave up. Along the way, he collected 8 Olympic medals, numerous National titles, and an induction to the Asian Hall of Fame (in recognition of his outstanding achievements and Japanese heritage); he guest-judged on *Project Runway*, and both entered and won the fourth season of *Dancing with the Stars* with his partner, Julianne Hough.

In contrast to this ambitious side of Apolo is the soft and compassionate one: he also takes the time to work with worthy and humanitarian causes. For example, he has worked with Product Red to help fight AIDS in Africa; the

Salvation Army to assist those less fortunate; and the Ronald McDonald House to help fund a home stay in Seattle, to mention but a few. Apolo is an interesting blend of drive and ambition and faith and spirituality.

The following is the visual of Apolo Anton Ohno's numbers.

A P O L O	A N T O N	O H N O
1 8 7 3 7	1 5 4 7 5	7 5 5 7
=26	=22	=24
=8	=22	=6

Sub #	Total Name #
72	
36	9

A P O L O	O H N O
1 8 7 3 7	7 5 5 7
=26	=24
=8	=6

Sub #	Daily name #
50	
14	5

MAY	22	Sub #	Lifepath #
5	22	27	9

Day: Master 22: The Builder

The connections in Apolo's name became apparent immediately and grew as I continued formulating his chart. The first and most obvious connection is to be found in his middle name and his day of birth: both show Master 22 energies, which can take the dreams and fantasies of the Master 11 and make them real and tangible in this Earth plane. The Master Builder (or Architect) has the fundamental power to create a rather large life—to amass and achieve and to, well, *build* his reality and surroundings and arrange their contents according to his desires. This super-charged energy is already making itself known. He *has* set an Olympic World record, so the balance of his life is akin to an open playing field (or ice arena, as it were).

The other main connector is to be found in his Total Name Number of 9. As you know, this complete read of any name indicates the Universal potential held within that name, and Apolo's gift vibrates exactly to his Number 9 Lifepath. Remember when I mentioned that the above connection is *ideally* what one wants to see and that the Total Name energy matching the Lifepath is quite auspicious? Here is a perfect example of this unification and proof of the power of aligned energies. Further, this 9 appears once more as the "sum of all he is," as represented by his Identity Initial Code of AAO (1+1+7 =9).

The following is what Apolo's energies look like when broken down into categories.

Whole Name Numbers
Social Energy
APOLO (A/1, P/8, O/7, L/3, O/7) = 26/8

Apolo's Cornerstone is the perfect expression of the pure and Original Force that the letter A and number 1 represent: both are "starter" energies, both are driven to succeed, and both pave the way for others to follow. The A/1 is the pioneer, the leader, the one who never gives up. In its positions as Cornerstones for both his Social energy and his

Inner Soul energy, the A/1 doubles in strength and potency. Apolo is a force to be reckoned with.

The energies that complete the essence of his social energy include the P/8, which means he will be direct and determined in his undertakings and committed to his goals, and that success will be drawn to him, especially materially. The key to its lasting power will be dictated by his spiritual development and his level of compassion.

Connected to this energy is the power and opportunity presented in the openness of the O/7. Since he has two of these energies in his social essence, this makes an incredibly strong statement about how far he can go and how much he can accomplish—if he is open to it. Squeezed between these impressive vibrations sits the loving L/3. This indicates that no matter how involved Apolo may become in projects, organizations, and sports, he will always make time for family, friends, community, and assisting or motivating others. The 3 energy shows that his life is filled with activity and that his mind is never still.

Apolo is a rare blend of assertiveness, control, determination, receptivity, and attentiveness. Three 7 symbols appear in his first name—one in the upside-down L—and this can produce an interest in the unusual, the mysterious, or the metaphysical... an interest that pops up again and will likely grow over time.

While he may suffer a few drawbacks and controversy along the way, chances are good that Apolo will stand up to opposition and achieve his goals, an ability he has already demonstrated.

His Whole Name Number of 8 within the social arena can mean that some may view him as too focused on achieving and not enough on just *being*. The sub number here is 26, which speaks to a need to connect and be connected to people, places, or things in a deep and devoted manner. What others may occasionally perceive as controlling behavior is actually based on genuine concern for the people, places, and things he loves. Apolo likes things to be in order, which is also a characteristic of the 8. Given enough time and experience, he carries the potential to reach that rare level of spiritual and material balance that is inherent to the fully developed 8.

Inner or Soul Energy
ANTON (A/1, N/5, T/4, O/7, N/5) = **22**
Master 22: The Builder
Apolo's Inner or Soul energy is *wired* to his Lifepath and states fairly succinctly that the desire and motivation to build something of lasting value is exactly matched by his potential to *do so* while he is on this Earth plane. Since he has accomplished much in his life thus far, I would say that these two Master Builder vibrations are incredibly accurate and hold tremendous promise for future undertakings. The 22 has the ability and talent to design its own life, but must take care not to "color outside the lines" or build castles on sand. Foundations must be afforded the same amount of attention as the building itself; it will only be as secure as its pilings. This 22 also carries the same warning regarding careful observance of moral and ethical boundaries connected to *successful* 22 energies.

The A/1 Cornerstone of Apolo's Inner Self holds the same drive and determination as his Social energy. (These two A/1 Cornerstones form a double whammy of originality, pioneering strength, tenaciousness, focused energy, and the natural inclination to keep going no matter what.) The conviction to achieve goals literally begins in his *soul.*

The energies that complete his Inner Soul include two N values, which fortunately soothe and calm the changes and eventfulness of their 5 values (despite the chaotic conflicts these outrageous number energies can cause) while the T and O just keep adding more thoughts, ideas, and options. The number 5 values emphasize the freedom that motivates Apolo—this is a base and core need that he will always have and in some odd way, always search for.

There is something else I must mention here and it concerns the double-2 values in the number 22. As oft-mentioned, double numbers have the potential to increase their energetic meanings or to create conflict in that particular area. In this case, the 2 theme in all of his subs and as a Master here can suggest difficulties in relationships; close, personal, and usually formative connections may hold challenging lessons. The Master vibration 22 has the power to *sup*press or *ex*press emotions, and they tend to *sup*press when they get the chance, which can lead to problems years later when foundations begin to crack. (I have noticed that major lessons are learned after the *second* run-through of name energies [unless the name is short], for the simple reason that we have been around a little longer and are a bit wiser by then by virtue of experience.)

Apolo's Inner Self is the nucleus of his actions and paths taken on a social level. There is a deep and abiding conviction that his "building" *will* be built, which gives him a deep and abiding sense of self—as such, he will likely come across as confident, cheerful, receptive, and outgoing. He will have a fantastic imagination and enthusiasm to spare. This is a soul energy that is loyal, responsible, methodical, and dedicated.

Domestic Energy
OHNO (O/7, H/5, N/5, O/7) = 24/**6**
As you already know, last names are not as important as the first two names but can influence the formation of character, ethics, and so on. The ideal number vibration to have in this position is Apolo's—his Domestic influence is the loving and nurturing number 6. This energy shows that there is a consistent and constant offer of support and caring, and a place to regroup when needed. The 6 is warm and safe and enduring; it is indeed the place of domestic bliss, which doesn't mean everything was always peaches and cream—rather, it means that home was and will continue to be safe for Apolo.

The Cornerstone here is the O/7. We have already said enough about this letter and number energy; the only thing I want to add here is that since this is a *domestic* influence, the opportunities would have originated from within the family structure itself, in particular, from the male essence of the family unit. This is a natural salutation to Apolo's father, Yuki.

The energies that make up the balance of the Ohno name are the H/5, N/5, and a final O/7. What is held in this essence is independent choice (H); freedom, artistic communication, sensory stimulation, changes and risk-taking (5); and the ongoing portals (O) or opportunities that seem to be awaiting Apolo.

Daily Name Number

APOLO OHNO (8+6) = 14/5

First sub numbers: 26+24 = 50

Apolo's Daily Name is composed of the sub numbers 50 and 14 and total to 5. The sub number of 50 indicates that changes, freedom (personal and financial), communication, sensory input, and stimulation are important elements to him. The one thing that pops out here is the potential for fame—the 5 stands for this alone, but when the intensifier of the cipher is added, this potential becomes even more likely. Looking at his second (and most important) sub number calls to mind breaking ground, as the 14 reads as "force through foundations", but 14 can also carry difficult frequencies within its structure, as this same force can apply to foundations such as family, job, health, and other basic aspects of life. Suffice it to say that Apolo Ohno as a Daily Name holds many changes that involve originality, determination, and pioneering breakthroughs as well as the sometimes chaotic changes and ongoing searches for sensory stimulation that the number 5 heralds. These ongoing changes are part and parcel of Apolo's path and will assist him in getting where he wishes to be; the freedom-seeking 5 does not usually settle for a run-of-the-mill existence, and his life will entail a theme of changes, so anyone who contemplates hitching up to Apolo's wagon had best understand and accept this before doing so.

Total Name Number
APOLO ANTON OHNO (8+22+6) = 36/**9**

First sub numbers: 26+22+24 = 72

Apolo's Total Name Number is 9: Beginnings and Endings. What this means is that Universe gave him a heavy load to carry when he arrived—some emotional baggage may have accompanied him and manifested in the early years of his life. The 9 is the highest on the evolutionary scale before graduating to the Masters (a potential already present in the Master 22), holds all of the lessons to be found in the previous grades 1 through 8 and provides the toughest subjects and homework.

Number 9 is the artist, the empath, the spiritualist. It moves through life gathering different experiences, passing through circumstances, and joining and releasing friendships and other connections. This is a "moving on" kind of energy as its nature is to seek out more knowledge and more experience. There is a spiritual element here that is different in tone than the balance of the other energies in Apolo's read—it suggests to me (again) that there may be a curiosity about the hidden side of life, which must be investigated if he is to realize the entire spectrum of the 9 essence. As mentioned previously, when there is a match between the Total Name energy (or the complete picture of one's potential) *and* the Lifepath number, well, all I can say is that Apolo has the proverbial world by the tail. It is up to him what he does with it.

Lifepath Number

May (5) + 22 = 27/**9**

Day: **22 Master Builder**

Apolo's Lifepath number 9 shows that beneath the outer composure lies a soft, sensitive, and aware person. He may need to come to terms with an element of the past that involves immediate family and understand that all was as it should have been. He is destined to be a leader of some type: perhaps within his natural habitat of the worlds of art and vision and performance. While his head can *appear* to be in the clouds, his heart will always be in the right place and somehow, his feet will always be on the ground.

Born on May 22, Apolo's Lifepath sub number is 27 (an interesting "mirror" of the sub for his Total Name Number) which was also his age when he won his 8th Olympic and record-breaking medal at the 2010 Games in Vancouver, British Columbia.

His sub number of 27 is interesting in that it shows the softer side of Apolo: the number 2 (which is oft repeated in his subs) represents friendliness, approachability, concern, kindness, and compassion. This is a nurturing essence, one who places considerable importance upon loyal friendships. Connections of 2 will likely permeate his work and personal life. The presence of the 2 indicates that heartfelt connections are as important as "reaching the goal." The connected 7 points once more to the brain and its functions—logic and mystery are its primary interests. This 27 also holds the potential of units of 2 working together, using the functions of the brain to create something unique and memorable. This is something he has likely not yet fully realized because of his age.

Lifepath Day

Born on the 22nd of May makes Apolo's specific entry energy 22—the Master Builder, which is identical to the energy vibration gifted to him by Universe on a Soul or Inner level. This kind of match, as I have already said, is ideal and fairly rare, and in this case, presents tremendous potential for success and material/spiritual gain because it springs from his Inner self and is propelled by a core desire or need. This gives Apolo extra intensity when it comes to creating, chasing, and actualizing his dreams. There is, however, a warning attached to this Master Number that calls for careful awareness of ethical and moral guidelines, which must be observed lest all that is built comes tumbling down. This message is doubled in his Inner Soul energy.

Highest Letter and Number Count

The highest volume of letter energies in Apolo's chart is the O—he has 5 of these in his complete name. To say that so many O values in one name is unusual would be an understatement. This offers Apolo so many opportunities and doors to choose from that someone less focused may well be overcome by the voltage held therein. Once again, it would appear that the world is his Oyster … providing he commits to finding his pearl.

The highest volume of a number energy in Apolo's chart is 7, which predictably connects back to the O values. Since 7 rules the brain, thoughts, plots, ideas, research, and anything else can make its home there. Apolo is sure to think things through very carefully before taking action. This would translate into someone who is highly intellectual and rational; however, the flip side of the 7 calls to the perhaps less scientific and controlled side of thought patterns. This call involves using his intellect to investigate the more mysterious side of life—a connection that keeps showing up.

Identity Initial Code

AAO (A/1, A/1, O/7) = **9**

This set of initials displays the sheer drive of the first letter in the alphabet and the first number in the scale and brings to mind the speed and power and force of direction that Apolo's chosen sport epitomizes. The A is the winner—the champion, the striver, and the one in motion—and two A charges in a row intensifies this force. However, here we also have an example of double energies (the two 1 values form a sub 11) and because of the possibilities of conflict of force, Apolo may occasionally fall down or crash or go off the rails and into the ditch, so to speak. These double A/1 values can create problems, setbacks, and misdirections along the way, especially if Apolo becomes distracted by the temptations of sensory stimulation that can be found throughout his name energies (5). The saving grace of this unit comes in the form of the O/7, which can be read as his destination: Open to all. The meaning of the O is almost unlimited; Apolo can look forward to opportunities that are "Olympic" in nature and, unlike the Games, hold no distinct parameters or time limits, other than those nature imposes.

The total of his initial code is 9 (which ties to his Total Name Number and his Lifepath number) and is illustrative of the theme "beginnings and endings" and also of deeply ingrained sensitivity, compassion, artistic talent (dancing, for instance), intuition, and spiritual awareness.

Words within Names

The most obvious connection here is the presence of the Greek God's name (although it is spelled slightly differently; the double L values reflect the difficult love life of the mythical god Apollo) and also of Mount Olympus, the home of the Pythias Games. Those games are considered the forerunner to the modern Olympics and were, according to legend, created in honor of the god Apollo after he slew the giant Python at Delphi with his bow and arrows.

This energy vibration suggests skill and swiftness and is certainly applicable to Apolo's social energies.

A rather humorous link exists in his middle name as well. Remember I mentioned all of the activity that goes on within Apolo's brain and Inner Self? Well, the "Ant" is often noted as being one of the most industrious and organized creatures in the world—again, this energy matches the activity and construction held in his Soul energy.

And last but not least: "Oh, No!" This is a phrase most likely uttered when events like crashes into boards, disqualifications, and less-than-stellar performances occur—and most likely by his dad. Speaking of his dad, Yuki supposedly named his son based on Greek translations of "steering away from" and "look out—here he comes!" How absolutely true that application of energy became ... it all but encapsulates the image of a speedskater.

Connecting Numbers

Since I do not have access to Apolo's private number assignments, I can only comment on the 8 Olympic medals he has won and the name of his new line of health products, *8Zone*. I would be remiss if I did not also add that it has been reported that he considers 8 to be his lucky number.

I wonder if he already knew that his Social energy vibration is an 8?

Leonardo da Vinci— Artist, Inventor, Scientist: The Renaissance Man

This famous artist (the *Mona Lisa* and *The Last Supper* to name but a few of his contributions to the world of painting) was much more than a painter—he was a multi-talented and multi-layered gentleman whose interests ranged from dissecting and "mapping" the interiors of cadavers to the more sublime study of the movements, currents, and properties of water (which he also "mapped" in his treatise "Codex Leicester," currently owned by Bill Gates). Leonardo was also an accomplished sculptor, draftsman, illustrator, architect, musician, scientist, and engineer whose desire for knowledge combined art with science, and produced wondrous results, all of which he attributed to "knowing how to see."

Leonardo began his apprenticeship while still young and learned all about making canvas and brushes; grinding and mixing paints; carving in wood, clay, and stone; and casting in metal, silver, and gold.

After his apprenticeship, Leonardo went on to create his own history, which is still regarded with tremendous respect hundreds of years later.

The interior workings of things fascinated Leonardo— the investigation of those cadavers I just mentioned were done to expose the body's functions and were based on curiosity and a genuine desire to *know*, rather than morbidity. The exact same level of care and attention were applied by Leonardo, whether creating intricate machinery or calculating the mathematical angles inherent in the creation of three-dimensional images on canvas.

His was an interesting, informative, and unique life, to be sure, but Leonardo also faced setbacks and disappointments: at least two of his major paintings remained unfinished because of suspected difficulties in the quality of the paints (since the restoration of *The Last Supper,* it is an acknowledged fact that very little of the original paint remains intact), including a commissioned piece for the Council Hall in Florence (1503) called *Battle of Anghiari* (which was to have greatly surpassed the size of *The Last Supper*) and another called *Ledo,* the sister painting, some say, to the *Mona Lisa.*

Another likely crushing disappointment had its beginnings with a commissioning from the Sforza dynasty around 1482: a gigantic horse was to be rendered and then cast in bronze. Leonardo spent approximately twelve *years* designing and molding the massive sculpture. It was eventually ready to be encased in bronze and would have been the largest sculpture of its kind at the time—a historic moment—when the threat of war intervened. Instead of the bronze being assigned as the crowning glory of Leonardo's magnificent sculpture, it was instead used to fill cannon molds. The project was aborted and the war reduced the majestic clay horse to a pile of rubble. How painful that must have been for him.

Although Leonardo created thousands of pages of text and illustrations, none were ever published; consequently, the natural assumption was that Leonardo did not care one way or the other about publishing his works. However, marked in the margin of one of his last anatomy drawings is a notation regarding exactly that—an expressed desire for his works to be published. His devoted student, Melzi, *did* publish abridged versions of some of da Vinci's work, but only after his death. This was perhaps another dream or desire he never realized.

So, here is a number 1 force who had to face challenges and new beginnings time and again—but who never gave up.

In true keeping with his double 7 values (see below), Leonardo was almost two-sided: he even wrote backwards ("mirror" writing, with his left hand); this duality was evidenced in many different ways. As an example, Leonardo loved beauty, art, and animals in all their forms and *despised* war, yet he also designed and invented intricate weapons specifically intended for *use during war*.

Further indication of Leonardo's philosophical understandings of the worlds of science and the spiritual are echoed in his own words about his conceptions of forms, objects, and particular uses of anything within the realm of Universe as being dictated through "physical and *spiritual* motion." It is almost as though he viewed everything from an objective point of view that just naturally incorporated the logical and the spiritual.

Perhaps the most telling statement on record regarding his view on painting (and likely his view of overall reality) is to be found in the following quotation:

The mind of the painter is transformed into a copy of the divine mind, since it operates freely in creating many kinds of animals, plants, fruits, landscapes, countrysides, ruins, and awe-inspiring places.
—Leonardo da Vinci (1452–1519)

This run through of his name essences will not go into quite as much detail as Apolo's—I just find Leonardo's numbers to be quite reflective of the man, his interests, his contributions, his art, and the impressive legacy he left behind—a primary goal of the number 1.

L E O N A R D O	D A	V I N C I
3 5 7 5 1 2 4 7	4 1	6 1 5 3 1
=34	=5	=16
=7	=5	=7

Sub #	Total Name #
55	
19/10	1

April	15	Sub #	Lifepath #
4	6	10	1

Once again, we are looking at a Total Name Number energy that matches the Lifepath Number energy. Energies like this are rarely held down; the Universe supports their endeavors in ways that are out of the ordinary, noticeable, and lasting. Considering this main energy is the Original Force of the number 1, this person who was Leonardo da Vinci had *something,* or a series of somethings, to do, be, or create, and he did so with admirable determination and over a vast domain and a period of many years. His life consisted of starts and stops and beginnings and endings

(19), yet he was a force unto himself; everywhere he went or anything he did always left a legacy, one way or the other. Because of the strong influence of the 10, his was also a life that was destined to leave a mark, an imprint upon man in some way, big or smal—which he did.

Something worthy of mention is his first sub number: the Master 55 or the Master Genius, because he *was* a Master Genius in so many ways—even today, many of his illustrated mechanical "blueprints" and ancient devices can be copied and built, and they work just fine. Indeed, many of the items and products we consider relatively commonplace today actually began in Leonardo's head and were first birthed under his pen. Found among his papers were sketches of (the first) motorcars, bicycles, (3-shot) machine guns, parachutes, tanks, and swinging bridges.

Whole Name Numbers
Social Energy

LEONARDO (L/3, E/5, O/7, N/5, A/1, R/2, D/4, O/7) = 34/**7**
Leonardo's Cornerstone energy is the L/3, which means he experienced the love of something at an early age; this love could have come in any form and we do know from his history that it took the form of art and design. The numeric value of 3 lends the force of activity to both the brain and the body—Leonardo was likely always thinking about creation, even as a youngster. His curiosity about the things around him was probably intense and may have left him in a world of his own—others may not have been able to follow his endless changes in focus and shifts in attention.

The balance of the energies in Leonardo's name begins with the sheer energy of the E/5, which simply exaggerated the love of his chosen topic(s), and such intensity could have easily become obsessive (this can manifest in relationships as well, but history shows that this was not Leonardo's focus). The L is a forward-reaching and helping energy; it wants to "make better" and even heal. It was from this place that Leonardo observed the life around him—seeking its secrets by using his senses and learning how to translate or communicate what he saw, and the O/7 allowed him to see things from an entirely unique perspective (this energy phase would have been highlighted before and around age 15—the same time frame during which he began his art apprenticeship). The N/5 that follows would have introduced a variety of interests and fascinating sensory stimulations that would have been, fortunately, influenced by the calming nature of the N— many subjects would be introduced and all would have been given logical and impartial assessment—until the A phase kicked in. This "fresh start" offered Leonardo the experience and knowledge to begin his own career—he would have a direction upon which to focus (painting) thanks to the presence of the A/1. Unfortunately, the R/2 does indicate disappointments along the way, as already touched on, and also can indicate difficulties in intimate or loving relationships; Leonardo never married, nor is there mention of a significant other in his life. The follow-up D/4 points to doors opening and closing: relationships that are short, if at all, and projects ending before they were begun. It is said that Leonardo became quite disillusioned towards the end of his life (perhaps due to the emergence of younger, talented artists) but the final O/7 of his social energy speaks to the considerable legacy of knowledge and subjects of study he left to us.

Leonardo's Whole Name Number is 7 and perfectly epitomizes his incredibly intelligent mindset, his logical thought processes, and his scientific outlooks. It also encompasses his spiritual side—this man looked at things from all sides and used both logical and spiritual angles when drawing, sculpting, or undertaking any expression of the thoughts and images in his brain.

It is likely that Leonardo was not readily understood by others. While they may have been impressed with his intellect and creativity, chances are good that he kept to himself and did not place too much value on the political side of social interactions. He may not have had much of an interest in socializing for its entertainment or social-status values, although he certainly did have ongoing and loyal relationships with both mentors and students. The descriptions of reserved, dignified, and well-respected most likely applied to this Italian Renaissance man quite nicely.

His Social sub number of 34 is a raw expression of the force of activity (3), which has the ability to "run through" or "destroy in order to rebuild" the foundations of the 4. This energy is one that can (and did) introduce new concepts, ideas, and practical applications that changed the conceptualizations and directions of mankind.

Inner or Soul Energy

Note: This is not actually his middle name; translated, this Italian word means "from," and here it refers to where Leonardo lived—but it is part of his name energy and so must be looked at in analysis.

DA (D/4, A/1) = 5

The placement of the Door as Leonardo's Inner Self is very appropriate here: the D/4 offers new vistas, concepts, inventions, and ways of relating to the other side of our normal perceptions, and the A/1 energy that follows applies solid force to projects found on the other side of the (opened) door and the determination to understand and master them.

The Whole Name Number of da totals to a 5, which underscores the two already found in his social nature. The Inner self of Leonardo da Vinci was likely filled with changing thoughts, sense impressions, and the desire to attain the "ultimate" in freedom through Universal truths and visions—images that were forever changing shape and content.

The inner soul of Leonardo was seeking and knocking; he likely did not think of himself in an overly personal way—as in *my* needs and wants. His sense of self was larger than most and was centered in his surroundings and what he could find there.

Domestic Energy
Note: Once again, this is not Leonardo's birth name—it refers to the place he lived; however, its energies still apply.
VINCI (V/6, I/1, N/5, C/3, I/1) = 16/7
The Cornerstone of V/6 seeks victory and unity: it lifts up to the heavens, and its essence is loving and warm. Leonardo sought this kind of victory—the kind that opened all doors and allowed access to the perfection of the Universe. This is not to say that he attained it, merely that he never stopped reaching for it. One other significant meaning connected to the V is the search for the perfect mate—something da Vinci likely found in his love for science and art rather than in a particular person.

The balance of this name energy includes two I factors: here is the power of the intuition in full bloom. The connection between "out there" and "down here" is emphasized and, to Leonardo, this must have been an accepted part of his psyche, as the N/5 is once again present to offer calm in all undertakings. The C/3 calls for communication of all that is seen, perceived, intuited, and sensed, through whichever medium available, and the final I value at the end of the name energy ties back to the final O in Leonardo—the aim does not falter, the goal remains the same—to access and express all that lies within the human and the Divine brain.

Again, the Whole Name Number is a 7—more of the same energy that is held in his social energy. It all goes back to the brain, time and again—and that is where Leonardo lived, in his brain.

The sub number is 16, an energy that is motivated or pushed (1) through love or emotion (6). In this case, it would read as a positive force in search of positive energies, perhaps at the expense of intimate and domestic love such as that found between husband and wife.

Total Name Number
LEONARDO DA VINCI (7+5+7) = 19/10/**1**
First sub number (34+5+16) = **55 Master Genius**
It seems so very fitting that this Renaissance Man's gift from Universe came in the form of the breakthrough vibration of the numbers 19/10, 55/10, and 1. Certainly original, inventive, curious, and a force unto himself, Leonardo as a name energy embodies the diversity and electrical charge

that drives this number's Lifepath, which is to seek, comprehend, achieve, and create.

The 19 reads as one of the more forceful and barrier-breaking vibrations known; it is the combination of the beginner, the starter, the one who knocks on doors and is not held back by fear. The 9 indicates the various stages and projects explored and investigated; therefore, these two thrusting and cyclical energies come together to create new starts, pioneering developments, and insatiable curiosity, which is present in both the 10 and the 1 energies.

Leonardo was a force unto himself and to mankind as well, and may have been almost heaven-sent (or a gift from Universe?) in a way: his very essence, which is reflected in his Total Name Number and its subs is an exact match to his Lifepath and its subs. Because of the nature of the number involved, Leonardo da Vinci was simply power supreme when it came to forging the way.

Lifepath Number

April (04) + 15 = 19/10/**1**

Here again is the main connector between the Total Name Number and the Lifepath Number. When these two vibrations are on the same wavelength, anything is possible. Leonardo da Vinci is a prime example of what can happen when dynamic and identical energies merge. He also illustrates the truth of a numeric rule of thumb: number 10 energies tend to leave something behind that is of considerable value to mankind or even just to a select few.

His Day of Birth number 6 suggests that he was a loving soul who seemed to be undergoing constant shifts in his life. To me, it feels like his was a focused search for love, but not in a physical way—more in a spiritual or altruistic way.

Highest Letter and Number Count

Leonardo was interested in almost anything, and the energies in his name reflect a broad coverage in range as well. Five of his letter energies repeat themselves while each of the others counts as one each. The doubled energies of the A, D, I, N, and O comment on his unending curiosity, his seeking of knowledge, his intuitive connection, his calm nature, and his thirst for new and fresh options, information, and projects.

The highest number count goes to the 1, 5, and 7, which are also the exact numbers assigned to his Total Name, his Inner and his Social energies, respectively. These numbers speak to an original freedom seeker whose search involved the untried and unusual.

Identity Initial Code

LDV (3+4+6) = **13/4**

Leonardo's Identity Initials are LDV (3+4+6) and total to 13/4. The number 13 suggests unusual forces at play. Sometimes it has to do with karma, and other times it can indicate unusual and even mysterious forces. Remember the number 13 is a force of activity that is beyond powerful and that its electrical forces can produce fundamental changes for good and for ill—the 13 is *that* potent. In this event, Leonardo's force of activity produced fundamental and lasting changes in the development and direction of humanity. A grandiose statement, but one that seems applicable here … which is a nice way to conclude my look at Leonardo's energies.

Leonard DiCaprio—
Producer/Actor and Environmentalist

Many years ago, a young expectant mother wandered through the Uffizi Gallery in Florence, Italy, marveling at the shadows and subtle depths in the art of Leonardo da Vinci. As she studied and wondered, the child in her womb reportedly delivered a kick worthy of an award. Perhaps this was a prediction of some sort, considering what her child went on to do with his life.

Apparently she didn't forget that kick, either, for when the child came, she named him after the Master painter she had been studying at the time of this memorable kick. However, baby Leonardo's path, though similar in many ways to the painter's, would take him down very different roads—the first of which began in a drug-infested and environmentally polluted area of Los Angeles known as Echo Park, where life as a kid, to put it mildly, could be rather challenging. Leonardo even credited living in a neighborhood that overflowed with drug addicts and prostitutes with helping him form aversions to drugs and for highlighting and ingraining the realization that we as a people needed to become more aware of the damage we were doing to our Earth and her environment: his neighborhood was a smaller version of the bigger picture.

Although his parents separated shortly after he was born, they were both active in his life and encouraged him to pursue his interests, one of which became acting or performing. In fact, Leonardo's first gig was on television's *Romper Room* at the age of five. He was obviously enthusiastic about performing, for he went on to make plenty of commercials and several educational shorts throughout his teens.

Leonardo kept auditioning until winning the lead in a low-budget, straight-to-video horror film called *Critters 3*, which served as a springboard into landing a recurring role on the struggling sitcom *Growing Pains*, which succumbed to its slumping ratings the following season. But Leonardo's reel was growing and that earned him an audition for *This Boy's Life*, a true story based on the memoirs of Tobias Woolf and his abusive stepfather, played by Robert De Niro. Leonardo won the part over hundreds of other young hopefuls and, with the release of the film in 1993, he proved beyond a doubt that he was a seriously talented actor... and one to watch.

This was only the first in a series of roles that involved complex, confused, and conflicted characters. The kicker was and continues to be that the majority are centered more on *true stories* than on fictional ones, and the fictional ones are undoubtedly real somewhere in the world.

In 1993's *What's Eating Gilbert Grape*, Leonardo portrayed a mentally handicapped teenager with such conviction that he earned a nod from the Academy Awards as Best Supporting Actor. Two years later, he took on *Total Eclipse*, the true story of Arthur Rimbaud, a poet whose tortured life centered around his sexual preferences. Yet another character based in truth came to life on screen during that same time frame: *The Basketball Diaries* grew from the journals of Jim Caroll, a young basketball player who seemed destined for NBA success but who became addicted to drugs instead. Then came a role as a stylishly seductive gunslinger in the 1995 movie *The Quick and the*

Dead, which offered yet another glimpse into the many faces of Leonardo the actor. His chosen roles were, to say the least, diversified and challenging, and with his shift in direction as Romeo in a modernized version of William Shakespeare's *Romeo and Juliet* in 1996, Leonardo became a sexy and convincing romantic leading man as well. His credentials grew, as did his fame; he seemed well on his way to success.

Then, in 1997, a gigantic steam ship named the *Titanic* plowed into Leonardo's life and changed it forever. This time, his role was more traditional, as in a "boy meets girl, girl loses boy" kind of way, and for a while, Leonardo was literally on top of the world, and on the top at the box office. *Titanic* became the highest-grossing movie ever made at that time and currently sits second only to *Avatar* (2009).

A string of unremarkable "how the heck do we match *that*" films followed until 2002, when Leonardo delivered a remarkable portrayal of a real-life con artist in *Catch Me If You Can.* Once again, Leonardo landed at the top of the A-list, a position he cemented two years later by winning a Golden Globe award for his role as Howard Hughes in *The Aviator.*

Leonardo's lifelong passion for environmental aware-ness, education, and protection began to take firm physical form as well. After narrating two films about environmen-tal issues, he followed up by co-writing, co-producing, and narrating *The 11th Hour,* a full-length film that explores how human kind is negatively affecting the health and equilibrium of our planet. This film was previewed at the 2007 Cannes Film Festival and won favorable reviews. In March 2008, *The 11th Hour* was honored with the 22nd

Annual Earthwatch Film Award. Leonardo has further demonstrated his commitment to this cause by serving on the boards of the Natural Resources Defense Council and Global Green USA and by forming websites that foster awareness of the true circumstances of our environment and its direction if change is not implemented and sustained soon. More recently, the World Wildlife Fund joined with Leonardo in a campaign called "Save Tigers Now," which is specifically aimed at saving a small tiger family that stands on the edge of extinction, which, to me, offers a peek at his love for animals as well.

Leonardo is a thoughtful, pragmatic, reserved, talented, and focused man who has remained true to his lifelong interests in acting and in the environment and has transformed them into things that we can see and relate to as genuine. He has turned his childhood dreams into his reality. The one thing that really stands out for me is that Leonardo is *substantial.* He seems to prefer portraying *real* people with real challenges and real stories, yet his career is all about creating an effective illusion. This is the perfect illustration of the developed 7: the world of the intellect is tapped into just as deeply as the world of the imagination.

Leonardo DiCaprio is also the ideal example of the Master 22 energy at work: he has built a strong foundation from which to act, so to speak. This is a man with yet much to accomplish—things that have little or nothing to do with acting. This is a man to watch, for he is building his life into one worthy of note, which is exactly what his Lifepath number forecasts.

Here is a visual look at Leonardo's energies.

L E O N A R D O	W I L H E L M	D I C A P R I O
3 5 7 5 1 2 4 7	6 1 3 5 5 3 4	4 1 3 1 8 2 1 7
=34	=27	=27
=7	=9	=9

Sub #	Total Name #
88	
25	7

L E O N A R D O	D I C A P R I O
3 5 7 5 1 2 4 7	4 1 3 1 8 2 1 7
=34	=27
=7	=9

Sub #	Daily Name #
61	
16	7

November	11	Sub #	Lifepath #
11		11 22	22

Month and Day are both:

Master 11: The Intuitive Imager

Lifepath: **Master 22: The Builder**

Whole Name Numbers
Social Energy

LEONARDO (L/3, E/5, O/7, N/5, A/1, R/2, D/4, O/7) = 34/7

Have you ever wondered how two identical name energies might compare to one another? There will be many similarities between the two Leonardos, however, the true distinctions in personalities will become evident as we look at DiCaprio's additional names, totals, and Lifepath energies.

That said, here comes Leonardo DiCaprio's Social signature, and don't be surprised if it sounds familiar. Quite familiar, in fact—but the difference lies in the details.

Leonardo's Cornerstone energy is the L/3, which means, like the other Leonardo, that he knew early in life where his interests lay, and in his case, it was in the direction of performing and also in protecting the environment. The numeric value of 3 lends the force of extra activity to both his brain and his body; Leonardo was likely always thinking about creating or creation, even as a youngster. His active curiosity about the things around him was likely intense and may have been part of the reason he was politely kicked out of *Romper Room* at age five.

Both as a child and as an adult, Leonardo has always been influenced by the Cornerstone of the L/3. His instinct to be involved and active and to motivate or assist in any way will always be a strong part of his personality. Others will find him quite helpful, friendly, and open without being too aggressive or too personal. A deep part of the L/3 is not visible to outsiders, nor does it wish to invade the privacy of others.

The balance of vibrations in his name continues with the sheer energy of the E/5, which adds an extra boost to anything (or anyone) that he likes (L) and can lead him to make connections based on impulse or the desire to help. The L is notorious for helping the right people for the wrong reasons and the wrong people for the right reasons, which can understandably lead to crossed wires and, sometimes, hurt feelings. By the same token, this LE combination can give LEnding a hand a whole new meaning. Similar to da Vinci, Leonardo relies on his senses when learning how to translate or communicate what he sees or feels (5), and the O/7 allows him to see things and express himself from an entirely unique perspective (this original energy phase would have peaked around age 14, which would tie in with the time he began to be taken seriously in the world of performing—and it is also around that time that he landed his first agent). The N/5 that follows introduces a variety of possibilities and exploration of emotional and sensory stimulations that are, fortunately, influenced by the calming nature of the N; many directions are possible and all are always fully investigated and given careful and logical consideration and assessment before any commitment is made. The placement of the A/1 energy indicates that certain projects or plans can affect the direction of Leonardo's life. The first time this energy kicked in was when he was 21—the year of the *Titanic*. The A/1 energy allowed him to "pull ahead" of the masses—in this case, using a ship rather than more traditional methods of transportation.

However, the follow-up R/2 phase does indicate disappointments along the way, particularly in the relationship department, and the D/4 doesn't help matters.

Like da Vinci, Leonardo does not seem anxious to marry (by his own admission), and the RD energy might go a long way in explaining why and might have something to do with being slightly disillusioned. And again, like Da Vinci, the final O/7 of Leonardo's social energy speaks to the considerable legacy he is building and the opportunities that still lie ahead; it is almost as though there are more important things on Leonardo's mind than marriage and its parameters.

Leonardo's sub number is 34—a steamroller kind of energy that can kick the legs out from under a chair and find a new way to build it that makes more sense. This is the same kind of energy as our first Leonardo and holds the same raw expression of the force of activity (3) driving straight through firm foundations (4). This energy is one that can introduce new concepts, ideas, and practical applications (7)—ones that can alter the direction of mankind or their behaviors and practices. Same message, different Leonardo.

Leonardo's Social Whole Name Number is a 7 (as are both his Total and Daily Name Numbers), and strongly suggests someone who is intellectually developed and who looks primarily to logical thought processes when considering various actions and reactions. But it also encompasses his spiritual side: in order to bring his complex characters to life, Leonardo would have had to access a deeply emotional and spiritual well—something he has already proven to be quite adept at doing—but on a social level, it would appear that this is one well he keeps closed, or at least well guarded, unless he is with trusted friends. Then the lid might come off.

Inner Energy
WILHELM (W/6, I/1, L/3, H/5, E/5, L/3, M/4) = 27/**9**
While Leonardo DiCaprio, like most others, is not generally known by his middle name, it does give indications about his inner workings and essences. Here is a quick look at those energies.

The Cornerstone of W/6 speaks to riding the waves and the ups and downs of life while maintaining a stoic and even temperament, but it also shows the deep desire for closeness, as the 6 refers to love in all its forms. This energy indicates that Leonardo will likely have a solid circle of friends and intimates, most of whom will be lifelong or long-term connections.

The remaining energies that combine to form his Inner or Soul desires can be read as follows: the I of the intuition says that he reacts to those ups and downs by following his gut reactions and tries to appreciate the highs and lows of the roller coaster for what they are—part and parcel of life and lessons to be learnedL although the combination of L, H, E (double 5 values), and L can present a few interesting situations that might even set off a firework or two. (Notice the anagram within those letters?)

Looked at from an Inner, or emotionally-based point of view, the L/3 is, among other things, very connected to friendship, love, assisting, and moving forward, and since there are two in this letter run, these qualities are emphasized. When the first L leads to the H, it faces a choice: positive or negative (up or down), and because the L is usually a positive energy, it would tend to go with the flow, meaning Leonardo would be open and willing to engage emotionally. Once the connection is made, the E is encountered. This dynamo throws excitement, risk, challenge, change, and stimulation of the senses into the picture. The more contrary double 5 vibrations of the HE will introduce an element of conflict into any relationship, as its chief meaning is one of independence. Hence, loving and caring emotions may indeed be engaged, but whether Leonardo wants to *become* engaged may be another matter entirely.

There is an indecision of sorts within this name energy: part of it *wants* to climb that ladder, and the other part most definitely does not. The freedom of the 5 plays a key role—this is not an energy that performs well when tied down or hindered in any way, yet the Cornerstone of Leonardo's Inner Soul energy seems to contradict this in that it holds domesticity as important and even necessary to inner satisfaction. As a concluding energy, the M/4 pictures someone who might prefer to remain on the emotional sidelines; helping out when necessary, but ultimately more comfortable keeping his emotions under wraps. I will just say this: it is likely that Leonardo's affections have been both up the ladder to Heaven and down the ladder to Hell.

The Whole Name number for Wilhelm is 9 and signifies the theme of beginnings and endings. It reflects all of the soul experiences Leonardo has had and will have and points to a time when he will be ready to end something significant and begin something equally significant: the 9 is all about learning to understand that life itself is composed of a series of beginnings and endings that are designed to create and sustain the development of a truly good person. Once this threshold is reached, a certain freedom results. Leonardo is still a young man with plenty of room to grow; being the best he can be will take on many shapes and forms, and those will be up to him.

The sub number for this name energy is 27, which shows an ongoing connection of pairs—whether they be people, places, or things—that are attached to the investigation of thoughts or anything sourcing back to the operations of the brain, logical or otherwise. Leonardo is not what I would normally call overly impulsive, but he is someone I would normally call logical. Hence, deep thought will be assigned prior to any important decisions. This number shows that Leonardo's peak performances will come through connections with others (2), and that an element of intellectual illusion and mystery (7) is also present. There is something here I have seen before, and it relates to two elements (or groups of pairs) coming together to produce something of note. This could easily be read as a joining of minds whose focus is on the bigger picture in which logic, science, and spirituality are combined. I am not sure exactly how this will manifest in Leonardo's life, but it will definitely be something of note and perhaps of consequence that reaches far beyond the parameters of his own life.

Domestic Energy
DICAPRIO (D/4, I/1, C/3, A/1, P/8, R/2, I/1, 0/7) = 27/**9**
And here we have yet another unusual energy aspect: Leonardo's Domestic energy is an exact match to his Inner or Soul energy. While not normally viewed as overly important in analysis because of the connection to the male hierarchy of the family unit, this match does indicate an influence that steadfastly supported Leonardo's goals and interests. His domestic energy is like a mirror of sorts that is connected to his sense of identity. However, the essence of beginnings and endings also lends a continuous theme of separation from the family unit—and it is known that although his parents did divorce while Leonardo was still young, they also continued to play active parts in raising him and in honoring his desires and predispositions.

The Cornerstone for this domestic name is the D/4, an energy that presents choices in terms of which direction to pursue and which door to raise a fist to. This is a firm and grounded vibration (by virtue of the 4) that can be as stubborn as it is loyal.

The letter energy that follows the D suggests that when opportunity knocked, the door was answered rather than ignored, and revealed a land of imagination, esoteric knowledge, and illusion in which the intuition played a key role (I/1: this energy is confirmed and strengthened by later repetition). This world of the imagination in turn reaches the C/3, which almost demands communication through its "open mouth": any form of entertainment falls under its domain, but focus is required in order to bring this entertainment to life—that is supplied by the A/1, and the potential for success and power is on offer via the P/8.

Unfortunately, the R/2 also shows trials and tribulations in close relationships, which can manifest in intimate or family realms, especially during formative years; this is when later adult patterns are set. The saving grace of this name energy is to be found in the second I/1 and in the O/7: these two energies are intuitive, progressive, open-minded, incredibly smart, discriminating, and objective.

The Whole Name energy for DiCaprio is another 27/9, which shows an advanced energy at work within this unit despite the theme of starts and stops, or separations. It almost reads as a blueprint that was drawn out once, then attempted again at a later point in time.

Leonardo succeeded based on the general blueprint laid down by his domestic name.

Daily Name Number
LEONARDO DICAPRIO (7+9) =16/**7**
First sub numbers: (34+27) = 61

Total Name Number
LEONARDO WILHELM DICAPRIO (7+9+9) = 25/**7**
First sub numbers: (34+27+27) = **88 Master Success** (16/7)
The reason I have listed these two calculations together is because they both total to the same number energy. The 7 is magickal in its applications. It can bring very good luck and very bad luck. In Leonardo's case, its influence is positive, and with the supportive sub number of 88, the sky's the limit.

Either way you slice it, Leonardo DiCaprio is a 7 energy—a very close link to our first Leonardo, whose Social and Domestic energies are also 7. What this means is that the gifts Universe gave DiCaprio when he arrived are being perfectly pursued in his daily life. He is following his path rather faithfully.

The 7 is ruled by the brain and is very articulate, intellectual, reserved, and dignified. Those who fall under its influence are often not truly known by others and are very private in general. The 7 has an exceptionally vulnerable interior that it works very hard at hiding or sometimes manages to suppress altogether. So, despite an outer appearance that may seem a little distant, Leonardo is actually very sensitive and compassionate. He is also, in many ways, very much like his namesake.

The sub numbers here are reversals of one another: his Total Name sub number shows as 16 while his Daily Name sub number (the one more commonly used) shows as 61.

What this means is that the same vibrations are present in each; however, his Universal gift shows the *force of love, the ability to break through emotional walls* (16), while his work on the Earth plane shows the *love from which a new force flows* (61).

Lifepath Number
November (11) + 11: **22 Master Builder**
Day: **11 Master Intuitive**

Once again, the Master Number energy potential is made evident and, in this case, quite directly. This Master 22 is actually formed by two Master 11 vibrations. The Master 11 (or Intuitive/Visionary) lives in the world of imagination, illusion, esoteric truths, progressive tactics, and mystery; *doubling* this energy affords the 22 a phenomenal reach in terms of visions and plans and their implementation here in the Earth plane. Translated, this means that Leonardo has the ability to implement change on a vast and considerable level; he could well become one of the leading forces behind the movement to protect the planet.

Once again, the Master 22 warning assigned to all who carry this energy must be mentioned. Awareness of the boundaries and parameters of proper conduct is paramount, as the high-level material wealth and success this vibration holds can lead to dramatic downfalls should this power be misused in any unethical way. Not that I think Leonardo needs this admonition. It just has to be said.

Lifepath Day
Leonardo's specific entry is marked by Master 11. Quite frankly, this means that he is naturally connected to energies other than his own. It will be his lesson and challenge

to harness and direct his intuition and to honor the unseen
and his own (perhaps suppressed) desire to investigate the
mysteries of life.

Highest Letter and Number Count

Leonardo's highest letters show a tie between the energies
I, L, and O. This would translate into a man who is more
intuitive than he would perhaps care to admit and that
this instinct guides him in many conscious and even subconscious ways. He is motivated to motivate; he is a born
leader who would support his words with actions. More
than that, Leonardo is an open soul and a natural helper
and sees opportunities or options that are perhaps sometimes not visible to others.

Leonardo's highest number count shows a tie of 5 each
between numbers 1 and 7, which increases the strength of
each number five times. Thus, the Original Force of the
number 1 is akin to hurricane-force winds, and the activity in the brain is equal to the brainstorm of the century.
Put in gentler terms, these numbers read as someone who is
actively seeking the truth in all things.

Identity Initial Code

LWD (3+6+4) = 13/**4**

And here is yet another connection back to Leonardo da
Vinci—both Leonardos share the identical Identity code:
13/4, which allows access to the considerable power and
mystery of the number 13: its presence usually suggests a
frequency force that can produce quite noticeable results,
both for good and ill. The number 13 is a force of activity
that is beyond powerful, and its electrical forces can produce fundamental and permanent changes. In this case,

Leonardo's force of activity is only beginning to produce fundamental and lasting changes in the area of greatest concern at the moment and could very well develop into a game plan that affects and directs the future habits of humanity. Another grandiose statement perhaps. Or perhaps not. Look at how this letter code can be read: the *activity of body and mind* (3) that is *motivated by love and concern* (6) and is of a *foundational and fundamental nature* (4). The result? A super-charged activity level (13) that effects/changes/improves the very elements of our home, the Earth (4).

Words within Names

This is just too much fun to pass up—aside from the obvious "Leo," which makes me think of a lion—Leonardo also shows something interesting in his Inner name. Think of being at the HELM of a ship. Then think of the famous *Titanic* shot. The word CAP in DiCaprio also caught my attention and Leonardo *is* known for wearing baseball caps, but in particular, for wearing different caps to different games—and their selections seem to have more to do with their design appeal than with supporting either team playing. It just seems that he picks the one that matches his mood on any given game day.

> *If you can do what you do best and be happy, you're further along in life than most people.*
> —Leonardo DiCaprio

Drew Barrymore—
Producer/Actor/Director/Model/Spokesperson

Here is someone who became a superstar by age seven and a drug addict by age ten. Drew Barrymore presents the most remarkable success story—one that began when most kids are still playing childish games in school.

Drew Blyth Barrymore was born February 22 (there's that Master Number again), 1975, in Culver City, Los Angeles, to separated-and-later-divorced parents Jaid, an aspiring actress, and John Barrymore Jr., an addicted actor who lived the life of a hippie.

With her birth into the Barrymore clan came instant mini-celebrity status and an almost-preordained entry into the world of show business. At eleven months, Drew completed her first television commercial, and at five earned her first big-screen credit alongside William Hurt in *Altered States*. But it was not until the release of the blockbuster *E.T.: The Extraterrestrial* (1982) that she gained national exposure. The cherubic and charming darling of this larger-than-life fantasy not only became an overnight sensation, she also began attending evening parties and popular nightclubs (often in the company of her mother) such as Studio 54 and the China Club, a turn of events that hardly missed the ever-attentive eyes of the media. A youngster out partying with adults was rather conspicuous, to say the least. After a few years of this mystifying behavior, Drew was labeled by the press as a "bad girl," an out-of-control "wild child," and she became more of a curiosity than anything else.

During the years that followed, Drew grew from pre-pubescent child to complicated teen, and the two were hardly alike. While she might have found the over-the-top attention delightful to begin with, these celebrations had soon taken on nightmarish overtones. Drew had become addicted to the readily available "party favors" and eventually found herself fighting an apparently losing battle.

At the age of fourteen, after a few failed attempts at sobriety, Drew communicated her distress in a rather straightforward manner: she cut her wrists. Fortunately, not only did she survive, she went on to gain control of her addictions within the year and followed up by petitioning the court for a "divorce" from her mother. Once recognized as a legal adult, Drew was free to manage her own career, financial affairs, and life in general.

By the age when most teens are tentatively exploring the real world beyond the rather sheltering walls of school, Drew Barrymore had already achieved super stardom, partied with celebrities galore, traveled to the core of addictions, been exposed to all manner of negative media publicity, survived a suicide attempt, conquered her dependencies, divorced her mother, and co-written a bestselling book entitled *Little Girl Lost*, about her life and her addictions. It was published just three weeks shy of her seventeenth birthday.

Her sheer strength of will and determination to gain control were key to her successes of the time—successes that were destined to continue.

In a rather shrewd move, Drew followed the release of her book by capitalizing on her bad-girl image: she took on her first leading role by portraying a beautiful, bewitching, seductive, and *very* bad girl in 1992's *Poison Ivy* (which also featured Leonardo DiCaprio). Although it did poorly at the box office, it did spawn two additional Poison Ivy films, but most importantly, at the time, it did what it had been designed to do: it re-introduced Drew to the public, but as an adult this time. Indeed, the child had morphed into a sexpot. To fortify this new image, Drew went on to pose nude for *Interview* magazine and continued to accept roles that required nudity and sensuality like *Doppelganger* (1993) and *Bad Girls* (1994). Also in 1994, Drew married bar owner Jeremy Thomas, a union that lasted less than two months.

Her notoriety spiked when on April 12, 1995, during a guest appearance on the David Letterman show, she hopped onto the host's desk, did a little dance and, with her back to the audience, flashed her (unwrapped) birthday present at the rather stunned but gracious birthday boy.

During that same year, Drew appeared nude in *Playboy*, which her godfather, Steven Spielberg, appeared to take serious exception to. For her twentieth birthday, he sent her a quilt, a note, and the spread from *Playboy* ... all three bearing the same theme. The quilt read "cover yourself up," as did the note, and the pictures spoke for themselves— they had been artistically altered to cover her up. Almost by design, Drew's focus did seem to shift shortly thereafter.

Within months, Drew had formed her own production company called Flower Films with her friend Nancy Juvonen. After 1996's *Scream,* she began to aim at lighter roles, romantic comedies like *The Wedding Singer* (1998) and *EverAfter* (1998), which showcased her talents in completely new and refreshing ways while also revealing her penchant for comedy. She bumped it up a notch in 2000 with her role as Dylan Sanders in a revival of the old television series *Charlie's Angels,* which her company co-produced. The film was a smash hit with audiences and helped to establish Flower Films as a viable entity and Drew Barrymore as a woman of distinction.

Drew's second attempt at marriage took place in 2001, when she wed comedian Tom Green. Unfortunately, it too did not prove lasting: they divorced a short time later. More films and projects followed as well, and, in February of 2004, Drew was recognized as a Barrymore in her own right—she was awarded a star on the Hollywood Walk of Fame. This was also the year during which Drew reconciled with her dying father, whom she had rarely seen as a child or while growing up; some things had come full circle.

Since then, Drew has been involved on various levels in various projects and is acknowledged and recognized as a multi-talented, irrepressible, and creative force in the entertainment industry.

In 2007, Drew became the new face of Gucci, signed a lucrative deal with Cover Girl as a model/spokesperson and as co-creative director of the initial campaign, and was featured on the cover and in the top spot of *People*'s 100 Most Beautiful. Later, she directed her first film, 2009's *Whip It,* which Flower Films also co-produced. Already the recipient of dozens of nominations and independent awards, in 2010 Drew saw sophisticated acknowledgment of her talent: she won both a Golden Globe and a Screen Actor's Guild award for her part in HBO's *Grey Gardens.*

One of the most important aspects of Drew's off-screen life began in 2005 when she made the first of two journeys to Kenya to view the plight of those living there. In 2007, the World Food Programme (WFP) named Drew as their Ambassador Against Hunger and on March 3, 2008, during an appearance on Oprah, Drew announced a personal donation of one million dollars to the organization, which suggests a heart that is obviously as open as her pocketbook. She also works with Much Love Animal Rescue. Compassion for the less fortunate is evidently a built-in commodity when it comes to this Piscean heart, but so too is promoting personal power, which she has done by working with organizations focused on encouraging young people to vote.

Despite dealing with situations and emotional trenches deep enough to drown a full-grown adult, this sweet child star went on to become one of the most captivating, charming, recognized, respected, admired, and successful women in the world. Here are the reflections of this resolute energy in numbers and letters.

D R E W	B L Y T H	B A R R Y M O R E
4 2 5 6	2 3 1 4 5	2 1 2 2 1 4 7 2 5
=17	=15	=26
=8	=6	=8

Sub #	Total Name #
58/13/4	
22	22

D R E W	B A R R Y M O R E
4 2 5 6	2 1 2 2 1 4 7 2 5
=17	=26
=8	=8

Sub #	Daily Name #
43	
16	7

February	22	Sub #	Lifepath #
2	22	24	6

Day of Birth: 22 Master Builder

As in previous samples, I am immediately drawn to the two Master Number elements in Drew's chart: one as her Total Name Number or Universal Gift, and the other as her Day of Birth, or the specific energy upon which she was "delivered." These Master 22 Builder essences are undoubtedly responsible for her ongoing drive to *create*: to build and to manifest what she sees as appropriate for her and for others. (You have surely noticed the many 22 energies contained in these sample reads? This serves to underscore the validity of the power held in Master Numbers: oftentimes, chosen careers or actions will result in fame; 22 is the architect who just cannot stop building, and the primary goal is to reach a level of achievement that allows assistance to be offered to others.)

If one looks further into the elemental 4 that the 22 operates as when not "on," it becomes evident that this energy carries significant impact in Drew's life and its construction. In addition to standing as her Social Cornerstone, it is also doubled to 8 in several places (including in her Identity Initials and her Social and Domestic Whole Name Numbers) and elevated to Master 22 in others. The 4 refers to the basic fundamentals of life and how strong they are or become—it plays with the building blocks of life. This feels as though Drew had to lay her own foundations in spite of or perhaps because of the strength of her family name. And she has done so. And will continue to do so.

A final connective note comes in the shape of the 6. This loving, nurturing, compassionate, and caring energy sits at the core of Drew's being (in her Soul energy or middle name) and is also her Lifepath Number. Drew is here to learn how to pinpoint, define, and experience personal true love—and will have to undergo all of the pain, confusion, and joy such a journey entails.

Whole Name Numbers
Social Energy
DREW (D/4, R/2, E/5, W/6) = 17/8

Drew's social Cornerstone energy assigns her the resoluteness, strength, and tenacity the D/4 represents. As you know, the D is the Door and it can stand open just as easily as closed; it represents the ins and outs of opportunity while its companion, the 4, often refers to family and foundational issues. Since this energy is her "welcoming" one, so to speak, it can portend difficulties in terms of fundamental issues within the home—for Drew, some doors were open while others were closed and destined to remain that way. The divorce of her parents and absence of her father kept two of those doors firmly closed (she rarely saw her father before their already-mentioned reconciliation and therefore did not have the opportunity to watch healthy interactions between loving parents).

Since the Cornerstone will always exert influence over the entire energy dynamic, this D will both help and hinder Drew. It is not an overly movable essence, but it can instill the Drive and Determination required to break down obstacles and blocked passages. Despite her cheerful demeanor, Drew is actually very much influenced by the 8 (a double 4) of her Whole Name Number. This gives her the power, authority, and intelligence to succeed materially, and by jumping ahead to her Inner Soul energy, which is that of the loving number 6, it becomes clear that Drew has the ability to reach a rare position: that of a spiritually and materially balanced energy, which is the goal of the developed 8. When engaged, this is the energy state in which anything becomes possible and, indeed, probable. Having two of these energies (Social and Domestic) can introduce some conflict, yes, but that is on a more personal familial level and is something Drew herself will come to terms with in her own way . . . and maybe she already has.

The balance of her Social energies are the R/2, E/5, and W/6. The presence of the R/2 is not an initially overly optimistic vibration: this is the one that refers to the successful formations of lasting and resilient relationships—from family members to friends to lovers—and the conflicts, tests, and indecisions attached to them. The R/2 cores back to our very first (usually parental) connections and relationships and the forms they took, or didn't take. These core patterns are reflected in our adult relationships and can put us through rather severe challenges until we make peace with their role models.

Drew's first run-through of these energies would have taken place from birth to around age 6, and then came the E/5 or an explosion of epic proportions (*E.T.*). But that was then. On a *daily* basis, this E represents Drew's bubbly, excited love of life and her eager embrace of new and different things, ideas, and even people. She values her independence, likes to be self-supporting, and enjoys stimulation of all kinds. Her life is and always will be prone to changes, which she actually welcomes. Boredom is not something Drew will put up with for long; she really is the free spirit that she seems to be. This love of life and certain impulsiveness is likely what led her to agree to two brief marriages and supports the fact that the R/2 and E/5 is not an overly fortunate combination of energies, especially on the romantic front. The E takes the "testing" of the R (partnerships, marriages, close connections) to new levels, and experiencing these periods is not what I would call particularly reassuring. But once Drew has been through a variety of different styles and types of relationships and has learned her likes and dislikes and her rights and wrongs within them, she will find her place and her true-love connection; for once the lessons have been learned and accepted, the R rolls in Recovery, Redemption, and Refreshing Rewards, which normally manifest as newfound relationships that make the whole lesson worthwhile.

The final W/6 brings us to the emotional ups and downs of its proverbial roller coaster and refers to the peaks and valleys, the negatives and positives that are found in all emotional attachments. Drew is all about connections made and connections lost, but she is not one to give up. She will hang on and ride it out, but only if it is something she feels is *worth* hanging on to, for whatever reasons. The most common of these will be out of loyalty. The W sticks around if trust is involved no matter how rough the trip. Not surprising since the W is represented by the Waters of love and emotional ties. Its presence is reassuring in this name energy, as it is indicative of long-lasting companionships that are based on cooperation and dedication. Drew is likely to have several committed friends and even business connections who will stick around through thick and thin—like Drew herself will.

Drew's Social Name Total is an 8, as is her Domestic, or last name. Double 8 values carry enormous power and potential; however, as already touched on, there is also the probability of conflict (which in this case would be carried between her Social persona and her Domestic roots), which can only be neutralized if the balance point between the two is found. Despite the power held in both names, I feel there is a need for complete distinction between the two, and therein may lie the contradiction or conflict.

Drew likes to be in control, but in a gentle way, and she does not respond well to those who tag onto her because of her name rather than who she is as a person. So there can be a bit of a conflict for Drew herself—between who she is as a person and who others might expect her to be because of the Barrymore name.

The goal of the developed 8 is to reach a plateau upon which the elements of life are equally distributed, or balanced, and that includes everything from Drew's friends to her relationships to her (spiritual) state of mind. Mind over matter. And her Social Number energy *is* supported by her brain, her mind, and her thought processes. The sub number 17 (the force of the brain) lends Drew the ability to detach emotionally and to apply logic to any given situation or circumstance—an admirable ability for one so soft-centered. While the 17 is hardly a weak-willed number, it is also one that invites investigation into the deeper and quieter realms of the imagination: reality and illusion; fact and fiction; life and death. Drew will likely find her interests in those areas growing over the years; after all, her Daily Name is the magickal number 7.

Inner Energy
BLYTH (B/2, L/3, Y/1, T/4, H/5) = 15/**6**
Again, this is not a name that Drew is commonly known by, but it does reveal a more detailed look at her Inner or Soul energies.

The Cornerstone of this name is the B/2, which translates into the search for the "other half" or the perfect union. However, since it is also a "closed' energy, there can also be a certain withholding when it comes to relationships (the number 2 is the strongest number element in Drew's chart, which we will see later). So while at heart Drew is ruled by the duality and normal disagreements that arise in any kind of union, she is also a very loving and giving energy (L/3).

At the very core (or heart) of her Inner essence is the Y/1, that fork in the road. The first time she would have experienced this change in direction would have been just prior to the release of *E.T.*—an event that changed her life and its direction in no uncertain terms, which is the precise meaning of the Y. But this letter energy can also indicate another situation altogether. The Y can point to an uncertainty, a confusion; a "which way do I go" type of energy. Since it follows the BL, it almost reads as in order to find her true BLiss, Drew may well choose an untraveled or just different road or direction at some point in her life, and this will likely involve something to do with her personal life and its contents. (The B and L are emotionally charged and loving energies having to do with expressions of caring and the willingness to give.)

The balance of her Inner Soul energies are the T/4 and the H/5. While the T throws additional and increasing forces into the mix and thereby underscores the undeniable changes any shift in direction might bring, the H is where she will likely face something having to do with commitment to her chosen direction, however it might manifest.

The Whole Name energy of Blyth is an exact match to Drew's Lifepath: the domestic and nurturing number 6. However, her sub number here is quite telling in that it forecasts the "force of changes" (15), which are necessary in order for this love energy to fully manifest itself. Since 5 is also connected to fame, it is likely that she will find her soul mate within that realm, but this sub number can influence the 6, making it more likely that a soul connection will take time simply because its essence is one of constant change.

Drew is nothing if not a true "love bug," which is my favorite expression for one under the domain of the 6. She is kind, soft-hearted, sensitive, open, approachable, compassionate, and generous, and because her Lifepath is also a 6, she is here to experience the truths about *love in all its forms,* whether they include art, music, fine foods, nature, or people. Drew is destined to seek out and experience the best of the best.

What makes her different from other 6 energies is that she is ruled by its formative energies of 2, which means people are important to her—and this means *all* people, not just those within her circle. The following L is, as already mentioned, a giving and helpful energy. She will want to (and already has) reach out to help others. Not because she feels obligated, but because helping others lies at the core of who she is.

Domestic Energy
BARRYMORE
(B/2, A/1, R/2, R/2, Y/1, M/4, O/7, R/2, E/5) = 26/**8**
Once again, we are looking at yet another B/2 as a Cornerstone, so the same energy of Drew's Inner Soul is connected to her family hierarchy—in particular, to the male history attached to the name. The duality and sometimes "closed" energy of the B points once more to the process of finding and blending with the perfect mate and achieving balance in relationships by learning how to compromise. There are four 2 values in this name and three of them are the relationship-oriented R. (Worthy of note is that two of these form a Subtle Master 22, a possible indication of conflict within the family's core unit and also of the position of

the family within its community, which would mean that the outside view of the family was likely one of status and accomplishment.)

So while the Domestic name is not usually of major import in analysis, this case stands as a bit of an exception, the reason being that the family history itself is significant and that Drew also carries the identical Total Name energy in her Social or first name: double 8 values show a power struggle of sorts. It is as though, on some level, Drew may feel the need to establish herself in no uncertain terms as a breed apart (from her famous relatives)—to establish herself as her own unique entity and talent that is not connected to or spun-off from another thread. This does not mean she desires to separate from her family or its history, rather, that she is her own person with her own history and talents and wishes to be accepted and recognized as such.

The presence of *four* 2 values (one of them a Cornerstone) makes a strong statement regarding core relationships and the patterns set long ago and their affects upon Drew when it comes to forming new and successful ones. This theme was introduced to Drew even before she was old enough to understand what was missing from her young life and has shown up so many times in her read that it is impossible to ignore.

One likely cause of relationship issues is to be found in the center of the Barrymore name itself: the Y/1 is the fork in the road and reads as a point of departure or separation, whether by choice or by force, and often manifests as break-ups and divorces. The Barrymore clan shows a history of divorces, including Drew's great-grandfather, Maurice Costello (who shares Drew's birthday, by the way), who married twice; her grandfather, John Barrymore, who married four times; and her own father, John Drew Barrymore, who married three times. Drew herself followed suit by marrying and divorcing twice before the age of 28. When found in the center of a Domestic name, the Y/1 is not representative of a stable core energy.

The balance of the vibrations in Barrymore include the A/1, M/4, O/7, and E/5. The A offers focused ambition; the M can gloss over details and hide many things; the O presents plenty of opportunity; and the E just adds extra energy to the entire picture. But the one thing that is consistent within this name energy is its commitment to love, as shown in the sub number 26.

Once more, the final comment on this name energy is summed up in the powerful and oftentimes controlling vibration of the 8, which can be read two ways: one will either have the control and lose it or have the control and keep it, something that seems to apply especially to the male figures in this family as both scenarios have occurred.

Drew Barrymore has the power, the control, and the means to attain material evidence of success, and she also has the compassion the fully developed 8 requires in order to keep it. If the spiritual road is further pursued, she is poised to step into its fullest and finest spiritual potential, and as such, she is, indeed, a breed apart.

Daily Name Number
DREW BARRYMORE $(8+8) = 16/7$
First sub numbers: $(17+26) = 43$
Drew's Daily Name is a unique combination of double 8 values, as already noted. This supplies her with vast

310 · *Chapter Six*

opportunities for both material and spiritual gain, authority, and status. It also forms a Subtle Master Number (88—Master Success). Similar to Leonardo DiCaprio, Drew has the ability to succeed beyond her own wildest dreams. Anyone who has seen Drew on film or being interviewed already knows that her heart is as big as they come, which is a necessity before the positive and fully formed 8 will realize the immensity of the fortune laid at its feet. Drew does carry the capacity to understand the temporariness of "things," and since her Lifepath reflects the open and true heart of a lover (as opposed to a fighter), she has one of the highest chances of experiencing the awesome serenity and success that accompanies true and lasting personal satisfaction.

The first sub number of Drew Barrymore totals to a 43, which suggests foundations already in existence (4) that are rearranged, recreated, and rebirthed (3). This is indicative of mind over matter. Drew's presence of mind helped her to restructure her life in spite of patterns and examples already set.

Her Main sub number of 16 shows the gentle undercurrents that will tend to lead her *towards* her goal rather than away from it; the "force of love and ability to break through walls" of the 16 energy is what motivates her. Drew is a force unto herself who has the power and determination to break through cycles and boundaries. This is one lady who has the ability to do tremendous things, and is another worth watching since she is still young and her future is unwritten.

Drew's Daily Name is a 7, fitting, I think, as that was her age when everything changed—forever. On a more contemporary note, she is at once a blend of enticing mystery and careful planning, which is evident when one looks back over the decisions she made and the directions she took following her near fall from grace as a child. The mind is a compelling tool and Drew knows how to use hers. She is much more intellectual than she perhaps lets on and can be reserved and somewhat distant at times, but that is when she does her deepest thinking. Since the 7 is of a dual nature and its lesson is to honor both sides of the brain, she is likely as open to her intuition as she is to the unusual, the unique, and the esoteric. There is an odd contrariness to the 7: one half is strictly practical and proper while the other is fascinated by the world of metaphysics and spirituality. There is much more to this lady than anyone realizes or can even see. Beneath her bubbly exterior lies a brilliant, imaginative, and highly progressive mind that is intrigued by many more topics than anyone might ever suspect.

Total Name Number
DREW BLYTH BARRYMORE (8+6+8) = **22 Master Builder**
First sub numbers: (17+15+26) = 58/13/4
We have seen the Master 22 fairly often in this short list of samples; often enough to gain a clearer understanding of its elevated energy potentials and the results thereof. This is indeed the number of building, of constructing, of foundations that are firm enough to hold whatever is added to them. This number is often found in the lives of celebrities, whether they belong to the entertainment world or another department of social interaction. When utilized correctly and not taken for granted or ignored, this vibration will leave an imprint upon our reality. The potential for

larger-than-life impressions and legacies is likely and even probable among strong 22 energies.

Universe gifted Drew Barrymore with the ability to dig deep, to manifest, to deliberately use her brain and her will to create something real and tangible for others to enjoy. In her case, this translates in a variety of ways, from entertaining to providing a role model for those addicted. Her struggles of youth and her victory over them provides an upstanding example of courage, dedication, and faith while her continued personal achievements and work with the less fortunate cements her growing reputation as a person of moral and ethical standards who is worthy of note and respect.

Her sub numbers of 58, 13, and 4 are commentaries that can be read thusly: the fame game was one she needed to, at a young age, gain control over in a lasting way (5 = fame and 8 = control) and the 13 offered her two options—to follow the karmic lead of her forefathers or to gather the "force of actions/activities" close to her heart and make her own decisions.

The final message of the 4 brings us back to the observations made at the start of Drew's read. The number 4 and its various shapes found throughout her analysis indicate that Drew Barrymore had a choice: build her own foundations or follow the blueprints laid out by some of her ancestors.

Thankfully, Drew chose to lay her own foundations.

Lifepath Number

February (02) + **22** = 24/**6**

Day: **Master 22 The Master Builder**

Drew's Inner Soul essence is firmly anchored to her Lifepath, which means, in simple speak, that her heart's desire (experiencing the reality that love is found through helping/loving others) is exactly in line with the reason she is here—to understand the various intricacies of love and the many forms it takes and to learn that attempting to label or organize or compartmentalize love is a losing proposition. It is what it is.

Drew is destined to follow her heart wherever it may choose to lead her, and although she must surrender to those inclinations, she must also recognize her own limitations. Put another way, she must also learn not to lose herself in the process.

The sub number of 24 comments further on the foundations created by units of 2—Drew has built her world into large groups of connections, each with its own function but to which the same loving energy of the 6 is applied.

The number 6 is very appreciative of and drawn to all things beautiful. They value a splendid painting as much as a fine piece of crystal and often prefer to present themselves as nicely as possible. Drew Barrymore is a work of art—one that has yet to be completed.

Day of Birth: 22 The Master Builder

Much has been already addressed in regard to this Master Number Universe gifted to Drew (as reflected in her Total

Name Number). It is also the specific energy upon which she traveled into this world. Drew has the tools and the imagination required to build her life as she sees fit, and fame and fortune have already found her. The only direction she is likely to continue building is *up,* which is why the following caveat bears repeating.

Since Drew has done a large amount of her own life construction, I doubt there is cause for concern; however, one final time, it must be said. The warning is simple and to the point: once significant achievements have been made, attention must still be paid to the base (or basement) structures, which are commonly seen as ethics or morals. These base elements, if not properly maintained, can easily shift, and we all know what can happen if buildings shift off of their bases. Again, not something I believe Drew has to worry about, but worth mentioning. The extreme powers held in Master Numbers can swing both ways—sometimes unexpectedly.

Highest Letter and Number Count

The most potent letter energy in Drew's name is the R/2. The Barrymore name, which is heavy in R energy and points to difficulties in relationships, has been recognized and celebrated for over a century, and its energy influences witnessed by millions. The high rate of divorces and separations and battles with drugs and alcohol within the family were common knowledge. Drew is also under the R/2 influences, but she has traveled through them several times and has come out a survivor.

The one thing I do want to reiterate about the R is its resuscitative and restorative qualities. Once the root lesson of understanding the rights and wrongs involved in any personal relationship (whether it be with the self or with another) is at long last learned and assimilated, the R can also present a time of refreshing rebirth and release. This usually occurs a little bit later in life as the R transits are difficult ones to truly master. However, it is also usually then that most hard-working R energies will finally find their soul mates ... in the mirror first and then in the physical form of another.

Fittingly enough, the highest number energy is the 2, which ties in with the R/2 but with an additional message. The 2 is not complete if it is only 1. The 2 *needs* its other half. That is the focus of the 2: to join, to unite, and to balance the picture. Drew is a people-person who likely has an extended family, which is perhaps even larger than her own. She needs to love and, like everyone else, to be loved. As such, she is open and willing to learn about interactions and emotional intimacies and stands the best chance at reaching the rewards at the end of the R challenge.

Identity Initial Code
DBB (4+2+2) = **8 Balance: Matter vs. Spirit**
The two 8 values found in Drew's Social and Domestic Total Name Number energies are reflected here, too. It's as though the feeling I had while doing this read, that Drew Barrymore's name energy is larger than the sum of its parts, has been confirmed. The 8 represents the lemniscate, the symbol for eternity and infinity, and Drew's name is filled with direct and indirect references to this essence and its symbol. She may well be one of the first Barrymores to truly understand the concept that true peace is only gained

through the release of control and the embracing of Faith, the healthiest infrastructure known to man. Drew seeks eternal balance in all things, and chances are good that she will find it.

> *I believe in fate. I believe that everything happens for a reason, but I think it's important to seek out that reason—that's how you learn.*
> —Drew Barrymore

conclusion

Many years ago, I was given a gift and asked to pass it along, which I have now done—to you, dear reader. In honor of that initial request, I respectfully ask you to do the same. Sharing knowledge is the greatest gift of all and now that you are free to be who you are and to feel good about it, you have also become a gift to others. Mass consciousness is composed of people like you and me and if we feel good about ourselves, others will feel good while in our company and will transmit that same energy to those they cross paths with later, which essentially creates a domino effect— a smile in LA can lead to a hug in China.

Chaldean name analysis offers us the chance to explore ourselves and to accept what we find as intrinsic to who we are. As a result, we come into our own power and just naturally become happier people. Happier people think happier thoughts, and that energy is picked up and carried into the energy matrix, which produces a happier matrix.

Since we know that every thought and emotion registers with Universe, I invite everyone who reads this to send out their own form of positive energy—it can be to someone specific or to the world in general. It just takes a moment, and if you doubt its effectiveness, I promise you that Universe doesn't; energy is energy and you are a conduit, just like everyone else. Imagine how the atmosphere on Earth would change if routinely charged with loving and positive ions, and then imagine how that might reflect back upon us and our environment—literally.

The Chaldeans seemed focused on rising above the limits of the physical mind and body to become closer to the Divine. I say that Heaven is right here on Earth and that it is up to us to do some gardening—starting in our own back yards. So pull some weeds and plant new seeds, and I will do the same. Together, we can bring the dream to life.

Until we meet again, I leave you in light, in love, and in peace.

Happy people are beautiful. They become like a mirror and they reflect that happiness ... if someone is giving of their spirit and they make you laugh and feel good, that's a whole other level of beauty.
    —Drew Barrymore, *People* magazine, April 2007

glossary

Acceptance: Spiritual term referring to the personal under-standing that we are all created exactly according to plan. Perceived imperfections are not flaws; they are inherent to our individual designs.

Alchemy: Ancient practice of attempting to transform base metals into gold and ideally creating an "elixir" of immortal life in the process.

Alpha and Omega: The first and last letters of the ancient Ionic Greek alphabet. Also used in spiritual terms to describe the "be all and end all," the entire picture, the beginning and the end, and all points in between.

Astrology: Literal practice of tracking the positions of the stars and using these celestial bodies as tools of divination or forecasting. This is where the signs of the Zodiac are "drawn" as sky patterns. (*See* Divination.)

Awakening: Spiritual term that refers to becoming aware of other levels of energy and the existence of a "higher" power.

Bermuda Triangle: Plenty of ships and planes have disappeared without apparent reason within the boundaries of Miami, Bermuda, and Puerto Rico. The term was coined by the media around 1964, and it stuck. Some say the lack of debris, the clear weather, and the calm seas are proof that something about the disappearances within this triangle is mysterious and dangerous, while others say many of these occurrences can be scientifically explained and that there is nothing mysterious about them at all.

Blueprint: The fundamental elements of our human and spiritual auras as reflected in our names, numbers, and Lifepaths. Another form of this aura can also be seen in the colors surrounding our bodies.

Butterfly Effect: This theory suggests that a small action can alter the course of events some distance away and is linked to the idea of cause and effect: all energy is connected, and every action has a *re*action. Therefore, the flap of butterfly wings in British Columbia might be linked to a hurricane in the Tropics.

Cornerstone: The first letter of any given person, place, or thing. The Cornerstone shows the strongest overall essence of the word itself and is what your Identity Initial Code is made up of.

Cosmic Catalog: Often used in conjunction with the Law of Attraction to reference the willingness of the Universal or Cosmic mind to give us that which is needed to improve the life. Our positive thoughts (and even magickal undertakings) are sometimes likened to "placing an order" with this catalog.

Cosmic Mind: This is another way of addressing the power of God, the Divine, Spirit, or Universal Consciousness.

Cosmic School: This relates to the idea that we are all here to learn a specific set of lessons and are actually attending a learning center which, while of this Earth plane, is actually "run" by higher level energies.

Cuneiform: This is one of the first forms of writing, or rather, printing. Used in Babylonian times, its symbols look rather like nails with wedge-shaped heads.

Current Energy Phase: A method of counting through each name until you reach your current age. These letters are then grouped to form a code, totaled, and studied for the letter and number energy messages they hold, and for which vibrations are affecting you the most at present.

Cycle or Pattern: Situations and/or relationships that repeat themselves in style and content. For example, if you are in your *third* abusive relationship, you are in a cycle that needs to be broken before you can move on.

Daily Name: The name you are most commonly called, for example, John Smith. The Daily Name does not include the middle name.

Déjà vu: Déjà vu refers to that odd feeling of having experienced an event before or having been in a particular place before—even if you know this is not so. The term originates with the French and translates as "already seen."

Direct Number: This happens when a name does not have more than a total value of 9; there are no sub numbers prior to the Whole Name Number. For example, "Amy" is 1+4+1 and equals a direct 6.

Divination: Divination methods include gazing into crystal balls, throwing runes, and pulling Tarot cards, and all are aimed at seeking guidance from a higher source. We ask for signs from the Divine, hence, *divin*ation. (*See* Divine.)

Divine: This is another way of saying God, Spirit, or Universe and connects to unexpected blessings and the absolute trust placed in something unseen. Also used when referencing information whose source cannot be readily explained.

DNA Activation Code 11:11: Because of the number 1's connection to original forces, four of these energies in a row would point to fundamental and foundational changes that are caused by a combination of powerful but separate forces. It is believed that while we now function on two strands of DNA, we once did so with twelve, which would have allowed for a much more advanced state of health in the body, mind, and spirit. Some believe this advance in our genetic structure (from two to twelve or more) will occur naturally over time. Others believe the time for activation is now and that 11:11 is a "code" and that activation can be encouraged through energy work that cleans and reprograms our belief systems. (*See* DNA Helix.)

DNA Helix: Deoxyribonucleic Acid (DNA) is our individual genetic information code that is contained within a twisted ladder-type shape called a double helix. These codes are passed down to our children and help to explain why a son looks so much like his dad or why a daughter sounds just like her mom.

Dowsing (Rod): Here is another ancient practice that involves a forked branch held by the forked end and used to locate things that are hidden. It is believed that the user or seeker energetically connects to that which is sought and that the rod moves to indicate its placement or location. (*See* Pendulum.)

Easter Island: This tiny island (approximately 15 miles long and 10 miles wide) lies thousands of miles off the coast of Chile in the South Pacific Ocean—literally in the middle of nowhere. When it was discovered by a Dutch captain in the 1700s, it was completely deserted save for hundreds of massive stone statues, some of which stood at least thirty feet tall and weighed several tons. Who lived there, how the stones were moved and erected, and why still remains a mystery.

Ego: The ego is our sense of self. It allows us to set and pursue goals, to develop personalities in which many things can manifest—not the least of which are pride, greed, envy, and also confidence, consciousness, and personality. It allows us to feel in control of our own lives and even superior to others. The ego is one of the main detractors in the search for spiritual connections, as it must be released (or at least subdued) in order to find true serenity and faith.

Energy: Energy is everywhere: it is electrical, radiant, nuclear, and spiritual. Energy is the flow of creation and movement and must be balanced to be positive. That applies to the human form as well—as above, so below. Allowing yourself to be an open conduit for energy flow is the key to spiritual growth.

Esoteric: That which is hidden or not immediately available to all. Mystic, occult, and spiritual knowledge that is specific to certain groups or subjects.

Faith: The unfailing belief in that which cannot be seen or proven, as in God or the Divine, and that "everything happens for a reason"—reasons we may not be aware of but nevertheless take "on faith." One of the major spiritual support systems of mankind.

Flower of Life: Sacred Geometry sits at the base of this venerable design, which consists of a series of overlapping circles and can be found in various places throughout the ancient world. It contains mysteries beyond what can be discussed here, but this circular maze is our picture of how the mind of the Universe might look. It is said that wearing a Flower of Life pendant can improve one's mental and physical state of well-being.

Frequency: This is used in reference to the energy levels projected by individual groups of letter or number energies, as in "what's your vibe?"

Hieroglyphics: One of the first forms of writing. Ancient Egyptian symbol script often used actual images or pictures while detailing a story or transcribing historical events. The idea of picture images is closely tied to the "reading" of symbols in our current alphabet and therefore to Chaldean numerology.

Holistic: Often heard in healing circles, holistic includes the whole picture. The condition of body, mind, and spirit are included and considered when choosing or performing healings.

Identity Initials: Simply put, your initials and their numeric total. This total presents an overall view of your vibrations.

Immortality: To gain eternal life; to never die. This can refer to the human form or to continued existence after the death of the physical body.

Intuition: This is that inner feeling that warns us of impending danger or that something is not quite right about a situation or person. The intuition is our sixth sense, is connected to Universe, and is never wrong.

Kaleidoscope: In spiritual terms, this word refers to the beauty and adaptability of the human spirit. In the mundane world, this is a long optical device that displays brilliant colors when rotated.

Karma: As you sow, so shall you reap. Karma is from the Sanskrit and means *to do, to make—action, word, or deed*—and refers to past life actions within these parameters. Negative karma is believed to remain attached to the soul after death and is thus carried into new incarnations, where reparations must be made, or balance re-instated.

Kundalini: Once again of Sanskrit origin, the Kundalini is often pictured as a sleeping snake curled at the base of the spine. The objective of spiritual healing and other modalities is to awaken this sleeping giant so it may support the quest for enlightenment.

Law of Attraction: An age-old concept that was given a modern name, the Law is simple in that what you think and what you say will attract and dictate your circumstances. Positive to positive and negative to negative. Becoming aware of your thoughts does take some practice, but it does work.

Lemniscate: The symbol for infinity or perfect balance; it looks like the number 8 on its side. The lemniscate is endless; it travels the same graceful curves forever and forms two loops that are mirror images of each other. Its meaning is balance in all things and therefore, perfect control.

Letter Energies: These are symbols (similar to hieroglyphics) that stand for particular things—like characteristics, tendencies, and sometimes events. Each letter stands for something different and forms a "picture" when linked together in a word or name.

Ley Lines: This term refers to a series of ancient areas—such as Stonehenge and the Pyramids—that are reputed to be highly charged with energy and to be interconnected via invisible energy strands, or ley lines.

Lifepath: The combination of your day and month of birth reduces to the number essence of your Lifepath, which suggests the reasons why you are here and what to do about it. The Lifepath is the lesson (or set of lessons) you must learn in order to graduate to the next level or phase of existence.

Magick: This is beyond magic—this is magic that is kaleidoscopic in nature. It takes the element of mystery and elevates it to one of awe and wonder. At the core of this magick is nature and working with its energies in a productive and respectful manner.

Major Arcana: Refers to the twenty-two cards of the tarot that represent major life events.

Manifest: This is what happens when you learn how to focus your thoughts upon something needed. There is definitely something magickal about seeing something manifest just as you pictured it. (*See* Law of Attraction.)

Master Numbers: Refers to double-digit numbers 11, 22, 33, and so on that have the potential to create or motivate in more powerful ways than their root numbers. Master numbers are the movers and shakers of the number scale and are the only numbers not reduced in name analysis.

Matrix: While the proper description of a Matrix is usually a series of interconnected lines and rows, to me, this is a grid of either electricity or mass consciousness or spirituality or all three that encompasses the Earth. Something about this Matrix feels mysterious and powerful and esoterically tied to the Flower of Life. (*See* Flower of Life.)

Meditation: My personal form of meditating is to sit outside under the trees or in front of my work area or even in my favorite easy chair while being still and quiet, allowing my mind to go where it wants to go and to show me images along the way. Some of these images make no sense, but some do. Of course, there are more traditional ways to meditate, but they are all aimed at accessing the spiritual plane.

Metaphysical: "Meta" means "beyond" (from the Greek *meta*). It is the study or subject of all the elements that lie beyond or "after" our physical bodies and senses.

Minor Arcana: While the Major Arcana provides the twenty-two major life events, the fifty-six remaining Minor Arcana cards speak to specifics in the different areas of life as indicated by the four suits of Pentacles, Swords, Wands, and Cups. In other words, they "flesh out" the stories and address, among other things, the areas of money, love, health, and success.

Number Energies: These symbols dictate types of energies, whether they be fast or slow or powerful or passive. When combined with the characters of letters, these number flows will also form a picture when linked together and play an integral role in the practice of Chaldean numerology.

Numerology: The practical application of number energies to the path or pattern of one's life. It is not a traditional divination system, but it is revelatory in a deeply personal way and can indicate times when certain events are likely to occur. Chaldean is but one form of numerology; some others are Pythagorean and Kabalarian.

Occult: Used here only in the positive sense. This term comes from the Latin *occultare* (to "hide" or to "conceal") and refers to the mystical and unknown and the revelation and understanding thereof.

Omen: A bird flies into the room and we think someone is going to die. That's an omen. Or, at least, that is one that I know of. Anything can be viewed as an omen, but I tend to listen to my intuition rather than start looking for omens because you can find them everywhere if you are actively looking. Having said that, there *are* times when repeated odd events will combine with messages from your intuition and present what can be seen as an omen, the meaning of which will be personal to the observer.

Oracle: Any device or tool that is used to peek into the placement of future energies.

Paranormal: This is something that travels past the boundaries of what we consider "normal" (*para* is linked to the Latin and carries a similar meaning to the Greek *meta*, which is to "go against, past, beyond, or above") and includes hauntings, possessions, telepathy, and UFO sightings. Paranormal events or subjects are those that challenge or defy scientific explanation.

Pendulum: Usually a crystal suspended on a chain, these are also in the oracle family and are used to indicate yes or no answers. (*See* Dowsing.)

Pentagram: This is another symbol that goes back in time and always makes me think of the stars in the sky, maybe because it is the five-pointed star and holds the power of God and man within its frame. It is a positive symbol, unless worn or drawn upside down. Then it is sometimes viewed as connected to Satan worship or the misuse of energies.

Personal Power: This is the willingness to set goals and pursue them without allowing fear to intervene. Personal power is self-confidence that is gained through faith in your own abilities as gifted by a higher power. It is not overly connected to the ego.

Pineal Gland: This is a pea-sized gland that sits in the middle of your brain and regulates the secretion of melatonin, which helps us sleep. It is connected to the mystic "third eye," which points to psychic abilities. When "opened" (through meditation, yoga, and reiki, to name a few methods), it is purported to offer a portal that sees beyond the physical and connects to the universal truths. (*See* Intuition.)

Prophets (Soothsayers): These have been around since the dawn of recorded history. Genuine practitioners are spiritual and intuitive and can indeed speak the "soothe." This word is linked to Old English and basically means to tell the *truth*. Only over time did this change to cast doubt upon the words spoken. Otherwise known as seers, fortunetellers, and psychics, these are people who are just more naturally open to messages and visions than others. To supplement their visions, some also use tools (such as the Tarot) to decipher the likelihood of specific events occurring in the future.

Psyche: This is the deep and inner core of our emotions. This is where we are extremely vulnerable. For example, if we suffer an emotional wound that is penetrating and lasting, it can become ingrained into our very essence or soul, or *psyche.*

Psychic: Psychics are able to *see*, but not always in the same direction and usually without any control over images. Some see the past; some see the future. Being psychic is one big step up from being intuitive; it can be an uncomfortable way to live, but it can also prove very helpful. For example, despite their sometimes fallible reputations, psychics are often consulted by police in cases involving missing persons. (*See* Prophets.)

Pyramids of Egypt: Seemingly without the means to do so at the time, the people of ancient Egypt managed to build the Great Pyramids at Giza so that they aligned almost exactly with the astral Belts of Orion. Questions swirl around these mystical structures: how they were built; where the mathematical knowledge required to do so came from; how they knew the astrological aspects and how to apply them to construction; and perhaps one of the most perplexing—why? Why would these people have cared about the astrological alignments of their structures?

Roadblocks: Roadblocks are repeated and determined attempts by Universe to stop you from doing something or from going somewhere, and there is always a reason. We just don't always know what it is, nor do we need to.

Runes: Runes are a set of symbols (originating with an old Germanic language) that formed a little-known alphabet, which was used when a document needed protection from prying eyes. But the primary use of runes even then was divinational; each symbol was marked or carved onto a small piece of rock, wood, or leather and used for divining the future. When thrown, only the runes falling face-up were considered. (*See* Divination.)

Soul Mate: We all dream of finding our soul mate, right? You may rethink that after reading this; not all soul mates are positive. Some are quite destructive and tie back to unfinished business; karmic debts and payback can come in forms other than romantic. So be careful that the soul mate you think you have found really *is* the soul mate you think you have found. Trust your intuition!

Stonehenge: Stonehenge, at least from a strictly structural point of view, always struck me as a giant circle within another made of huge rock dominoes with a smaller horseshoe in the center. Some of these dominoes have fallen down, but the rest remain standing, as they have done for thousands of years. There is undoubtedly mystery surrounding these monuments, why they were built, what was done there, and so on, but the largest mystery (just like Easter Island and the pyramids) involves how the people who built them knew enough about astrology to align its structure with lunar and solar solstices.

Sub Numbers: The most important subs are the ones just before your final number for any name. There can be a number of double digits found when reducing a Whole Name, and while these may hold messages for you, it is the last or main subs that will tell you the most about yourself.

Symbology: This means being aware of symbols around you that seem to play into what you were just thinking or answer questions you were just asking… similar to a stop sign appearing when you've just wondered about having that second hamburger.

Synchronicity: Often mistakenly called coincidence, synchronicity occurs when two elements come together in a surprising or unexpected way. A typical example is when you are thinking about someone you have not spoken to in a long time and an hour later, the phone rings and guess who's on the line? Synchronicity is energies that meet and ride the same path for a short time, often resulting in a meeting of minds or people or ideas.

Tarot: The tarot is a very old and very well-used system of divining and advising that can offer spiritual insight and growth as well as a peek at potential upcoming events. (*See* Divination, Major Arcana, and Minor Arcana.)

Total Name: The Total Name Number is your entire name (including your middle name) and shows your "proper" and governmental essence as well as the potential gifted to you by Universe upon your "delivery" here.

Tree of Life: Although the natural connection is to the Tree in the Garden of Eden and forbidden fruit, this Tree is more concerned with human, plant, and animal existence. It performs many functions that are intrinsic to the cycle of life and is honored as such.

Universe/Source/Spirit/Divine: All refer to God; the Almighty; the One Who Creates. I think of God as a consciousness—one that contains all knowledge and wisdom of the past, the present, and the future.

Whole Name: Each of your individual names adds up to a Whole Name—like the name John totals to number 9. Each Whole Name Number is descriptive of the category in which it falls: if "John" is a first name, it will reflect Social aspects.

Wicca: Wicca is based on worship of the Goddess (and her consort) and involves ritualized ceremony, strict codes of conduct, and beliefs and ethics, and is positive in tone. It is not the same thing as witchcraft, which can be practiced by anyone in any way and can be positive or negative in intention. (*See* Witch.)

Witch: The origin of the term *witch* is not exact but is suspected to come from the Anglo-Saxon word *wicca*, which is believed to have meant "wise." So from there, it is not hard to imagine an old wise woman of an ancient village who grew herbs, knew how to mix healing balms, and occasionally threw twigs or stones on the ground to study their patterns as the true core origin of the now-mixed meaning of the word *witch*. To my mind, this term means someone who works with and honors the power of nature and the energy/spirit of all things.

Yin/Yang: This ancient term sources back to China and is their version of how things work in the Universe. One half of the symbol is white and the other black, which is meant to reflect the fact that nothing ever is truly black or white. Their swirling action represents the continuous flow and changes of nature and life itself.

recommended reading

Allen, James. *As a Man Thinketh.* Britain: 1902. http://jamesallen.wwwhubs.com/

Bodine, Echo. *Echoes of the Soul.* Novato, CA: New World Library, 1999.

———. *A Still, Small Voice.* Novato, CA: New World Library, 2001.

Braden, Gregg. *The Divine Matrix.* Carlsbad, CA: Hay House, 2008.

———. *Spontaneous Healing of Belief.* Carlsbad, CA: Hay House, 2008.

Buckland, Raymond. *Practical Candle Burning Rituals.* St. Paul, MN: Llewellyn, 1970.

Cunningham, Scott. *Earth Power.* St. Paul, MN: Llewellyn (reprint), 2002.

———. *Divination for Beginners.* St. Paul, MN: Llewellyn (reprint), 2003.

Goodman, Linda. *Love Signs.* New York: St. Martin's Press, 1978.

Hay, Louise. *You Can Heal Your Life.* Carlsbad, CA: Hay House, 1984.

Hicks, Esther, and Jerry Hicks. *The Law of Attraction.* Carlsbad, CA: Hay House, 2006.

———. *Ask and It Is Given.* Carlsbad, CA: Hay House, 2006.

Peck, Scott. *The Road Less Traveled.* New York City, NY: Simon and Schuster, 1978.

Thompson, Leeya Brooke. *Chaldean Numerology: An Ancient Map for Modern Times.* CA: Tenacity Press, 1999.

bibliography

Blavatsky, H.P. (Collated Articles). "The Chaldean Legend," *Theosophy Magazine,* Vol. 52 No. 6 (1964): 175–182, http://www.blavatsky.net.

Dafoe, Stephan. "Philip 1V—1268–1314," accessed June 21, 2011, http://blog.templarhistory.com/2010/03/philip iv-1268-1314/.

Mock, Janet, ed., and Julia Wang, ed. "Celebrity Central—Top 25 Celebs—Drew Barrymore," *People Magazine,* accessed June 21, 2010, http://www.people.com/people/ drew_barrymore/biography/0,20007949,00.html.

Russell, Rusty. "Ancient Babylonia—History of Babylonia," accessed June 21, 2011, http://www.bible-history.com.

Saba, Charles. "Chaldean Numerology," Charles Saba Natal Charts & Timing of Events, accessed June 21, 2011, http://www.chsaba.com.

The Biography Channel. "Apolo Anton Ohno Biography," accessed June 21, 2011, http://www.biography.com/articles/Apolo-Anton-Ohno-226021.

———. "Drew Barrymore Biography," accessed June 21, 2011, http://www.thebiographychannel.co.uk/biographies/drew-barrymore.html.

———. "Leonardo da Vinci Biography," accessed June 21, 2011, http://www.biography.com/articles/Leonardo-da-Vinci-40396.

———. "Leonardo DiCaprio Biography," accessed June 21, 2011, http://www.biography.com/articles/LeonardoDi-Caprio-9273992.

———. "Phil Spector Biography," accessed June 21, 2011, http://www.biography.com/articles/Phil-Spector9489973?part=1.

The Internet Movie Database. "Drew Barrymore," accessed June 21, 2011, http://www.imdb.com/name/nm0000106/.

The website of Apolo Anton Ohno; http://www.apolo antonohno.com.

The website of Drew Barrymore; http://www.drewbarry more.com/index.html.

World Food Programme. "Drew Barrymore announces a US\$1 million donation on 'The Oprah Winfrey Show,'" published March 3, 2008. http://www.wfp.org/node/212.

Of the dead sciences of the past, there is a fair minority of earnest students who are entitled to learn the few truths that may now be given to them.
—H. P. Blavatsky